# Organizational Behavior Management and Developmental Disabilities Services: Accomplishments and Future Directions

*Organizational Behavior Management and Developmental Disabilities Services: Accomplishments and Future Directions* has been co-published simultaneously as the *Journal of Organizational Behavior Management*, Volume 18, Numbers 2/3 1998.

The *Journal of Organizational Behavior Management* Monographs/"Separates"

*Current Topics in Organizational Behavior Management*, edited by Phillip Duncan

*OBM in Multiple Business Environments: New Applications for Organizational Behavior Management*, edited by Brandon L. Hall

*Improving Staff Effectiveness in Human Service Settings: Organizational Behavior Management Approaches*, edited by Lee W. Frederiksen and Anne W. Riley

*Computers, People, and Productivity*, edited by Lee W. Frederiksen and Anne W. Riley

*Job Stress: From Theory to Suggestion*, edited by John M. Ivancevich and Daniel C. Ganster

*Organizational Behavior Management and Statistical Process Control: Theory, Technology, and Research,* edited by Thomas C. Mawhinney

*Promoting Excellence Through Performance Management*, edited by William K. Redmon and Alyce Dickinson

*Pay for Performance: History, Controversy, and Evidence*, edited by Thomas C. Mawhinney and Bill L. Hopkins

*Organizational Culture, Rule-Governed Behavior and Organizational Behavior Management: Theoretical Foundations and Implications for Research and Practice*, edited by Thomas C. Mawhinney

*Organizational Behavior Management and Developmental Disabilities Services: Accomplishments and Future Directions,* edited by Dennis H. Reid

These books were published simultaneously as special thematic issues of the *Journal of Organizational Behavior Management* and are available bound separately. Visit Haworth's website at http://www.haworthpress inc.com to search our online catalog for complete tables of contents and ordering information for these and other publications. Or call 1-800-HAWORTH (outside US/Canada: 607-722-5857), Fax: 1-800-895-0582 (outside US/Canada: 607-771-0012), or e-mail getinfo@haworthpressinc.com

# Organizational Behavior Management and Developmental Disabilities Services: Accomplishments and Future Directions

Dennis H. Reid, PhD
Editor

*Organizational Behavior Management and Developmental Disabilities Services: Accomplishments and Future Directions* has been co-published simultaneously as the *Journal of Organizational Behavior Management*, Volume 18, Numbers 2/3 1998.

The Haworth Press, Inc.
New York • London

*Organizational Behavior Management and Developmental Disabilities Services: Accomplishments and Future Directions* has been co-published simultaneously as the *Journal of Organizational Behavior Management*™, Volume 18, Numbers 2/3 1998.

The Haworth Press, Inc., 10 Alice Street, Binghamton, NY 13904-1580 USA

Cover design by Thomas J. Mayshock Jr.

**Library of Congress Cataloging-in-Publication Data**

Organizational behavior management and developmental disabilities services : accomplishments and future directions / Dennis H. Reid, editor.
     p. cm.
     "Co-published simultaneously as the Journal of organizational behavior management, volume 18, number 2/3 1998."
     Includes bibliographical references and indexes.
     ISBN 0-7890-0662-6 (alk.paper)
     1. Developmentally disabled–Services for. 2. Organizational behavior I. Reid, Dennis H.
HV1570.O74 1998
362.3'86–dc21
                                                    98-39134
                                                      CIP

# INDEXING & ABSTRACTING

Contributions to this publication are selectively indexed or abstracted in print, electronic, online, or CD-ROM version(s) of the reference tools and information services listed below. This list is current as of the copyright date of this publication. See the end of this section for additional notes.

- *ABI/INFORM Research (basic coverage indexing & abstracting data-base available in both print & CD-ROM from University Microfilms International (UMI), 300 North Zeeb Road, P.O. Box 1346, Ann Arbor, MI 48106-1346)* UMI Data Courier, Attention: Library Services, Box 34660, Louisville, KY 40232
- *Academic Abstracts/CD-ROM*, EBSCO Publishing Editorial Department, P.O. Box 590, Ipswich, MA 01938-0590
- *Academic Search: data base of 2,000 selected academic serials, updated monthly,* EBSCO Publishing, 83 Pine Street, Peabody, MA 01960
- *Biostatistica*, Executive Sciences Institute, 1005 Mississippi Avenue, Davenport, IA 52803
- *Business Education Index, The*, Delta Pi Epsilon National Office, P.O. Box 4340, Little Rock, AR 72214
- *Business Source: keyword access to abstracts for over 530 business-related journals, and selected newspapers in the business field; updated monthly,* EBSCO Publishing, 83 Pine Street, Peabody, MA 01960
- *Central Library & Documentation Bureau,* International Labour Office, CH-1211, Geneva 22, Switzerland
- *CNPIEC Reference Guide: Chinese National Directory of Foreign Periodicals,* P.O. Box 88, Beijing, Peoples Republic of China
- *Current Contents: . . . . . see: Institute for Scientific Information*
- *Ergonomics Abstracts*, School of Manufacturing & Mechanical Engineering, The University of Birmingham, Birmingham B15 2TT, England
- *Human Resources Abstracts (HRA)*, Sage Publications, Inc., 2455 Teller Road, Newbury Park, CA 91320
- *IBZ International Bibliography of Periodical Literature,* Zeller Verlag GmbH & Co., P.O.B. 1949, d-49009 Osnabruck, Germany

(continued)

- *Institute for Scientific Information,* 3501 Market Street, Philadelphia, Pennsylvania 19104-3302. Coverage in:
  a) Social Science Citation Index (SSCI): print, online, CD-ROM
  b) Research Alerts (current awareness service)
  c) Social SciSearch (magnetic tape)
  d) Current Contents/Social & Behavioral Sciences (weekly current awareness service)
- *INTERNET ACCESS (& additional networks) Bulletin Board for Libraries ("BUBL") coverage of information resources on INTERNET, JANET, and other networks.*
  - <URL:http://bubl.ac.uk/>
  - New locations will be found under <URL:http://bubl.ac.uk/link/>.
  - Any existing BUBL users who have problems finding information on the new service should contact the BUBL help line by sending e-mail to <bubl@bubl.ac.uk>.
  The Andersonian Library, Curran Building, 101 St. James Road, Glasgow G4 0NS, Scotland
- *Management Abstracts*, T & T Management Development Centre, P. O. Box 1301, 2nd Floor, Frederick Street, Salvatori Building, Port of Spain, Trinidad and Tobago, West Indies
- *Management & Marketing Abstracts*, Pira International, Randalls Road, Leatherhead, Surrey KT22 7RU, England
- *Management News*, Institute of Management, No. 2 Savoy Court, The Strand, London WC2R 0EZ, England
- *MasterFILE: updated database from EBSCO Publishing,* EBSCO Publishing, 83 Pine Street, Peabody, MA 01960
- *Mental Health Abstracts (online through DIALOG)*, IFI/Plenum Data Company, 3202 Kirkwood Highway, Wilmington, DE 19808
- *Operations Research/Management Science,* Executive Sciences Institute, 1005 Mississippi Avenue, Davenport, IA 52803
- *Personnel Management Abstracts*, 704 Island Lake Road, Chelsea, MI 48118
- *Psychological Abstracts (PsycINFO)*, American Psychological Association, P. O. Box 91600, Washington, DC 20090-1600

(continued)

- *Sage Public Administration Abstracts*, (SPAA) Sage Publications, Inc., 2455 Teller Road, Newbury Park, CA 91320
- *Social Science Citation Index .... see: Institute for Scientific Information*
- *Sociological Abstracts (SA),* Sociological Abstracts, Inc., P.O. Box 22206 San Diego, CA 92192-0206
- *UP-TO-DATE Publications,* 2900 Steeles Avenue East, Suite 212, Thornhill, Ontario L3T 4X1, Canada

## SPECIAL BIBLIOGRAPHIC NOTES

*related to special journal issues (separates)*
*and indexing/abstracting*

❏ indexing/abstracting services in this list will also cover material in any "separate" that is co-published simultaneously with Haworth's special thematic journal issue or DocuSerial. Indexing/abstracting usually covers material at the article/chapter level.

❏ monographic co-editions are intended for either non-subscribers or libraries which intend to purchase a second copy for their circulating collections.

❏ monographic co-editions are reported to all jobbers/wholesalers/approval plans. The source journal is listed as the "series" to assist the prevention of duplicate purchasing in the same manner utilized for books-in-series.

❏ to facilitate user/access services all indexing/abstracting services are encouraged to utilize the co-indexing entry note indicated at the bottom of the first page of each article/chapter/contribution.

❏ this is intended to assist a library user of any reference tool (whether print, electronic, online, or CD-ROM) to locate the monographic version if the library has purchased this version but not a subscription to the source journal.

❏ individual articles/chapters in any Haworth publication are also available through the Haworth Document Delivery Service (HDDS).

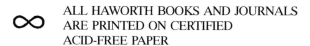

# ABOUT THE EDITOR

**Dennis H. Reid, PhD,** is Director of the Carolina Behavior Analysis and Support Center, Ltd., in Morganton, North Carolina. With over 25 years' experience as a management practitioner, researcher, and author in developmental disabilities, he has earned awards from the American Association on Mental Retardation and the North Carolina Chapter of the Association for Behavior Analysis. Dr. Reid is the author of over 75 journal articles relating to managing and providing human services and currently is an Associate Editor for the *Journal of Organizational Behavior Management* (The Haworth Press, Inc.).

# Organizational Behavior Management and Developmental Disabilities Services: Accomplishments and Future Directions

## CONTENTS

# Introduction

## Dennis H. Reid

An area of major impact of Organizational Behavior Management (OBM) since the inception of its flagship journal, the *Journal of Organizational Behavior Management,* has been the human services sector. In particular, organizations providing supports for individuals with developmental disabilities have been the focus of numerous OBM investigations. According to a 1995 bibliography (Reid & Parsons, 1995), over 270 articles, book chapters and books have been published on OBM investigations and applications in developmental disabilities agencies. As such, arguably more OBM research attention has been directed to supervisory and management practices in agencies for individuals with developmental disabilities than any other type of organization.

In light of the attention given to OBM in human service agencies for persons with developmental disabilities, what have we learned about the utility of OBM in these important organizations? This special collection attempts to provide some answers to this question. In eight invited papers, nationally recognized OBM researchers and practitioners in the human services provide commentary on what OBM has accomplished. Each paper provides a review of relevant OBM research in a specific area related to human service organizations for individuals with developmental disabilities. Based on the literature reviews, a very considerable amount of information is provided regarding what OBM research has accomplished, as well as where gaps currently exist in the research data base. Using their knowledge of the existing research combined with extensive experience applying OBM in the human services, the authors also provide insightful comments regarding future directions for OBM research and application.

There is far too much information within the papers comprising this

[Haworth co-indexing entry note]: "Introduction." Reid, Dennis H. Co-published simultaneously in *Journal of Organizational Behavior Management* (The Haworth Press, Inc.) Vol. 18, No. 2/3, 1998, pp. 1-5; and: *Organizational Behavior Management and Developmental Disabilities Services: Accomplishments and Future Directions* (ed: Dennis H. Reid) The Haworth Press, Inc., 1998, pp. 1-5. Single or multiple copies of this article are available for a fee from The Haworth Document Delivery Service [1-800-342-9678, 9:00 a.m. - 5:00 p.m. (EST). E-mail address: getinfo@haworthpressinc.com].

volume to adequately summarize each paper here. However, there are three themes that run through essentially all of the papers. These themes, derived independently by the authors of each paper, will be briefly summarized in the remainder of this introduction. The intent is to help focus the reader on what appear to be the primary accomplishments, existing gaps and future directions in OBM research and application in agencies for people with developmental disabilities.

## DEMONSTRATED EFFECTIVENESS OF OBM

The most consistent outcome among OBM investigations in agencies serving individuals with developmental disabilities is the demonstrated effectiveness of OBM supervisory and management strategies for improving aspects of staff work performance. Such an outcome has occurred in essentially every type of agency in which OBM has been investigated. Although the majority of successful OBM investigations have involved large residential settings, even investigations conducted less frequently in other settings (e.g., community living arrangements, preschools, vocational centers) consistently reported significant improvements in staff performance with the OBM procedures that were investigated. The majority of these investigations demonstrated means of improving the work performance of paraprofessional personnel such as residential direct support staff. Investigations targeting work performances of professional personnel have likewise reported success with OBM approaches, although the latter investigations have occurred much less often than research involving paraprofessional staff. In short, within the parameters in which OBM procedures have been investigated, results of numerous research undertakings have indicated that such procedures are quite effective for improving and managing staff work performance in developmental disabilities services.

## RESTRICTED SCOPE OF OBM APPLICATIONS

The second theme, that appears across the majority of the invited papers, pertains to the somewhat restricted scope of most of the reported OBM investigations. Specifically, although OBM research applications in developmental disabilities have been numerous and effective as just summarized, the investigations have typically addressed relatively restricted aspects of agency operations. Most OBM research has focused on using behavioral supervisory procedures to alter selected work performances of a respective group of personnel within a given agency. Often the targeted work performances, albeit very important, represent a small part of the staffs' overall job responsibilities. Few investigations have evaluated use of OBM procedures to affect all or even a major portion of an agency's operations.

The lack of investigations on the utility of OBM for managing an entire agency limits the degree to which OBM can be validly offered as a means of enhancing provision of supports and services in agencies for persons with developmental disabilities. A hallmark of OBM is its reliance on applied research and scientific evidence to substantiate the efficacy of its component procedures. By OBM's own standards, there currently is insufficient evidence to conclude definitively that OBM is a viable and effective means of operating an entire developmental disabilities agency in a top quality manner. This does not mean that OBM cannot necessarily fulfill such a role, only that there have been too few investigations in this area to draw data-based conclusions. Among the few cases in which OBM has been applied on an agency-wide basis though, the results have been supportive of this approach to large-scale agency management.

## NEED FOR RESEARCH ON COMPREHENSIVE APPLICATIONS AND WIDER-SCALE ADOPTION

A third theme that emerges from the invited papers pertains to two areas in which future OBM research seems warranted in agencies for individuals with developmental disabilities. The first area relates to the relative lack of investigations on comprehensive applications of OBM across major agency operations as just noted. In order to determine the extent to which OBM can be effective on a large-scale basis, more research is needed to demonstrate and evaluate comprehensive OBM applications. The second area warranting research relates to wider adoption of OBM procedures among human service agencies. In one way or another, every paper in this volume notes that OBM is used routinely in only a small number of developmental disabilities agencies relative to the thousands of such agencies in the United States and abroad.

In considering the need for research on comprehensive applications and wider-scale adoption of OBM, several issues warrant attention. One major issue is that research in these areas is likely to represent a complex and labor-intensive undertaking. Examples of the primary difficulties in conducting such research are discussed in the invited papers. Individual authors also offer useful suggestions as to how the research might proceed, and especially in regard to increasing use of OBM in a larger number of human service agencies.

A second issue related to research on comprehensive OBM applications and wider-scale adoption is that this type of research should complement and not replace the need for continued research on smaller-scale OBM applications. In one sense, a management system can be effective only to the degree that its component procedures are effective and the procedures are effectively applied. Hence, prospective and current OBM researchers should not be dissuaded from developing new and/or refined supervisory procedures for managing selected areas of staff work performance. Researchers should likewise not be discouraged from investigating ways of ensuring that supervisors apply existing OBM procedures in a skillful and effective manner. Research that improves specific aspects of the OBM technology and its likelihood of being effectively applied in typical human service agencies is likely to enhance the probability that OBM will be used on a wider scale with agency operations and used by more agencies.

A final issue related to investigations on comprehensive applications and wide-scale adoption of OBM is that the current lack of such research should not necessarily be viewed as troublesome for the OBM field. A pervasive characteristic of management in human services is susceptibility to popular fads. Many approaches to human services management have stimulated national interest and investment of considerable resources only to quickly fade away without any apparent improvement in the provision of agency services. Although there are a number of reasons why various management approaches are short-lived in the human services, experienced managers would likely attest to two primary reasons. First, the management approaches fail to specify what constitutes their component procedures–leaving working supervisors uninformed over how to apply the approaches within their day-to-day jobs. Second, the models are not sufficiently effective once applied in typical human service agencies. Supervisors and managers invest time and energy in the new management approaches and then find that their work place operations are no different as a result of their efforts. When considering the nature of OBM though, these reasons for the temporary tenure of many management approaches are not very relevant. Essentially by definition, OBM consists of an ever evolving technology stemming from research that demonstrates the effectiveness of procedures constituting the technology. The technological aspect requires careful specification of management procedures, and the research aspect provides for documented effectiveness. These characteristics act against the two primary reasons why management approaches tend to be short-lived. However, these two features of OBM also are likely to have contributed to the lack of research on more comprehensive applications and wider-scale adoption. The development of an effective, well-articulated technology through applied research takes time and effort–time and effort that has occupied the research endeavors of most OBM investigators in the human services. To have attempted to market and disseminate OBM on a large-scale basis prior to the establishment of an effective technology could easily have subjected OBM to the faddish nature of other management approaches.

If concerted effort is undertaken in the future to apply and evaluate OBM in a more comprehensive manner and to better disseminate the technology, it seems the effort is more likely to be successful relative to not having taken the time to develop, evaluate and demonstrate the effectiveness of the technology. From this perspective, the conditions seem to be well established at this point to move forward with these ambitious investigatory and implementation endeavors. It is hoped the information provided in this special collection will help promote and guide those endeavors.

## REFERENCE

Reid, D. H., & Parsons, M. B. (1995). *Staff training and management: Bibliography of Organizational Behavior Management reports in developmental disabilities and related human services.* Morganton, NC: Developmental Disabilities Services Managers, Inc.

# SECTION 1
# OVERVIEW OF THE RELATIONSHIP BETWEEN ORGANIZATIONAL BEHAVIOR MANAGEMENT AND DEVELOPMENTAL DISABILITIES

## History and Contribution of Organizational Behavior Management to Services for Persons with Developmental Disabilities

Peter Sturmey

SUMMARY. This article traces the development of the field of organizational behavior management (OBM) from its origins in early behavior modification studies, the development of a technology for modifying staff behavior, to recent developments in the evolution of cultures. An ecological model of staff behavior is outlined using Bronfenbrenner's (1979) ecological model of human development. The technology used to modify staff behavior is briefly reviewed. In

Peter Sturmey, PhD, is affiliated with the San Antonio State School, San Antonio, TX 78214.

[Haworth co-indexing entry note]: "History and Contribution of Organizational Behavior Management to Services for Persons with Developmental Disabilities." Sturmey, Peter. Co-published simultaneously in the *Journal of Organizational Behavior Management* (The Haworth Press, Inc.) Vol. 18, No. 2/3, 1998, pp. 7-32; and: *Organizational Behavior Management and Developmental Disabilities Services: Accomplishments and Future Directions* (ed: Dennis H. Reid) The Haworth Press, Inc., 1998, pp. 7-32. Single or multiple copies of this article are available for a fee from The Haworth Document Delivery Service [1-800-342-9678, 9:00 a.m. - 5:00 p.m. (EST). E-mail address: getinfo@haworthpressinc.com].

the final section recommendations for managers and researchers are made. Managers should be aware that there is an effective technology for modifying a wide range of staff behaviors that can be implemented both in response to crises and during routine management. Future research on OBM should address three major concerns. First, OBM should broaden the scope of its enquiry beyond the immediate staff and consumer dyad to include analysis of and intervention upon the entire ecosystem within which the consumer's behavior occurs. Second, the issue of integrating theory with practice should be pursued more vigorously through fundamental research on supervisor behavior and through basing interventions on an analysis of the variables maintaining current supervisory behavior. Third, greater attention should be paid to developing training for middle managers as generalist users of the principles of OBM. *[Article copies available for a fee from The Haworth Document Delivery Service: 1-800-342-9678. E-mail address: getinfo@haworthpressinc.com]*

## HISTORICAL BACKGROUND

The 1950s saw an increase in publications demonstrating that the laws of learning could be applied to problems of social significance. These early studies demonstrated that persons with developmental disabilities had the capacity to learn skills and that the principles of learning could be applied to teach skills and to reduce maladaptive behaviors. Despite their promise, the applied significance of many of these early studies were limited. The behavior selected was sometimes not of any great social significance, and the studies typically involved a single subject. Further, the analysis of the behavior of a single person without reference to the behavior of the other people who are normally present is incomplete (Taylor & Carr, 1992). The agent of change was typically a research psychologist in a laboratory or specially designed classroom rather than direct care staff and parents in a regular residential, work or family setting. Thus, applied relevance of early studies appeared limited since they did not address the application of behavioral interventions within the context of a naturally occurring group of people. All of these limitations gave impetus to the development of Organizational Behavior Management (OBM) with persons with developmental disabilities.

By the 1960s several researchers identified the issue of staff performance as central to the progress of the application of behavior analysis in naturally occurring settings. Bensberg and Barnett (1966) wrote that ". . . employee turnover easily constitutes the most troublesome, most costly, and probably most unnecessary problem in the institutions . . ." (p. 157).

Their early monograph, *Attendant Training in Southern Residential Facilities for the Mentally Retarded*, identified many important issues in staff training. Tharp and Wetzel (1969) articulated the triadic model of intervention. In this model the *consultant* acts as an expert, and a *mediator* dispenses reinforcers to a *target*. This model was subsequently refined and developed as a more complex model of consultancy and staff training (Berstein, 1982; Loeber & Weisman, 1975). Tharp and Wetzel also included a broader analysis of 'resistances' to change as behavior maintained by naturally occurring contingencies that are more powerful than those that the behavior change agent can influence. These 'resistances' are in fact an early account of the ecology of intervention. Thus, in the 1960s the stage was set for a greater formalization (Tharp & Wetzel, 1969: Chapter 7) of methods for training and maintaining the behavior of staff.

### Early OBM Studies

Early OBM studies typically evaluated the efficacy of a specific intervention technique to change a specific staff behavior. For example, Panyan, Boozer, and Morris (1970) evaluated the effects of posted graphic feedback on the number of completed behavior modification projects by direct care staff. They found that posted graphic feedback was an effective method of increasing the number of completed projects. This result was replicated by Welsch et al. (1973), thus demonstrating the potential robustness of feedback to staff as a method of changing staff behavior. Panyan et al. described their study as using feedback to staff as a reinforcer for staff behavior, however, presented no descriptive or experimental analysis of staff behavior. Thus, it is unclear whether the mechanism of change in observed staff behavior was actually feedback functioning as a reinforcer for staff completing behavior management projects.

Blindert (1975) directly observed naturally occurring rate of interactions, prompts and reinforcement in an institutional setting for 15 children with developmental disabilities. He observed only two interactions per child in a 10 minute session, of which only about 0.5 interactions per 10 minutes were judged to promote learning. This study suggested that the naturally occurring contingencies operating on staff did not support staff behavior constituting a habilitative environment for the persons who lived in this setting. Repp, Felce, and De Kock (1987) present a review of this literature.

Following these early OBM studies the field has broadened. First, the complexity of interventions has increased. Intervention packages have included various forms of giving staff information such as live and video-taped lectures, readings, quizzes, discussion groups, and brief rationales for intervention. Some interventions have included modelling of staff skills through role play, observing trained staff work with consumers, and video-tape. Various forms of feedback such as verbal, graphic, written, and self-evaluation have been evaluated. Verbal and written feedback have included narrative feedback, numerical feedback through points, or percentage correct staff performance, a numerical measure of consumer behavior, or combinations of these. Feedback could be immediate or delayed. Maintenance mechanisms have also been evaluated. Common elements in maintenance mechanisms have included both antecedents and consequences of staff behavior. Antecedents have included memos, posted reminders, and verbal prompts from peers, supervisors or consumers. Staff consequences have included written or verbal feedback on either staff performance or its products, and performance-based lotteries and other consequence-based interventions. Some studies have encouraged staff participation in change through self-reinforcement, setting performance standards by staff, self-monitoring and self-evaluation (Burgio, Whitman, & Reid, 1983).

A second way in which the field has broadened has been the range of staff behaviors addressed. Examples can be found in Table 1. Third, the methodological sophistication and social validity of interventions has greatly improved over time. For example, in later studies greater attention has been paid to more meaningful, long-term interventions and maintenance over longer periods of time (Christian, 1984; Sturmey, 1995; Sturmey & Hughes, 1996). Larger scale interventions such as those by entire services for hundreds of consumers and staff (Saunders & Saunders, 1995; Sturmey & Hughes, 1996) raise issues such as multiple organizational problems (Christian, 1984; Jensen et al., 1984); the positive and negative effects of intervention on non-targeted aspects of staff and consumer behavior (Duus, 1988); the use of direct care staff and technicians as trainers (Sturmey, Ellison, & Stephens, 1996; Van Den Pol, Reid, & Fuqua, 1983); staff opinion about the acceptability of various methods of being trained (Reid & Parsons, 1995); and, staff perceptions of their own training needs (Sturmey & Stiles, 1996; Thousand, Burchard & Hasazi, 1986). Finally, there has been greater attention to interventions in a wider range of settings, using a wider array of change agents, a wider array of target behaviors than in early studies and more sophisticated experimental designs.

The following sections of this review will not attempt to provide a comprehensive review of all research papers in this area; they are too numerous and too diverse. Rather, the review will focus on the use of functional analysis as a general method of understanding and intervening with human behaviors of social significance (Sturmey, 1996) to develop an eco-behavioral model of staff performance. In the next section, a review of intervention studies will be presented within the framework of the eco-be-

TABLE 1. Some examples of the range of staff behaviors modified in the OBM literature in settings for persons with developmental disabilities.

| Target behaviors | Reference |
| --- | --- |
| Staff-consumer interactions | Burgio et al. (1983) |
| Active treatment | Sturmey (1995) |
| Age appropriate activities | Dyer et al. (1984) |
| Parent training skills | Hardy & Sturmey (1994) |
| Staff skill training | Greene et al. (1978) |
| Documentation by case managers | Horner et al. (1990) |
| Staff safety skills | Van Den Pol et al. (1983) |
| Reducing use of restraint | Jensen et al. (1984) |
| Unscheduled staff leave | Reid et al. (1978) |
| Supervisory skills | Clark et al. (1986) |
| Institutional reform | Christian (1984) |

havioral model. In the final section conclusions for both managers and researchers will be drawn. Areas future research should address will also be noted.

## AN ECO-BEHAVIORAL MODEL OF STAFF PERFORMANCE

There have been many studies of how to intervene and manage staff behavior. Relatively little has been done to develop a comprehensive model of staff behavior. This limits research in two ways. First, all interventions should be based upon an understanding of the environmental variables that influence the current undesirable behaviors regardless of the form of the problem, and whether the problem is pathological or non-pathological (Sturmey, 1996). Second, much of the concern over staff behavior is related to management and prevention of behavior disorders. Current models of behavior and psychiatric disorders are now expanding their analysis from the one-way contingencies operating on the consumer (Carr, 1977; Iwata et al., 1982) to the bi-directional contingencies that flow between consumer and staff or parents (Hastings & Remington, 1994; Oliver, 1993; Taylor & Carr, 1992). Interventions with staff and parents should therefore be based on an understanding of their behavior and its relationship to a wide range of environmental variables. These variables should include both those that are close in time and space to the staff behavior and those more distant variables which may still be important and influential.

## An Ecological Model of Staff Performance

Ecological models of human behavior have been developed both for normal human development (Bronfenbrenner, 1979), and atypical human development (Richardson, 1987), and have also been applied to OBM (Mawhinney, 1992 b). Bronfenbrenner (1979) defined the ecology of human development as "... the scientific study of the progressive accommodation between an active, growing human being and the changing properties of the immediate setting where the person lives ... and by the larger contexts in which the settings are embedded ..." (p. 21). Bronfenbrenner's model distinguishes four systems that surround the developing person: the *microsystem, mesosystem, exosystem,* and *macrosystem.* Figure 1 contains an ecological model of staff behavior using Bronfenbrenner's terminology to organize the literature on staff behavior. In this model it is the staff person as a developing adult who is located at the center of various systems of the ecology.

### Microsystem

Bronfenbrenner defines the *microsystem* as "a pattern of activities, roles, and inter-personal relations. . . in a given setting . . ." (p. 22). The microsystem encompasses the activities of the job including the informal social aspects of a job; the roles of being a trainer, peer of the person with mental retardation, and colleague of other direct care and other staff. Inter-personal relations include relationships with the person with mental retardation, staff peers, supervisors, and professional staff. Their activities are a crucial aspect of the microsystem in determining the behavior of staff.

Staff enter a setting with a learning history that may impede or facilitate performance on the new job. This may relate to both specific and general staff skills. Specific skills include documentation, interaction with consumers, peers, supervisors, and professional staff, and ability to teach a consumer and follow a behavior management plan. More general work-related skills include flexibility, ability to delay gratification, time and attendance, and perseverance. Lakin et al. (1983) found that staff without prior specialized training, who selected their job because of special interest in working with this population, and satisfaction with pay and promotion prospects predicted staff who would stay. Staff who selected a job for economic or convenience reasons, who were young, who had professional ambitions and who had specialized training were much more likely to leave. Hastings and Remington (1994) and Mawhinney (1992 b) have both suggested that staff's verbal representations of contingencies are the prime learning mechanism in much of staff behavior. These verbal representa-

FIGURE 1. An ecological model of staff performance.

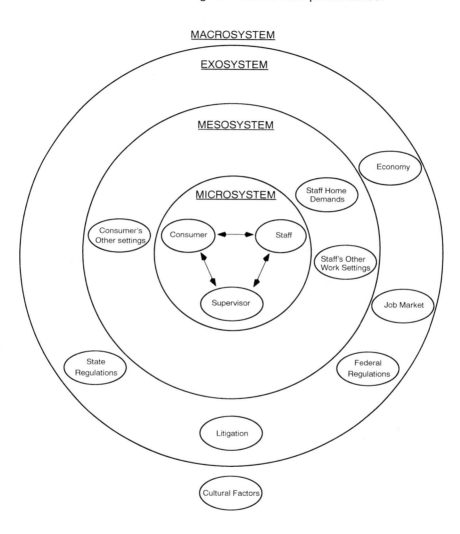

tions such as training and early social experiences on the job are modifiable through experience.

Staff may enter a job situation with or without specific skills and with a learning history related to their work effort and enjoyment. These factors can all be regarded as something that new staff members bring with them to the immediate microsystem. Staff can communicate to their peers and supervisor early their willingness to work, take on new responsibilities, and their ambitions within the new organization. These factors in turn will influence the behavior of peers and supervisors. New staff may be shaped up by peers and supervisors into poor work performance early on. Equally important can be the behavior of supervisors. Staff are explicit in the supervisor behaviors they prefer and dislike (Clark et al., 1986) indicating that supervisors do indeed control some relevant reinforcers and punishers for staff. The effects of modelling from a supervisor, although not researched to date, may also be very powerful, especially when there are also contingencies for following the model.

The behavior of persons with mental retardation can powerfully control staff behavior (Oliver, 1993). Interactions with consumers are very unevenly distributed (Duker et al., 1989; Grant & Moores, 1977) suggesting that they vary according to their reinforcing or punishing significance to staff. Factors such as maladaptive behaviors (Duker et al., 1989; Emerson et al., 1988; Grant & Moores, 1977; Hall & Oliver, 1992), ability to interact reciprocally, key social behaviors (such as smiling, vocalizing, speech, approaching staff) and other social behaviors that can effectively solicit staff interaction may all exert significant control over staff interactions. These variables may affect the pattern of staff interaction generally as well as staff's persistence in teaching a consumer and adherence to behavioral or other training protocols. Equally, a consumer's physical attractiveness, body odor, factors related to staff response cost, such as physical disabilities requiring greater physical effort, can all function to punish staff interactions. The literature on staff stress indicates that maladaptive behaviors can provoke stress (Bersani & Heifetz, 1985; George & Baumeister, 1981; Quine & Pahl, 1985), negative affect, and even verbal and physical abuse (Rush, Hall, & Griffin, 1986).

## *Mesosystem*

Bronfenbrenner (1979) defines the *mesosystem* as ". . . the interrelations among two or more settings in which the developing person actively participates . . ." (p. 25). The interaction between the various settings in which staff members find themselves has been addressed by Redmon and Lockwood (1987). They have suggested that the competition between work and home activities or competing activities from other settings can be conceptualized within the framework of the matching law. The matching law states that ". . . the relative amount of responding on concurrent schedules of reinforcement matches the relative amount of reinforcement obtained under the two schedules . . ." (Redmon & Lockwood, 1987 p. 57). They suggest that when both concurrent schedules are highly reinforcing, competition between them will occur. For example, if looking after young children at home is very reinforcing or failing to do so is very punishing, then effort and response rate may be reduced at work. They suggest that if both schedules can offer the same reinforcement, for example through child care at work, then competition between the two schedules will be reduced and work-related behaviors should increase.

There are many possible relationships between the different settings that a staff member occupies. Although the literature on stress and work performance could address the issue of how home-related stressors affect work and vice versa it has not yet done so. Other relevant examples of the effect of multiple settings on the behavior of a staff member at work include their allocation of time and effort between various settings within work, such as between a residential building, vocational building, staff training and break areas. Another common example of this includes the effects of working two jobs and the competition for staff time and effort between the two jobs. These aspects of the ecology of staff behavior have been relatively neglected.

### Exosystem

The *exosystem* ". . . refers to one or more settings that do not involve the developing person, but in which events occur that affect, or are affected by, what happens in the setting containing the developing person . . ." (Bronfenbrenner, 1977: p. 25). Settings outside of work can greatly affect staff behavior in a number of ways.

The *exosystem* influences the behavior of direct care staff through the relative economic value of a job. The relative economic value of a job is reflected in the relative value of the salary and benefits package compared to the relative value of alternatives such as unemployment or alternate forms of employment. The relative value of a job is also affected by the costs to an employee in undertaking the job duties such as, cost of travel to work, interference with other jobs, family, and social responsibilities. If alternate forms of employment are readily available then the relative value of the current job may not be great. In these circumstances the reinforcing or punishing value of the consequences that a supervisor can implement become very limited. If the response cost to the supervisors of attempting to deal with a performance issue is that the supervisors will have to do the work themselves and work is disrupted, then supervisors may be much more tolerant of poor employee performance.

Staff turnover has repeatedly been identified as one of the most important concerns of managers in both institutional and community services

(Bensberg & Barnett, 1965; Bruininks, Kudla, & Haubner, 1980). Factors in the *exosystem* can greatly influence staff turnover. High turnover means that services are disrupted, cohesiveness among staff groups does not develop, staff must be reassigned to do other staff's duties with consumers whom they do not know, the employer and supervisor get little return for their investment of time in training staff, services to consumers may be reduced (Pierce, Hoffman & Pelletier, 1974), and employers incur substantial costs of training new staff (Zaharia & Baumeister, 1978). The social validity of staff turnover is also attested to by interventions that have targeted this problem (Reid, Schuh-Wear & Brannon, 1978; Shoemaker & Reid, 1980).

Mitchell and Braddock's (1994) USA national survey of staff turnover in community and institutional settings illustrates the role of variables from outside the setting where staff work which relate to staff turnover. They found that the mean annual turnover (and range for all states) in institutions was 16% (range 12% to 69%) and in community settings was 43% (range 31% to 178%). Turnover was related to wages, health benefits, staffing ratios, and unionization. Turnover was greater in urban than rural areas for both institutional and community staff. This again suggests the role of competing schedules of staff reinforcement operating in rural and urban communities.

## Macrosystem

The *macrosystem* is the ". . . consistencies, in the form and content of lower-order systems (micro-, meso-, and exo-) that exist or could exist, at the level of subcultures or the culture as a whole, along with any belief systems or ideology . . ." (Bronfenbrenner, 1977: p. 26). Cultural factors can influence staff performance. If the expectations of staff performance or managers are alien or strange to the local culture then it may be less likely that staff will implement the desirable procedures that managers expect. Examples of the effects of subcultures or cultures include differences in belief systems held by groups of staff from different ethnic, social or educational backgrounds. The majority of behavioral research has been carried out in the United States and to a lesser extent north Europe. Much of the emphasis on target behaviors such as economic productivity, self-sufficiency, and conventional social behaviors may present a difficulty in exporting it to other cultures (Sturmey, Thorburn, Brown, & Reed, 1992) or even sub-cultures within one country.

The *macrosystem* can influence the behavior of direct care staff in the way that state, federal, and ideological belief systems develop. For example, over the last five years the ideology of consumerism, choice and outcomes for consumers has become influential nationally within the United States as it has influenced accreditation standards (The Accreditation Council on Services for People with Disabilities, 1993). These ideological changes that have taken place far removed in time and space from direct care staff and consumers are now beginning to influence their behavior in a number of important ways.

*Organizational culture and OBM.* Many non-behavioral theories of organizations use concepts of organizational culture and talk about the necessity of implementing a change within an organization's culture in order to improve profit and productivity (Demming, 1982, 1986). More recently OBM theorists have attempted to address this problem by using Skinner's concept of cultural evolution (Glenn, 1991; Skinner, 1953). Cultural evolution refers to the selection of units of behavior that are exhibited by members of a community, that can evolve, survive, or be extinguished. Mawhinney (1992 b) used this metaphor to describe the evolution of the "big three" in the car industry–General Motors, Ford, and Chrysler–from the 33 auto companies in existence at the turn of the century. Mawhinney (1992 b) has hypothesized that in some organizations decisions made early on in the history of the organization may have a fundamental, long lasting impact on the survival and flexibility of the organization to respond to changes. Results of these decisions made by top management are described as meta-contingencies, that is ". . . contingent relations between cultural practices and the outcome of those practices . . ." (Glenn, 1991, p. 62). In business the explicit outcome is profit and survival of the company. In human service organizations the outcome controlling top management is obscure (Reid & Parsons, 1995). Ostensibly the purpose of organizations for persons with developmental disabilities is their habilitation and well being. However, it is not clear that this is the one or only function they serve. It has been suggested that large human service organizations are not greatly motivated to fulfill their mission to consumers, if in so doing it threatens the survival of the organization or leads to adverse consequences (Baer, 1992). For example, if a service was completely successful in habilitating all residents to such an extent that all were discharged, what would happen to that organization?

In attempting to provide an analysis of organizational cultures from a behavior analytic perspective Malott, Shimamune and Malott (1992) have argued that much learning by staff in complex organizations is not contingency-shaped learning because there are too many contingencies to learn quickly. The consequences are often too small and remote in time to facilitate learning. Malott et al. argue that most learning by staff takes place through verbal mediation, or rules that staff learn to follow (e.g., "If I do this, my boss will leave me alone"). They argue that although almost all

OBM interventions use contingency management, the mechanism through which they operate is internalization of rules. In many OBM interventions the delivery of consequences is distant in time and could not explain behavior change. For example, when a contingency such as winning a lottery prize in three months time and subsequently getting an extra day off from work a month thereafter could not explain an immediate and rapid change in behavior such as deciding to come to work today when feeling a little sick.

Cultural differences between organizations are very apparent. Differences between organizations have been reported with respect to staff turnover (Mitchell & Braddock, 1994), level of staff stress and staff satisfaction (Buckhalt, Marchetti & Bearden, 1990; Haubner & Bruininks, 1986; George & Baumeister, 1981), and management strategies such as how major transitions like facility closures are managed (Kraushaar, Elliot, & Sturmey, in press).

## A TECHNOLOGY OF STAFF TRAINING AND MANAGEMENT

### Identifying and Validating Staff Competencies

A first step in any OBM intervention is identifying those staff competencies that are important (Thousand et al., 1986). Several empirical studies have identified important staff competencies. Clark et al. (1986) identified important supervisory skills by using multiple methods to generate and evaluate supervisory skills. Supervisor competencies were generated by a literature review, and ratings of role plays of facilitative, neutral, and detrimental staff-supervisor interactions. These competencies were then rank ordered by 200 direct care staff. Top ranked competencies included defining a task clearly, encouraging employees' abilities, and making clear work assignments. Low ranked competencies included listening, but ignoring staff suggestions, rambling during meetings, and making critical and comparative comments about other employees publicly. These extensive social validity data were used as the basis for subsequently training supervisors to exhibit these valued skills. Sturmey and Stiles (1996) generated training competencies for shift supervisors in a large residential facility. They found that the top five items were improving staff attendance, improving staff-consumer interaction, stress management, active treatment, and promoting team work between staff. The items that were rated most highly all reflected motivating and training direct care staff to perform active treatment, manage time, and establish priorities. The ten lowest ranked items mostly related to completing paperwork, and classes that were already currently available to shift supervisors. Looking at service-wide needs, Bruinincks et al. (1980) surveyed managers of community services who identified recruitment, training, and turnover as the highest priority problems for their services. An alternate approach to evaluate the importance of the staff behaviors selected for training is social validation and staff acceptability data. Social validation data are typically collected using Likert scale ratings of staff performance before and after training and how acceptable staff felt the training, or components of the training, were (Reid & Parsons, 1995). The majority of research on validating staff competencies has focussed on staff perceptions. The views of consumers themselves and family members have not been evaluated.

## Skill Acquisition

Reid and Parsons (1995) describe a seven step prototypical OBM staff training program as follows: "(1) Specify work skills to be taught. (2) Provide staff with a checklist description of the work skills specified in step 1. (3) Verbally describe the work skills on the checklist to staff along with the rationale for the importance of the skills. (4) Physically demonstrate the work skills for the staff. (5) Observe staff practice the targeted work skills. (6) Provide corrective/and or approving feedback to staff based on their demonstration of the targeted skills. (7) Continue steps 4, 5, and 6 until staff are observed to perform the targeted skills correctly" (p. 58). This framework usefully describes the basic steps in skill acquisition within an OBM framework. In contrast to traditional staff training there is no requirement for the staff to attend a class, pass a mastery quiz, or describe what they should do. Instead, emphasis is placed on the motor behavior of the staff and demonstration of the skill to mastery criterion.

## Maintenance

Organizational Behavior Management characterizes the traditional approach to maintaining staff behavior as 'train and hope.' In traditional approaches to staff training, behavior outside the classroom and maintenance are rarely addressed. OBM has developed a variety of approaches to maintain staff behavior after initial skill acquisition. These have typically included continued measurement of staff performance, usually combined with antecedent and consequential elements for staff such as reminders and various forms of feedback. It may be possible to gradually fade out the frequency and number of elements in the maintenance phase.

When applied consistently these methods can be very powerful in changing and maintaining the behavior of a large number of staff over an extensive period of time. Several studies have reported maintenance of active treatment in institutional settings for large numbers of staff and consumers for periods in excess of a year (Saunders & Saunders, 1995; Sturmey, 1995; Hughes & Sturmey, 1996). Dunn, Lockwood, Williams and Peacock (in press) used feedback to maintain implementation of a behavior management plan for a seven-year period.

## IMPLICATIONS FOR MANAGERS

### Scope of OBM

Organizational Behavior Management offers a wide range of methods for changing important staff behaviors. OBM can be used to address every day and crisis situations. For the majority of staff performance issues there is probably at least one or two studies that can be used as a model for intervention. Often, an OBM intervention can be readily embedded within routine management with little extra effort. For example, when I set up an injury review committee consumers with high rates of injuries were identified. We then conducted a fairly routine record review of the high risk consumers' treatment plans by a committee of middle mangers. *If this had been all we had done it is unlikely that staff behavior would have changed.* The OBM element in this project was that consumers were then assigned a priority reflected in when they were next reviewed by the committee. At that time, the case managers had to report back on their plans, the implementation of the plan, and the outcome reflected in the new injury data. Thus, there were both prompts for case managers to review their work, and consequences in the form of verbal feedback, additional work, and reduced frequency of committee monitoring if they were successful.

Organizational Behavior Management methods have a better scientific basis for their effectiveness than any other method of training and maintaining staff behavior. This includes Continuous Quality Improvement (CQI: Demming, 1982, 1986) or Total Quality Management (TQM: Saunders & Saunders, 1994). The training methods typically used include orientation classes, day-to-day management strategies, special projects, and responses to specific crises.

It is important to note that many early examples of OBM took place in institutional settings. However, the issues of staff performance are broadly similar in community services (Killu, 1994). Indeed, at times these problems may be exacerbated by higher staff turnover and poorer staff working conditions (Mitchell & Braddock, 1993, 1994). There is a growing literature on the application of OBM in community settings (Demchack & Browder, 1990; Harchick et al., 1992).

### Training of Managers

Being a manager has not traditionally been regarded as a professional status; there are no specific training pre-requisites, licensing requirements, or legal protection of the title. No specific supervisory skills are required. Managers are free to develop maladaptive supervisory practices that are ineffective, or that are effective in reducing some undesirable staff performances in the short term and ineffective in the long term. Consequently, some senior managers exhibit few, if any, supervisory skills. Not only does this lead to ineffective supervision of their staff, it can also lead to incompetent senior managers making poor decisions, and more skilled junior managers being frustrated, limited, or punished by their supervisor's lack of skill.

Managers who wish to become skilled should seek out training and supervision in OBM methods. Although reading and attending conferences may help, it is unlikely to change the supervisory behavior of a manager back in the work setting. Managers who wish to learn OBM skills should set up their own training schedule to shape up their own behavior. As an example, Table 2 illustrates a summary of my own acquisition of OBM skills, and, projects that I have undertaken over the last 10 years. It is notable that the earlier projects were discrete, if not trivial, in scope. Later projects have become broader, longer term, and have involved entire organizations.

## CHALLENGES TO RESEARCHERS

### Implications of an Ecological Model

The proposed ecological model of staff behavior encompasses a very broad range of variables that may lawfully affect staff behavior. This view is different than that typically implied by OBM intervention studies since they often focus on the social behavior within the microsystem. Temporally more distant variables such as shift patterns and number of consecutive days worked can affect important staff performances such as interaction rates (Duker et al., 1991). Typically, OBM studies have not intervened at a greater distance from the staff member and consumer and have not addressed issues such as rule governance (Hastings & Remmington, 1994; Mawhinney, 1992 b). An ecological model of staff performance has heuristic

TABLE 2. A chronological summary of the OBM projects that the present author has been involved with. Generally over time the number of staff and consumers have increased as has the duration of the intervention.

| Problem | Intervention | n Staff/Parents | n Consumers | Duration |
|---|---|---|---|---|
| #1 Staff not writing training objectives correctly (Sturmey et al., 1988) | Redesign form to prompt staff | Approx. 20 | Approx. 40 | Approx. 5 months |
| #2 Parents of preschool children with developmental disabilities lack teaching skills (Hardy & Sturmey, 1994) | Brief definition & modeling of teaching skills; weekly written feedback | 3 | 3 | 10 weeks |
| #3 Quality assurance system for residential services | Measure of service performance refined; data collection schedule developed; goal setting & monitoring procedure developed | Several hundreds; 30 homes/wards | Approx. 400 | 18 months |
| #4 Monitoring deadlines for psychology department | Written feedback on late work & tickler system | 8 psychologists | 280 | 30 months |
| #5 Monitoring of consumer injuries | Assign priority to consumer based on frequency and severity of injuries; bring case manager back on basis of consumer outcome | 35 case managers and 8 psychologists | 720 | 24 months |
| #6 Lack of active treatment in a home (Sturmey, 1995) | Brief training & verbal & written feedback | 30 staff | 35 | 1 year |
| #7 Behavior technicians not turning in work on time. | Written feedback on late work & tickler system | 6 staff | 80 | 2 years |
| #8 Lack of active treatment across entire facility (Hughes & Sturmey, 1996) | Brief training & verbal & written feedback | 600 staff | 310 | 27 |

value in directing attention beyond the immediate staff environment to broader areas for potential points of intervention, but creates the problem how to rigorously evaluate such interventions empirically within the paradigm of applied behavior analysis.

Although we have a fairly extensive literature on the functional analysis of staff behavior (Repp et al., 1987) there has not been a clear integration of this literature with the technology of intervention. Thus, it has been suggested that competition between the concurrent schedules of home and work may account for this problem (Redman & Lockwood, 1987) and it has been reliably shown that staff attendance can be impacted by contingency management (Reid et al., 1987; Shoemaker & Reid, 1980), presumably making staying at home more costly and attending work relatively more reinforcing. However, we have no data to support the notion that competition between concurrent schedules is an important or powerful variable in controlling staff attendance because we lack a powerful technology for measuring naturally occurring schedules of reinforcement that occur across the many settings of a staff member's entire life.

Although there is an effective technology to change staff behavior there has been relatively little integration of theory and intervention (Agnew & Redmon, 1992). For example, several authors have suggested that much of the operant paradigm used by authors to explain the effectiveness of feedback is explained in terms of rule governed behavior rather than contingency learning (Hastings & Remington, 1994; Malott, 1992; Eubanck & Lloyd, 1992). The task of integrating theory with intervention is indeed daunting. In discussing the application of the matching law to OBM Redmon and Lockwood (1987) lament that ". . . it is difficult to precisely identify schedules of reinforcement that are operating in a complex environment. These problems make literal extrapolations from the laboratory to less controlled settings untenable . . ." (p. 59). In a similar vein Mawhinney (1992) noted that meta-contingencies, a key concept in a behavioral account of cultural evolution, are ". . . complex, dynamic, organizational feedback functions, some of which can be quantified . . ." (p. 12). This statement seems to imply that some meta-contingencies can not be quantified: a severe limitation for an account of behavior based upon applied behavior analysis.

### Use of Staff Punishment

Many managers routinely use, or attempt to use, punishment as a method of changing staff behavior. For example, following a dramatic example of poor performance, such as returning from being sick for an extended period of time, a supervisor may humiliate a staff member in front of peers or assign him/her a difficult client for the entire shift. Some forms of punishment have been formalized into personnel manuals for adverse staff action. Typically, these strategies are reserved for the most serious staff performance problems such as client abuse, serious and chronic abuse of time, and severe, general incompetence that has not responded to less aversive staff interventions. Staff punishment may often be used inappropriately. It is not accompanied by procedures to support appropriate staff performance, such as clarification of performance expectations, and reinforcement of appropriate staff behavior, training in the relevant skills, is not contingent upon inappropriate staff behavior, or is applied inconsistently (Demming, 1982, 1986; Reid & Parsons, 1995). Yet, managers frequently use punishment. Changing staff behavior through punishment can have considerable social validity in certain circumstances. It therefore behooves researchers to understand the mechanisms that account for supervisors' use of punishment, to evaluate the use of both positive, effective alternatives to staff punishment, and to evaluate its rational and effective use.

### The Need for Dissemination Models

Organizational Behavior Management has addressed most important aspects of staff performance in services for persons with developmental disabilities. It is ironic that such an effective technology of staff management has not been adopted by services on a more widespread basis. Managers are more likely to know about less effective staff management methods such as their local performance review mechanism, quality circles, project teams and committees, and management philosophies such as CQI and TQM (Dey, Sluyter, & Keating, 1994; Demming, 1986; Saunders & Saunders, 1994). Researchers need to address issues regarding the extent to which OBM methods have been adopted, why they have not been adopted more readily, and what barriers stand in the way of its wide scale adoption.

Organizational Behavior Management has greatly emphasized training discrete staff skills in a specific context. This may be a highly effective strategy in solving a specific problem, but is very limited as managers may have great problems generalizing the solutions of one problem to another. The issue of generalization of managers' OBM skill has been greatly neglected in the research literature. Although accessible readable texts on OBM now exist (Reid & Parsons, 1995) these texts have not been evaluated as a means of training managers in generalized OBM skills. Presumably reading such texts would be relatively ineffective in changing managers' behavior in most circumstances. It would be useful for researchers to develop and evaluate interventions that can teach and maintain the generalized application of managers' OBM skills to a wide range of staff topographies, different management problems, staff groups and contexts.

Two articles were identified as possible models for this kind of endeavor. Maher (1984) described and evaluated a training program in OBM for seven educational administrators. The program consisted of two phases. In the first phase participants attended five three hour instructional sessions scheduled over a one week period. The instructional settings covered topics such as key concepts and methods of OBM, applying the skills to performance problems, evaluation skills, and involving staff in the change process. In the second phase participants undertook projects with supervision over a one year period. Data indicated that both classes and supervised projects were implemented as scheduled. Outcome data indicated that participants gained considerable skill from the classes as evaluated by their performance during role plays of simulated problems. Most impressive were the products of the supervised projects. All seven projects were completed over a one year period and addressed problems such as increasing parent participation in school meetings and increasing school counselling services. One school district administrator reduced staff non-attendance in 1,200 teaching staff using clarification of policy, monitoring of attendance by principals, a staff bonus scheme, and monthly written feedback. Staff non-attendance was improved by 30% to 40% in 10 schools and by 10% to 20% in two schools. A broadly similar approach was used by Nordstrom, Lorenzi and Hall (1991) to train 32 middle and upper level managers in city government in OBM methods who then conducted nineteen OBM projects. The average project changed the targeted staff behavior by over 50%. So far this two phase strategy to train supervisors in OBM and provide ongoing supervision has not yet been applied to services for persons with developmental disabilities but is currently the most promising paradigm for the large scale, diversified implementation of OBM.

## *Integration with Current Management Philosophies*

As noted in earlier sections OBM is not a widely used technology for management of staff behavior. Other approaches to management, such as CQI, TQM, and personalistic approaches to management have become very popular. One popular approach is Demming's "Theory D" (Deming, 1982, 1986). Theory D's 14 points consist of exhortations to give up old, ineffective management practices and '. . . create constancy of purpose . . . adopt the new philosophy . . . improve constantly . . . [and] . . . break down barriers between departments . . . .' Demming also recommends the use of statistical process control to identify sources of variation in product quality. Statistical process control is a procedure for graphing product output and identifying significant deviations from the typical by plotting control limits of one, two or three sigma deviations above and below a center line or time series mean. Demming criticizes poor managers for failing to use data, using inappropriate data, or reacting to usual variations in product quality as the basis for their decision making. Such practices foster blaming workers for product variation when there may be other systemic factors responsible for such variations, or, no actual significant deviation from the norm. Demming criticizes managers who use punishment methods to manage staff behavior in response to random variations in product quality and notes that, given the tendency of all data to regress to the mean, managers will suffer from the illusion of efficacy.

Continuous Quality Improvement has much that is compatible with OBM such as data-based and rational approaches to managing staff behavior, graphical presentation of data, staff education, and encouraging staff education and contribution to problem solving (Pfadt & Wheeler, 1994; Hantula, 1995; Mawhinney, 1987, 1992a). There is also considerable mismatch (Saunders & Saunders, 1994; Hopkins, 1995). Demming's exhortations are to stop current ineffective management practices; but he fails to specify what positive actions to take to remedy these problems. Many of his positive exhortations are couched in generalities such as 'Institute leadership . . . help people and machines and gadgets do a better job . . . Drive out fear . . . Put everyone in the company to work to accomplish the transformation . . .'' (Demming, 1986: pp. 23–24). Specific forms of intervention are lacking. A second area of criticism from behavior analysts has been from the lack of emphasis, if not outright aversion, to the use of contingency management of staff behavior (Mawhinney, 1992b). Third, it is unclear if implementing change based upon Demming's 14 points will actually increase the profitability of an enterprise or the quality of a product. Hantula (1995) notes that when change has been ascribed to the introduction of CQI methodologies it is not clear what the interventions were, and what the outcomes were for the companies. Thus, there is no substantial empirical evidence regarding the effectiveness of CQI methodologies and interventions. This point seems to be a significant barrier to the integration of CQI and OBM.

If methods of OBM are to be acceptable then it must be perceived that they are introduced in a compatible way that is complementary to existing management philosophies. If OBM methods are unnecessarily adversarial they are unlikely to be accepted. OBM methods can easily be perceived as methods that fill in the technological gaps that Demming explicitly eschews. Thus, they can serve a useful purpose to organizations trying to implement CQI, but that lack technological knowledge. However, explicit disagreement on issues such as staff performance targets and staff reinforcement may be hard to avoid.

## CONCLUDING REMARKS

Organizational Behavior Management has become the most powerful and empirically validated methodology for understanding and changing staff behavior. Future research should address three main issues: broadening the basis of analysis to include the entire ecosystem of staff behavior, integrating behavior analysis theory with the OBM technology of intervention, and, developing the large scale dissemination of OBM to managers in services for persons with developmental disabilities.

## REFERENCES

The Accreditation Council on People with Disabilities (1993). *Outcome based performance measures*. Towson, Md: The Accreditation Council.

Agnew, J. L., & Redmon, W. L. (1992). Contingency specifying stimuli: The role of "rules" in organizational behavior management. *Journal of Organizational Behavior Management, 13,* 67-76.

Baer, D. M. (1992). Much ado about something: Comments on papers by Malott and Malott, Shimamume, and Malott. *Journal of Organizational Behavior Management, 13*(2), 77-79.

Bensberg, G. J., & Barnett, C. D. (1968). *Attendant Training in Southern Residential Facilities for the Mentally Retarded*. Atlanta: Southern Regional Educational Board.

Bernstein, G. S. (1982). Training behavior change agents: A conceptual review. *Behavior Therapy, 13,* 1-23.

Bersani, H. A., & Heifetz, L. J. (1985). Perceived stress and satisfaction of direct-care staff members in community residences for mentally retarded adults. *American Journal of Mental Deficiency, 90,* 289-295.

Blindert, H. D. (1975). Interactions between residents and staff: A quantitative investigation of an institutional setting for retarded children. *Mental Retardation, 13,* 38-39.

Bronfenbrenner, U. (1979). *The Ecology of Human Development*. Cambridge: Harvard University Press.

Bruininks, R., Kudla, M., Weick, C., & Hauber, F. (1980). Management problems in community residential facilities. *Mental Retardation, 18,* 125-130.

Buckhalt, J. A., Marchetti, A., & Bearden, L. J. (1990). Sources of job stress and job satisfaction reported by direct care staff of a large residential mental retardation facility. *Education and Training in Mental Retardation, 15,* 344-351.

Burgio, L. D., Whitman, T. L., & Reid, D. H. (1983). A participative management approach for improving direct care staff performance in an institutional setting. *Journal of Applied Behavior Analysis, 16,* 37-53.

Carr, E. G. (1977). The motivation of self-injurious behavior: A review of some hypotheses. *Psychological Bulletin, 84,* 800-816.

Christian, W. P. (1984). A case study in the programming and maintenance of institutional change. *Journal of Organizational Behavior Management, 5*(1), 99-153.

Clark, H. B., Wood, R., Kuechnel, T., Flanagan, S., Mosk, M., & Northup, J. T. (1985). Preliminary validation and training of supervisory interaction skills. *Journal of Organizational Behavior Management, 7*(1/2), 95-115.

Demchack, M. A., & Browder, D. M. (1990). An evaluation of the pyramid model of staff training in group homes for adults with severe handicaps. *Education and Training in Mental Retardation, 25,* 150-163.

Demming, W. E. (1982). *Quality, Productivity, and Competitive Position.* Cambridge: MIT Press.

Demming, W. E. (1986). *Out of the Crisis.* Cambridge: Massachusetts Institute of Technology, Center for Advanced Engineering Study.

Dey, M. L., Sluyter, G. V., & Keating, J. E. (1994). Statistical control and direct care staff performance. *The Journal of Mental Health Administration,* Spring, 1994, 201-209.

Duker, P. C., Boonekamp, J., Brummelhuis, T. Y., Hermans, M., Van Leeuwe, J., & Seys, D. (1989). Analysis of ward staff initiatives toward mentally retarded residents: Clues for intervention. *Journal of Intellectual Disability Research, 33,* 55-67.

Duker, P. C., Seys, D., Van Leeuwe, J., & Prins, L. W. (1991). Occupational conditions of ward staff and quality of residential care for individuals with mental retardation. *American Journal of Mental Retardation, 95,* 388-396.

Dunn, J., Lockwood, K., Williams, E. E., and Peacock, S. (1997). A seven-year follow-up of treating rumination with dietary satiation. *Behavioral Interventions: Theory and Practice in Residential and Community-Based Clinical Programs, 12,* 163-172.

Duus, R. E. (1988). Response class in the organizational setting: The effects of location-Specific feedback. *The Psychological Record, 38,* 49-65.

Emerson, E., Cummings, R., Barrett, S., Hughes, H., McCool, C., & Toogood, A. (1988). Challenging behaviour and community services. 2: Who are the people who challenge services? *Mental Handicap, 16,* 16-19.

George, M. J., & Baumeister, A. A. (1981). Employee withdrawal and job satisfaction in community residential facilities for mentally retarded persons. *American Journal of Mental Deficiency, 85,* 639-647.

Glenn, S. S. (1991). Contingencies and meta-contingencies: Relations among behavioral, cultural, and biological evolution. In: P. A. Lamal (Ed.) *Behavioral analysis of societies and cultural practices* (pp. 39-73). Washington DC: Hemisphere.

Grant, G. W., & Moores, B. (1977). Resident characteristics and staff behavior in two hospitals for mentally retarded adults. *American Journal on Mental Deficiency, 82,* 259-265.

Greene, B. F., Willis, B. S., Levy, R. & Bailey, J. S. (1978). Measuring client gain from staff-implemented programs. *Journal of Applied Behavior Analysis, 11*, 395-412.

Hall, S., & Oliver, C. (1992). Differential effects of severe self-injurious behaviour on the behaviour of others. *Behavioral Psychotherapy, 20*, 355-366.

Hantula, D. A. (1995). Disciplined decision making in an interdisciplinary team environment: Some implications for clinical applications of statistical process control. *Journal of Applied Behavior Analysis, 28*, 371-377.

Harchick, A. E., Sherman, J. A., Sheldon, J. B., & Strouse. M. C. (1992). Ongoing consultation as a method of improving performance of staff members in a group home. *Journal of Applied Behavior Analysis, 25*, 599-610.

Hardy, N., & Sturmey, P. (1994). Portage Guide to Early Intervention III: A rapid training and feedback system to teach and maintain mother's skills. *Educational Psychology, 14*, 345-358.

Hastings, R. P., & Remington, B. (1994). Rules of engagement: Toward an analysis of staff responses to challenging behavior. *Research in Developmental Disabilities, 15*, 279-298.

Haubner, F. A., & Bruininks, R. H. (1986). Intrinsic and extrinsic satisfaction among direct-care staff in residential facilities for mentally retarded people. *Educational and Psychological Measurement, 46*, 95-105.

Horner, R. H., Thompsen, L. S., & Storey, K. (1990) Effects of case manager feedback on the quality of individual habilitation plans. *Mental Retardation, 28*, 227-241.

Hopkins, B. A. (1995). Applied behavior analysis and statistical process control. *Journal of Applied Behavior Analysis, 28*, 379-386.

Hughes, T., & Sturmey, P. (May, 1996). *Development and evaluation of a facility wide project to improve active treatment.* Paper presented to the American Association on Mental Retardation 120th Annual meeting, San Antonio, Texas.

Iwata, B. A., Dorsey, M. F., Bauman, K. E., & Richman, G. S. (1982). Toward a functional analysis of self-injury. *Analysis and Intervention in Developmental Disabilities, 2*, 3-20.

Jensen, C. C., Morgan, P., Orduno, R., Self, M. A., Zarate, R., Meunch, G., Reguers, R. A., & Shaley, B. (1984). Changing patterns of residential care: A case study of administrative and programmatic change. *Journal of Organizational Behavior Management, 6*, 155-176.

Killu, K. (1994). The role of direct-care staff. *Behavioral Interventions, 9*, 169-176.

Kraushaar, K., D. Elliot, & Sturmey, P. (in press). Program evaluation of state school closure: Parent perceptions. *American Journal on Mental Retardation*, in press.

Lakin, K. C., Hill, B. K., Bruininks, R. H., Hauber, F. A., & Krantz, G. C., (1983). Factors related to job stability of direct-care staff of residential facilities for mentally retarded people. *Journal of Community Psychology, 1*, 228-225.

Loeber, R., & Weisman, R. G. (1975). Contingencies of therapist and trainer performance: A review. *Psychological Bulletin, 82*, 660-688.

Maher, C. A. (1984). Training educational administrators in organizational behavior management: Program description and evaluation. *Journal of Organizational Behavior Management, 6*(1), 79-97.

Malott, R. W. (1992). A theory of rule-governed behavior and organizational behavior management. *Journal of Organizational Behavior Management, 13*(2), 45-65.

Malott, R. W., Shimamune, S., & Malott, M. E. (1992). Rule-governed behavior and organizational behavior management: An analysis of interventions. *Journal of Organizational Behavior Management, 13*(2), 103-116.

Mawhinney, T. C. (1987). Organizational behavior management and statistical process control: Theory, technology and research. *Journal of Organizational Behavior Management, 9*, 1-4.

Mawhinney, T. C. (1992 a). Total Quality Management and organizational behavior management: An integration for continual improvement. *Journal of Applied Behavior Analysis, 25*, 525-543.

Mawhinney, T. C. (1992 b). Analysis of organizational cultures as selection by consequences: The Gaia hypothesis, metacontingencies, and organizational ecology. *Journal of Organizational Behavior Management, 13*(2), 1-44.

Mitchell, D., & Braddock, D. (1993). Compensation and turnover of direct care staff in developmental disabilities residential facilities. I: Wages and benefits. *Mental Retardation, 31*, 429-437.

Mitchell, D., & Braddock, D. (1994). Compensation and turnover of direct care staff in developmental disabilities residential facilities. I: Turnover. *Mental Retardation, 32*, 34-42.

Nordstrom, R. R., Lorenzi, P., & Hall, R. V. (1991). A behavioral training program for managers in city government. *Journal of Organizational Behavior Management, 11*(2), 189-211.

Oliver, C. (1993). Self-injurious behaviour: From response to strategy. In: C. Kiernan (Ed.), *Research to Practice? Implications of Research on the Challenging Behavior of People with Learning Disability,* (pp. 135-189). Clevedon, United Kingdom: BILD Publications.

Panyan, M., Boozer, H., & Morris, N. (1970). Feedback to attendants as a reinforcer for applying operant techniques. *Journal of Applied Behavior Analysis, 3*, 1-5.

Pfadt, A., & Wheeler, D. J. (1994). Using statistical process control to make data-based clinical decisions. *Journal of Applied Behavior Analysis*, 349-369.

Pierce, P. S., Hoffman, J. L., & Pelletier, L. P. (1974). The 4-day work week versus the 5-day work week: Comparative use of sick time and overtime by direct care personnel in an institutional facility for the severely and profoundly retarded. *Mental Retardation, 12*, 22-24.

Quine, L., & Pahl, J. (1985). Examining the causes of stress in families with severely handicapped child. *British Journal of Social Work, 15*, 501-517.

Reddman, W. K. & Lockwood, K. (1987). The matching law and organizational behavior. *Journal of Organizational Behavior Management, 8*(1), 57-72.

Reid, D. H., & Parsons, M. B. (1995). *Motivating Human Services Staff. Supervisory Strategies for Maximizing Work Effort and Work Enjoyment.* Morganton, NC: Habilitiative Management Consultants, Inc.

Reid, D. H., Shuh-Wear, C. L., & Brannon, M. E. (1978). Use of a group contingency to decrease staff absenteeism in a state institution. *Behavior Modification, 2,* 251-266.

Repp, A. C., Felce, D., & De Kock, U. (1987). Observational studies of staff working with mentally retarded individuals: A review. *Research in Developmental Disabilities, 8,* 331-350.

Richardson, S. A. (1987). The ecology of mental handicap. *Journal of the Royal Society of Medicine, 80,* 203-206.

Rusch, R. G., Hall, J. C., & Griffin, H. C. (1986). Abuse provoking characteristics of institutionalized mentally retarded individuals. *American Journal of Mental Deficiency, 90,* 618-624.

Saunders, R. R., & Saunders, J. L. (1994). Edward Demming, quality analysis, and total behavior management. *The Behavior Analyst, 17,* 115-126.

Saunders, R. R., & Saunders, J. L. (April, 1995). *Organizational behavior management.* Workshop presented to the Texas Association for Applied Behavior Analysis, Dallas, Texas.

Shoemaker, J., & Reid, D. H. (1980). Decreasing chronic absenteeism among institutional staff: Effects of a low-cost attendance program. *Journal of Organizational Behavior Management, 2,* 201-205.

Skinner, B. F. (1953). *Science and Human Behavior.* New York: MacMillan.

Sturmey, P. (1995). Evaluating and improving residential treatment during group leisure situations: An independent replication. *Behavioral Interventions, 10,* 59-67.

Sturmey, P. (1996). *Functional Analysis in Clinical Psychology.* New York: Wiley.

Sturmey, P., Ellison, D., & Stephens, D. (June, 1995). *A simple, inexpensive and effective way of training direct care staff in skills training,* paper presented to the Texas Association on Mental Retardation, Corpus Christi, Texas.

Sturmey, P., Newton, T., and Crisp, A. G. (1988). An evaluation of a simple, inexpensive method of increasing nurse compliance with documentation for goal planning. *Journal of Advanced Nursing, 13,* 496-500.

Sturmey, P., & Stiles, L. A. (1996). Training needs of shift supervisors in a residential facility for persons with developmental disabilities: Shift superiors' and middle mangers' perceptions. *Behavioral Interventions. Theory and Practice in Residential and Community-Based Clinical Programs, 11,* 141-146.

Sturmey, P., Thorburn, M. J., Brown, J. M., & Reed, J. (1992). Portage Guide to Early Education: Cross cultural aspects and intracultural variability. *Child: Care, Health and Development, 18,* 377-394.

Sulzer-Azaroff, B., Pollack, M. K., & Fleming, R. K. (1992). Organizational behavior management within structural and cultural constraints. *Journal of Organizational Management, 25,* 117-137.

Taylor J. C., & Carr, E. G. (1992). Severe behavior problems related to social interaction. 2. A systems analysis. *Behavior Modification, 16,* 336-371.

Tharp, R. G., & Wetzel, R. J. (1969). *Behavior Modification in the Natural Environment.* New York: Academic Press.

Thousand, J. S., Burchard, S. N., & Hasazi, J. E. (1986). Field-based generation and social validation of managers and staff competencies for small community residences. *Applied Research in Developmental Disabilities*, 7, 263-283.

Van Den Pol, R. A., Reid, D. H., & Fuqua, R. W. (1983). Peer training of safety-related skills to institutional staff: Benefits for trainers and trainees. *Journal of Applied Behavior Analysis*, 16, 139-156.

Welsch, W. V., Ludwig, C., Radiker, J. E., & Krapfl, J. E. (1973). Effects of feedback on daily completion of behavior modification projects. *Mental Retardation*, 11, 24-26.

Zaharia, E. S., & Baumeister, A. A. (1978). Estimated position replacement costs for technician personnel in a state's public facilities. *Mental Retardation*, 16, 131-134.

# OBM and Quality Improvement Systems

Robert A. Babcock
Richard K. Fleming
Julianne R. Oliver

**SUMMARY.** A review of the empirical OBM literature on quality improvement systems in organizations serving persons with developmental disabilities (DD) suggests the current literature offers a small but growing number of studies of large-scale, long-term, applications of behavioral supervision to improve targeted areas of staff performance. One conclusion offered is that it may be possible to expand the scope of OBM interventions in DD organizations by integrating OBM into the development of total quality management (TQM) approaches to quality improvement. To illustrate how such an integration might be accomplished, the current paper discusses OBM research in four areas that are important in implementing TQM (organizational systems analysis, team effectiveness, measuring consumer responses, and data analysis). Recommendations for practice and future research in OBM within DD organizations are discussed. *[Article copies available for a fee from The Haworth Document Delivery Service: 1-800-342-9678. E-mail address: getinfo@haworthpressinc.com]*

The literature in organizational behavior management (OBM) offers a number of proven procedures for improving the quality of services for persons with developmental disabilities (Reid, Parsons, & Green, 1989;

Robert Babcock is affiliated with Emory University, School of Medicine. Richard K. Fleming and Julianne R. Oliver are both affiliated with Auburn University.

[Haworth co-indexing entry note]: "OBM and Quality Improvement Systems." Babcock, Robert A., Richard K. Fleming, and Julianne R. Oliver. Co-published simultaneously in *Journal of Organizational Behavior Management* (The Haworth Press, Inc.) Vol. 18, No. 2/3, 1998, pp. 33-59; and: *Organizational Behavior Management and Developmental Disabilities Services: Accomplishments and Future Directions* (ed: Dennis H. Reid) The Haworth Press, Inc., 1998, pp. 33-59. Single or multiple copies of this article are available for a fee from The Haworth Document Delivery Service [1-800-342-9678, 9:00 a.m. - 5:00 p.m. (EST). E-mail address: getinfo@haworthpressinc.com].

Fleming & Reile, 1993; Sturmey, 1998). In recent years, researchers have expanded the scope of OBM interventions in developmental disabilities to include larger-scale, longer-term applications. However, few investigations have reported the development of comprehensive (e.g., organization-wide) and flexible quality-improvement systems.

Total quality management (TQM), continuous quality improvement (CQI) and statistical process control (SPC) represent closely related systems approaches to developing quality improvements within organizations (hereafter, we will use TQM to refer to these various approaches). In contrast to traditional top-down, or management-directed structural approaches, TQM-type programs involve generating change from within the organization, relying heavily on cross-functional teams supported by upper-level management. Cross-functional teams consist of members from varying organizational levels or disciplines who bring specific skills to bear on complex organizational problems. Total quality management and OBM are compatible in many ways and recently OBM researchers have explored ways in which TQM approaches may offer a vehicle for extending the scope of OBM approaches in a range of organizations (e.g., Mawhinney, 1992; Redmon, 1992).

The purpose of this paper is to (a) review the empirical literature on systems-level OBM interventions in developmental disabilities; (b) describe critical components of quality improvement programs (e.g., TQM, CQI), with particular attention to how they might apply to human service organizations; and (c) present and discuss recommendations for OBM research and application that are relevant to the development of large-scale quality improvement systems in developmental disabilities.

## REVIEW OF EMPIRICAL LITERATURE

### Selection of Articles

Studies considered for review included large-scale and long-term staff training or management investigations in developmental disabilities published in the *Journal of Organizational Behavior Management* (JOBM), the *Journal of Applied Behavior Analysis* (JABA), and *Behavioral Interventions* (BI) (formerly *Behavioral Residential Treatment*). These three journals have traditionally published the largest number of OBM studies. However, additional studies were also identified through a search in Psych-Lit, using the key words "quality" and "mental retardation" or "quality" and "developmental disabilities." Studies selected for review were generally those that targeted staff performance at more than one level of position in the organization (e.g., supervisors and direct-care staff), addressed multiple staff performances (conducting assessments, implementing treatment programs, etc., thereby favoring possibilities of response generality), and were conducted over periods of six months or more. Applying these criteria necessitated making some subjective judgements and, as a result, a number of high quality studies that did not meet all three criteria were excluded, with the understanding, however, that they would be reviewed in other articles in this volume.

## Review of Empirical Literature

Ivancic, Reid, Iwata, Faw, and Page (1981) evaluated a supervision program designed to incorporate language training into care routines at a state facility for persons with mental retardation. A facility supervisor utilized prompts and feedback to train seven direct-care staff to use four language training behaviors. Increased language training behaviors were observed in six of the staff. Supervisory feedback was faded without decreases in staff performance during a maintenance condition. Questions raised by the authors included: how to establish the use of the supervisory procedure with direct line supervisors and, how to refine the language activities used to produce better consumer outcomes.

In another larger scale intervention, Coles and Blunden (1981) managed direct-care staff's instructional interactions with persons with mental retardation. Initially one direct care staff was assigned the jobs of providing residents with choices of materials, positive attention contingent on engagement, and providing prompts. After increased staff-consumer interactions and consumer engagement were observed, a second study was conducted that extended staff responsibilities for implementing the intervention across additional direct care staff, ward managers, the unit manager and the hospital administrator, and eventually the management team of the facility. Consumer engagement and staff-consumer contacts increased over the 33 weeks of intervention. Six weeks of follow-up data collected after a 30 week break in observations indicated the system had a lasting effect.

Christian (1983) described the five year development of the May Institute, a multifaceted residential program for autistic children. Although not a controlled study, many components of the developmental process involved embedded OBM projects. Many of these projects have been published and comprise an important body of research in OBM (e.g., Dyer, Schwartz, & Luce, 1984). (Also see Christian, 1996, for a review of OBM interventions in community programs.)

The goal of the organizational development program was to establish an administrative structure and set of policies and procedures to support wide-scale implementation and maintenance of empirically-validated behavioral treatment strategies. A comprehensive contract between the executive director and the agency's executive board supported work performance contracting that specified acceptable levels of quantity and quality of staff performance across all staff levels in the organization. Development of the organizational structure also included establishing formal rules for program operation, expert consultation and peer review, small spans of control for supervisors, and flexibility for program staff to work in teams on special projects.

Measurable improvements over the five year period included: increases in the operating budget, funding from grant sources, numbers of staff, staff salaries, publication of manuscripts and conference presentations, number of consumers discharged, number of consumers discharged into home environments and, decreases in staff turnover, the use of psychotropic medications and cost quotients. These and subsequent accomplishments (Luce, Christian, Anderson, Troy, & Larrson, 1992) provide a compelling illustration of what is possible when behavioral principles are applied systematically and in a coordinated manner across an entire human service agency.

Two features in particular should be emphasized. First, the executive director obtained an initial agreement by the Institute's board of directors that all treatment offered to consumers would be based on empirically-validated procedures. Second, changes in the organizational structure were based on the premise that clear and accountable management was absolutely necessary to provide effective behavioral programming services and protect the welfare of consumers served by the program.

In one OBM study conducted at the May Institute, Dyer et al. (1984) used posted definitions of functional materials and immediate written feedback to staff to increase the quality of planned staff-to-student activities in a residential setting. These authors noted a number of context variables that might have contributed to the results obtained. The study represented only one part of the multicomponent agency reorganization, 74.4% of the staff participating in the study held either a bachelor's or a master's degree, and, while no explicit contingencies were attached to the feedback, administrative staff supported the goals of the study.

In another setting, Parsons, Schepis, Reid, McCarn, and Green (1987) provided a large-scale, long-term OBM intervention. Thirty-nine educational staff working with 152 severely handicapped students across four schools received an intervention package provided by an experimenter who also served as the school's principal. The package included inservice training and self-management supported by prompts and verbal feedback from the principal. The intervention resulted in consistent increases in student engagement in functional tasks that were maintained over a two-year period.

Richman, Riordan, Reiss, Pyles, and Bailey (1988) investigated a self-monitoring procedure designed to increase work behavior and adherence to activity schedules among direct-care staff working in an ICF-MR. Staff recorded data daily on their own performances and provided the experimenter with the data. After three to four weeks of clear improvements in staff behavior, decrements in performance occurred among some staff. Supervisor feedback was then added with the desired results. This study also produced systematic change: Following the termination of the study the supervision procedures were reportedly continued for at least two years at the facility and adopted by 12 additional facilities in the state. Similar to previous studies of self-management by direct-care staff (Burg, Reid, & Lattimore, 1979; Burgio, Whitman, & Reid, 1983), the results of this study suggest that the supervisor-supported practice of having staff collect data (self-monitor) produced good results.

In another large-scale effort, Parsons, Cash, and Reid (1989) validated a behavioral observation system that yielded normative data on levels of involvement in active treatment among consumers in 22 residential living units across six state ICF-MR facilities. During observations used to establish normative levels, off task behavior occurred in 67% of observations while active treatment was recorded in only 19% of observations. Further, when active treatment was observed it was functional in only 56% of the observations.

In a second experiment in one of the six facilities, the authors implemented an intervention that structured time periods during which specific consumer activities were to occur, provided specific staff assignments, trained staff, and provided written feedback to individual staff at least weekly. Intervention data collected over 9 to 15 month periods reflected decreased consumer off-task behavior coupled with increased participation in active treatment.

Support for long-term maintenance of the intervention included weekly data-based reports on progress to a senior facility manager. The manager provided feedback to the next manager, who in turn provided feedback to living unit supervisors. The intervention in this study also provided a successful plan of correction for deficits in active treatment identified by Medicaid surveyors during the baseline condition. Parsons et al. (1989) noted that outcomes (i.e., active treatment) involving financial consequences for the facility validate the usefulness of OBM and could lead to greater opportunities for OBM interventions. They also concluded that the focus on consumer, rather than staff, behavior may have increased the acceptability of the intervention to staff and immediate supervisors, thereby supporting its long term application.

Reid, Parsons, Green, and Schepis (1991) examined the validity of what is perhaps the largest, longest standing, and most pervasive quality assurance program in the field of developmental disabilities, the Title XIX Medicaid ICF-MR reimbursement program. Noting that 49 of 50 states receive a total of $4.6 billion in federal reimbursement for services meeting the eligibility criteria for this program, the authors used direct observations of active treatment and nonadaptive consumer behavior to examine 60 units across 16 facilities in 11 states. Twelve of the units were not certified by Title XIX; the remaining 48 were. The average percentage of active treatment for the certified units was 17% compared with an average of 20% active treatment for non-certified units. The authors also compared data from direct observations of interaction activities and nonwork behavior of staff before, during and after an ICF-MR survey. The observations revealed a pattern of very low levels of interaction before the survey, high levels of interactions when the survey team was on site, followed by very low levels of interaction immediately following the departure of the survey team. In another facility under similar conditions, percentages of clients provided with leisure materials during leisure activity times were observed in pre-survey, survey, and post-survey three day periods on two units. Again, the availability of materials was much higher during the survey than during the pre- and post-survey observations.

Reid et al. (1991) concluded that there are problems with the methodology of the ICF-MR program and suggested that better observational definitions and measurement processes be developed and shared with providers. Providers could then be required to collect their own data on a much more frequent basis, using external surveyors to check for the quality of the data provided. Given reforms of the Title XIX program encouraging states to develop community programs for persons formerly or currently served in ICF-MR settings, and given the number of persons served in community programs without waiver funding, further research is also needed on how to support states in using direct observations of staff interaction, consumer engagement in functional behavior, and other important outcomes to evaluate the quality of community settings.

Selinske, Greer, and Seema (1991) investigated the application of an OBM program of student instruction, and behavioral staff supervision in a small school serving students with multiple handicaps. Supervisors, who had previously been trained at the doctoral level in behavior analysis and education, developed teacher training modules and trained teachers to mastery, observed teachers' performance, and provided feedback. A $1000 monetary bonus was provided to teachers for mastering 10 training modules by taking quizzes at an individualized pace.

Supervisors reliably logged those aspects of their own performance that resulted in permanent products resulting in verifiable data on many supervision activities. Following baseline, a teacher training condition and then a full treatment condition were sequentially introduced in a multiple baseline across groups of teachers over a two year period. The package produced mastery of training modules by teachers, increased supervisory activities and increased mastery of training objectives by 3 out of 4 groups of students.

Harchik, Sherman, Sheldon, and Strouse (1992) demonstrated the effectiveness of a long term consultation from a Ph.D.-level consultant to staff in a residential community program. After one year, consultation activities were continued by a middle manager (for six months) without graduate training in behavior analysis. This study supported the conclusion that behavioral staff management programs need to become a permanent part of the organization. However, differences between the consistency of positive results achieved by a highly experienced consultant and a middle manager suggested that some unidentified competencies may be needed for success in implementing structured behavioral consultation. In addition, multiple staff behaviors were targeted by consultation depending upon the staff's current performance and the needs of the adults in the group. Recommendations for future research included: developing methods of maintaining staff behavior change with less frequent consultation, addressing the conditions needed to maintain effective consultation, operationally defining and empirically validating technical skills and social skills needed by effective behavioral consults, and socially validating the importance of the consumer outcomes of these changes in staff training.

Pollack, Fleming, and Sulzer-Azaroff (1994) described an OBM case study with a 40-member psychology staff working in a large state run facility for persons with mental retardation. Bachelor's, master's and doctoral level staff were trained and supervised to set contextually relevant goals (e.g., conducting functional analyses, designing interventions, training staff). The staff members met biweekly in 10-member groups to discuss goal accomplishments, receive supervisory and peer feedback and praise, and set new goals. These "review and reinforcement" meetings had been conducted for approximately two years at the time the article was published, and close to 1800 professional goals had been accomplished. Although not a controlled investigation, this study demonstrated the feasibility of implementing and sustaining a large-scale intervention involving multiple levels of staff and performance goals.

In another study targeting supervisory performance, Parsons and Reid

(1995) assessed procedures for training residential supervisors to provide feedback to staff. Training in the content of the feedback (i.e., techniques for teaching consumers) established correct use of feedback procedures with only one out of seven supervisors. However, subsequent training in how to provide feedback resulted in consistent improvements in the quality of the supervisors' feedback to staff.

Using effective reduction programming procedures for individual consumers, Shore, Iwata, Vollmer, Lerman, and Zarcone (1995) investigated the effects of pyramidal training by supervisors following brief inservice training that was supplemented by videotaped modeling of program procedures. Pyramidal training from supervisors was arranged by providing supervisors practice in implementing the procedure with feedback to a criterion of 100% accuracy, providing instructions in how to train staff using a data sheet to assess staff performance and providing instructions to give feedback to staff twice weekly following training. Supervisors were then provided feedback by experimenters to verify that staff training occurred. The effects of each form of training were assessed in terms of both staff behavior and consumer responses. Pyramidal training by supervisors was highly effective in comparison with enhanced inservice training, which produced negligible improvements in staff or consumer behavior.

### Summary and Conclusions

In summary, there has been a relatively small but growing number of empirical studies reporting large-scale, long-term OBM interventions designed to improve quality in organizations serving persons with developmental disabilities. Two of the studies we reviewed (Coles & Blunden, 1981; Ivancic et al., 1981) and a large number of smaller scale studies not reviewed (cf. Sturmey, 1998) broke ground in demonstrating that behavioral approaches to supervision could be described and implemented in a controlled fashion. Subsequently, researchers have systematically replicated these procedures on a larger scale and over longer periods of time with excellent results (e.g., Parsons et al., 1989). Some of these studies documented a clear need to expand quality improvement efforts to include objective behavioral observations of active treatment (Reid et al., 1991), confirming the significance of earlier reports (Repp & Barton, 1980) on the failure of regulatory procedures to ensure adequate habilitation. In addition, large-scale quality improvement projects have been implemented in community group homes (Harchik et al., 1992), in private school systems (Selinske et al., 1991), and in private residential programs (Christian, 1983).

The findings that staff behavior in state-run facilities is highly reactive to external surveys (Reid et al., 1991) and that improvements in staff performance in group homes deteriorated when consultation was withdrawn (Harchik et al., 1992) suggest that *permanent* supports will be needed for the long-term maintenance of improvements in staff performance generated by behavioral contingencies. Consistent with this point, most of the larger-scale studies involved supervisors in providing performance feedback (combined with other antecedents and consequences) to line staff. For this strategy to work, supervisors must be taught specifically how to train (Fleming, Oliver, & Bolton, in press), supervise (Parsons & Reid, 1995), or consult (Harchik et al., 1992) with staff. Based on early evidence, the benefits of providing competency-based training to supervisors in these performance domains appear great, although such training is apt to be more costly than less effective alternatives (Shores et al., 1995). In calling for research on the variables affecting continued use of supervisory skills, Parsons and Reid (1995) have noted that it is unreasonable to expect supervisors to maintain newly acquired supervisory skills without an adequate organizational support system. Further, research on supervisors' use of feedback in another human service area suggests that supervisors may implement feedback only when doing so is systemically reinforced (Babcock, Sulzer-Azaroff, Sanderson, & Scibak, 1992). Consistent with this point, most of the large-scale studies have successfully arranged for such support (e.g., Coles & Blunden, 1981); or have provided it directly through one or more of the investigators serving in a position of authority within the organization (Parsons et al., 1987). The relatively limited number of large-scale and long-term studies in this review may be an indication of how difficult it is to generate and maintain such administrative support.

For behavior analysts, this may be a good reason for *carefully* joining the TQM movement. For example, consider that the TQM movement has captured interest as a vehicle for accomplishing the The Accreditation Council's (1993) Outcomes for Persons with Disabilities. If OBM procedures can be structured into large-scale, management-supported TQM initiatives for achieving such outcomes, the TQM system may provide significant opportunities ("teachable moments") for OBM practitioners to exert favorable influences on organizational practices. An example, noted previously, might be the opportunity to apply OBM procedures as a means of resolving ICF-MR deficiencies (Parsons et al., 1989). Other changes might include adoption of data analysis and interpretation skills used in OBM (see also the discussion on data analysis below), increased use of behavioral problem-analysis approaches (e.g., in team work), and perhaps even the "spontaneous" use of principles of behavior analysis among managers and other staff. Thus, OBM might offer quality managers a vehicle for better accomplishing TQM objectives in human service agencies. TQM, in turn, might provide a vehicle for gaining organizational control over reinforcement contingencies previously not available to behavior analysts.

In one other very important, and on-going, case study (Christian, 1983; Luce et al., 1992), a host of quality improvement objectives were achieved through the top-down development and implementation of a systems-wide effort to completely restructure an existing private residential organization. The results reflect multiple changes across all levels of the organization, led by a doctoral-level behavior analyst as the executive director of the organization. Comparing the scope and results of this study with the scope and results of most of the other studies we reviewed, one tentative conclusion can be offered: When it is possible to gain the full support needed to initiate a thorough OBM-based, structural transformation of the organization, this approach may result in improvement on a larger number of dimensions than would be accomplished with more incremental approaches.

This conclusion must be qualified, however, for two reasons. First, while most of the other studies involved supervisory support at one or more levels, it appears that with the possible exception of Selinske et al., (1991) none of the other studies was conducted in an environment in which the experimenter had the level of organizational support obtained in Christian (1983). Perhaps the other OBM approaches would have expanded from a smaller initial scope to address a growing number of performances within the organization had adequate support been available from the governing board of directors.

Second, future case studies at a level of Christian (1983) may reveal clues about the importance of a number of other intra- and extra-organizational context variables, only some of which may be identifiable from the existing literature. For example, the development of the May Institute was supported, in part, by grant funding and the development of university affiliations. In the development of another large-scale and long-term (exceeding 20 years) human service program, the Teaching Family Model of Group Homes for disturbed children, these same two factors also were identified as important (Fixsen & Blase, 1993). The continued expansion of the May Institute, to include a larger continuum of services and dissemination of literature on successful strategies (96 publications as of 1992), attests to the viability of this model (Luce et al., 1992). The development and publication of literature on comprehensive organizational development projects conducted by other behavior analysts, in other states, would extend the replicative history of such work and thus be more helpful to both consumers and program planners.

One important obstacle to developing an extensive published replicative history of very large-scale systems may be the differing mandates of research and service.

Fixsen and Blase (1993) noted that:

> Researchers devote their lives to looking for the necessary *and* sufficient conditions under which human behavior can be affected. Program developers devote their lives to looking for sufficient conditions under which treatment can be implemented to improve the lives of people. We hope that the *necessary* conditions will become apparent over time as more and more replications become functional. (p. 610)

The different requirements for research and service delivery may be an obstacle to the publication of large-scale quality improvement case studies if the editorial criteria for evaluating small-scale, highly-controlled, research are applied to manuscripts without appreciation of the scope and context of the study. For example, in large case studies, the scope of the phenomena investigated may necessarily limit the controls over threats to internal validity and thus require greater reliance upon interpretation instead of experimental control (see Malagodi, 1986, for a discussion of the need for radical behaviorism to include greater cultural analysis).

In assessing the extent to which the studies provided a system for accomplishing quality improvement it may be useful to consider the dictionary definition of the term "system." The Oxford English Dictionary (1971) provides 10 definitions of the word system. The most general of these includes, "a set or assemblage of things connected, associated, or interdependent, as to form a complex unity" (p. 3213). In the definition with the most relevant context, a system is "an organized scheme or plan of action, esp. one of a complex and *comprehensive* kind" (p. 3214, italics added). Thus, a complete quality improvement system would provide an organized, connected and interdependent set of efforts. These efforts would manage performance antecedents and contingencies with adequate complexity to identify and focus on quality improvement in *each* of the factors impacting upon important consumer outcomes.

Given this definition of a quality improvement system, it is no criticism of the growing number of the large-scale, long-term studies published to date to suggest that only one study published in the developmental disabilities literature (Christian, 1983) and one other model that we know about in the teaching group home literature (e.g., Fixsen & Blase, 1993) offer a fully developed system.

Rather than offering a number of examples of fully developed quality improvement systems, the current literature offers a large number of smaller-scale studies and a small number of larger-scale studies that have carefully examined, in a rather systematic fashion, effective approaches to behavioral supervision. They have also demonstrated, through systematic replication, that behavioral supervision is particularly effective for those performances related to "active treatment." Thus, system developers have a well established foundation from which to develop more comprehensive, iterative, and dynamic quality improvement systems. Such systems may be favorably influenced by a critical understanding of TQM.

## TOTAL QUALITY MANAGEMENT

Prior to the advent of TQM, traditional manufacturing approaches to quality assurance involved final inspections of products to identify failures to be rejected and possibly reworked. In human service organizations, a parallel approach exists in the form of annual Title XIX surveys. These surveys typically identify failures to meet certification standards on a yearly basis. Another source of failure in quality occurs in placements when consumers are sometimes rejected due to preventable organizational failures to meet individuals' needs. By contrast, in TQM environments, careful and ongoing management of molecular aspects of quality (using within-in-process outcome measures), combined with timely efforts to correct minor problems, appear to produce reasonably failure-free long-term outcomes. For example, in manufacturing tires, careful specification and monitoring of the critical product dimensions (e.g., the depth of tire tread to be cut), assessed during important steps in the process, permit timely interventions that virtually prevent defective tires from being manufactured (Brethower & Wittkopp, 1987). Further, product quality is defined in terms of key dimensions (e.g., performance, durability, cost, availability, ease of installation) relevant to the total satisfaction of the consumer.

Deming's approach to quality improvement systems (i.e., statistical process control or SPC) involves: (a) learning about quality characteristics critical to the customer; (b) defining product requirements in measurable terms; (c) training workers to use statistical tools to assess variability in repeated measures of mid-process results; (d) assigning sources of variability in process outputs to common versus special causes; and (e) arranging timely actions at the proper organizational level to resolve identified problems. This cycle, repeated in iterative fashion (e.g., the Shewart circle of plan, act, check, do, plan . . .) exemplifies the process of continuous quality improvement (Mawhinney, 1992).

Deming and others have expanded SPC to provide a management approach to altering organizational systems and cultures to focus pervasively on quality (see Saunders & Saunders, 1994, for a perspective on how Deming's management philosophy probably developed). TQM efforts involve workers in cross-functional teams designed to identify and eliminate problems in quality and to develop better ways of producing products and services that meet changing customer expectations. In TQM, quality becomes the primary mission of the organization, shared at all organizational levels. In human service organizations, TQM is frequently termed continuous quality improvement (CQI). For more detailed discussions of TQM, SPC, and their relationship to behavior analysis see Mawhinney (1986, 1987, 1992), Redmon (1992), Redmon and Dickinson (1987), and Brethower and Wittkopp (1987). For a detailed presentation of CQI which incorporates Gilbert's performance engineering approach in supported employment, see Albin (1992).

Cross functional employee teams are an important component of this approach. Employee empowerment in TQM involves making the design, measurement, management, and improvement of quality an ongoing daily part of each employee's job. This requires that employees learn to take measures, chart and interpret data, and in other ways contribute meaningfully to organizational efficiencies in their daily work. Time spent in off-line team activities that do not produce changes in daily tasks (i.e., talk about values without action) is viewed as a source of waste (Feigenbaum, 1991). Thus employees are involved in the team process as a means of solving problems that interfere with quality. In doing so, they come to improve their problem-identification and problem-solving skills, increasing the likelihood that they will contribute to improving an increasing number of organizational performance areas.

Successful TQM efforts in one company can have an influence on the market share of other companies. The development of TQM technology (including previous product designs, information management systems, just-in-time inventories, self-managed teams of skilled staff, and more efficient organizational structures) drives much steeper competition, creating a positively accelerating curve of customer expectation and competitor competence (Feigenbaum, 1991). Anyone needing a concrete example of this principle need only consider changes in the automotive industry during the last 30 years.

To foster America's response to the global competitive crisis produced by better quality practices in other parts of the world, Congress enacted the Malcolm Baldrige National Quality Improvement Act in 1987. As a national program for promoting TQM, the Malcolm Baldrige process provides awards for companies meeting stringent criteria reflecting accomplishments. A set of core values drives the Baldrige process (TQM). These include: (a) Customer-Driven Quality where quality is judged by the customer; (b) sensitivity to emerging customer and market requirements; (c) awareness of new developments in technology and rapid responses to customer and market requirements; (d) leadership that creates a customer orientation, clear and visible quality values and expectations, and reinforcement of those performances consistent with such values and expectations; and (e) creation of opportunities for growth and development throughout the work force.

Companies competing for the award must have a well-defined and well-executed approach to: (a) continuous improvement of products and services; (b) reducing errors, defects and waste; (c) improving responsiveness; and (d) improving productivity and effectiveness in using resources. Continuous quality improvement must involve regular cycles of planning, execution, and evaluation, preferably using quantitative measures, linking desired performance and internal operations. Companies are expected to create a close link (i.e., a "shared fate" relationship) between employees and customers, to reward individual and group quality performance, and to enhance employee satisfaction and other indicators of employee well-being. For a fuller description of these and other criteria of Malcolm Baldrige competition, see American Society for Quality Control (1993).

Returning to human services, we agree with Redmon (1992) that there are opportunities for applied behavior analysis in the total quality movement and that behavior analysis has a great deal to offer to TQM. This may be especially true in implementing TQM approaches to develop better services and supports for persons with developmental disabilities. In the remainder of this paper we will examine four topics which are important in implementing TQM (organizational systems analysis, measurement of consumer responses, teams, and data analysis), and offer a few recommendations for practice and some suggestions for research based on a selective reading of relevant OBM and behavior analysis literature.

## RECOMMENDATIONS FOR RESEARCH
## AND PRACTICE IN OBM

### Organizational Systems Analysis

The focus of OBM practitioners in developing quality improvement *systems* in organizations is very clearly shared by TQM. For example, descriptions of exemplary TQM practice typically describe methods for transforming an organization's processes such that they become systematically aligned with one another to achieve a well-conceived quality mission. Emphasis is placed on assessing and understanding the host of contextual variables operating inside and outside of the organization that might influence the accomplishment of mission-related objectives. The multitude of assessment tools used in TQM (e.g., Pareto diagrams, cause and effect diagrams) attest to its reputation as a systemic approach.

In a similar vein, most of the studies reviewed in this paper sought to impact more than a single organizational process and to endure as a permanent fixture in the organization's structure. In the case of Christian (1983), an entire organizational system was transformed and the processes developed were maintained. However, in contrast to what might be expected in TQM, very few OBM studies, even outside of human service organizations, have incorporated any type of data-based analysis of contextual variables. One exception is Green et al., 1991, who conducted, and later utilized, a scatter plot analysis to identify the best opportunities for direct care staff to perform instructional activities with consumers.

The importance of understanding the influence of, and interplay among, the various contextual variables that operate in a human service organization has been discussed in some depth in the OBM literature (e.g., Riley & Frederiksen, 1984; Sulzer-Azaroff, Pollack, & Fleming, 1992; Redmon & Wilk, 1991). Conceptual analyses of "metacontingencies" that might affect cultural practices, including organizational practices, have been conducted (e.g., Glenn, 1991; Redmon & Wilk, 1991; Mawhinney, 1992), as have conceptual analyses of the influence of rules in organizations (Malott, 1992; Agnew & Redmon, 1992). In addition, other systems-analysis approaches described in the OBM literature have been more specific in identifying classes of organizational variables and possible functional relationships that might exist between and among them. These approaches include Behavioral Systems Analysis (BSA) (Krapfl & Gasparotto, 1982), the Performance Engineering Matrix (PEM) (Gilbert, 1978), and the Total Performance System (TPS) (Brethower, 1982).

Despite this high level of conceptual activity there have been very few attempts in OBM to describe data-based methods (other than data generated from rating scales or other self-reports) for conducting systems analyses. Redmon and Wilk (1992) noted that references to the PEM or TPS were "virtually nonexistent" in the OBM literature, and that even guidelines for selecting performance targets were not provided. One exemplary component of some descriptions of TQM is the emphasis on collecting data to be used in problem analysis and intervention planning. In our view, OBM, with its otherwise rigorous methodology and conceptual underpinnings, holds tremendous potential for developing sophisticated, and functional, data-based analytic methods, perhaps parelleling the advances that have been made in functional analysis methodology with individuals exhibiting aberrant behavior.

In conclusion, we recommend the development of more systematic, data-based procedures for assessing influential contingencies in organizations. Tried and true analytic methods based on direct observation (e.g., narrative recording and sequence analysis, scatter plotting, analysis of conditional probabilities), review of permanent products (e.g., memos communicating organizational expectations, written feedback statements, goal statements), and, in some cases, behavioral interviews offer a start. Empirically testing hypotheses about organizational contingencies reflects a needed developmental step. This is an area in which behavior analysis can clearly benefit from the emphasis on these factors in TQM.

## Measurement of Consumer Responses

As discussed previously, one of the central goals of quality improvement systems is to meet the immediate and long-term needs of consumers. Accordingly, appropriate systems must be developed to ensure that valid and reliable data, reflecting individual consumer responses, are collected, and that these data are used in coordination with other measures of organizational performance. Applied behavior analysts have long been concerned about consumer satisfaction, particularly since Wolf noted the importance of "social validity" in applied behavior analysis in 1978 (Wolf, 1978). Wolf (1978) defined social validity as judgements made about three features of behavioral interventions: (a) the social significance and desirability of the established *goals*; (b) the social appropriateness, or acceptability, of the *procedures*; and (c) the social importance of the *effects*, or results, including unpredicted effects. A recent special issue of JABA (1991, Volume 2) revisited the issue of social validity, presenting multiple perspectives on the concept and its definition, current measurement approaches, and how assessment data are used.

Although a comprehensive review of the articles included in the JABA special issue is beyond the scope of this paper, several key points discussed in the papers have direct bearing on the assessment and use of consumer reaction data in developing OBM quality improvement systems in developmental disabilities. These points, discussed below, include: (a) the identification of consumers, (b) the purpose of social validity assessment, including the use of resulting data, (c) the relationship between consumer satisfaction measures and other more primary dependent measures (i.e., process and outcome measures affected directly by interventions), and (d) the development of more ecologically sensitive and systemically valid measurement systems.

We turn first to the identification of consumers. There are multiple consumers of services provided by organizations serving people with developmental disabilities, raising the question of whose reactions should be assessed and for what purpose? Clearly, clarity about the use of the term "consumer" is important. Schwartz and Baer (1991) noted the importance of assessing a representative sample (and the correct sample) of consumers when conducting a social validity assessment. They delineated four categories of consumers: (a) direct consumers [the "primary recipients of the program intervention" (p. 193)]; (b) indirect consumers (individuals who purchase a program for another individual, e.g., a direct consumer, or who are otherwise affected by the results of the program); (c) members of the immediate community ["people who interact with the direct and indirect consumers on a regular basis, usually through close proximity during work, school, or social situations" (pp. 193-194)]; and (d) members of the extended community ["people who probably do not know or interact with the direct and indirect consumers but who live in the same community" (p. 194)] (Schwartz & Baer, 1991).

According to Albin (1992), consumers, viewed from a quality improvement perspective, are individuals inside or outside of the organization who are the "next in line" recipients of organizational processes or products. For example, in human services, the most direct consumer of clinical interventions is the person receiving treatment. However, organizational staff who routinely implement interventions are also consumers; they are direct recipients of training and management procedures designed to ensure their clinical proficiency. Indeed, staff acceptance of and satisfaction with OBM interventions may be critical to the long-term viability of organizational interventions (refer to Parsons, 1998, in this issue, for a review of approaches to assessing staff acceptability of OBM procedures and staff morale).

Schwartz and Baer's (1991) categorization of consumers, combined with Albin's (1992) definition, which adds a focus on staff as critical consumers, are important from a behavioral systems analysis perspective. To the extent that such an analysis considers the full complement of individuals or groups within and outside of an organization who are recipients of the organization's processes, it may then be possible to better understand the various sources of influence over those processes (i.e., the larger natural community of stakeholders and contingency managers) in designing quality improvement interventions. The analysis would need to identify both active consumers and passive consumers (persons who do not currently exert influence, but who might under certain conditions) and attempt to understand their reactions (or potential reactions) to organizational change.

A second area of importance when considering assessment of consumer responses concerns the purpose of social validity assessment and the use of resulting data. In many OBM studies in developmental disabilities, staff participants are asked to complete a brief survey soon after the study is completed. The survey generally consists of a set of questions asking participants to rate the extent to which they felt they, and perhaps the consumers they served, benefited from the intervention. One of the implicit purposes of such an assessment is to evaluate whether the intervention might be adopted and supported by the organization as standard operating practice, certainly a worthy goal. Very few studies, however, have reported on how the results of the survey were used in subsequent program development, much less on how effective the revised interventions were. In addition, few authors reported conducting a survey prior to implementing the intervention. In fairness, OBM practitioners and researchers are often on safe ground in the sense that considerable empirical support exists for their selection of habilitative goals and procedures, e.g., when the target for staff training is to increase the use of proven procedures in order to improve skill acquisition, engagement, health conditions, and certain classes of maladaptive behavior among individuals with disabilities (Fleming & Reile, 1993). Still, there is a need for OBM researchers to report on the collection and integrated use of social validity data in subsequent research.

According to Schwartz and Baer (1991), the purpose of social validity assessment is to evaluate the viability or acceptability of the goals, procedures, personnel, results, and ease of implementation of a proposed or on-going intervention. Ideally, all relevant consumers of the program should be surveyed, not just the most direct program recipients. The resulting information may then be used to change components of the program, as needed, to enhance its viability for each group of stakeholders. It might pay for OBM researchers to reassess the nature and purpose of social validity assessment as it is now typically performed in applied research. This would undoubtedly result in the identification of a greater complement of consumers, as addressed above.

At this point, the reader might be concerned about the validity of survey data and might wonder, in considering how to develop data-driven quality improvement systems, about the relationship between social validity measures and other, more primary dependent measures, e.g., objective indices of learning or habilitation. Hawkins (1991) warned against blind acceptance of the notion that *typical* social validity measures are valid. While it is reassuring to learn that one has satisfied consumers, one must also be concerned about whether the services offered are valid in a larger sense. The example of facilitated "communication" may serve as an example. Some parents (indirect consumers) were highly satisfied with their childrens' new-found abilities to "communicate" with the help of a facilitator, only to later conclude that the facilitator's responses, not their child's, was really what was being communicated. Consumers will *stay* satisfied only when they are well served, and immediate satisfaction with a technically inadequate intervention is likely to eventually turn to significant dissatisfaction and well earned distrust.

Hawkins (1991) used the term "habilitative validity" to refer to the degree to which participating successfully in an intervention (i.e., individuals changing their behavior in the desired ways) enables an individual to maximize the benefits and minimize the costs experienced in their current and future natural environments. Accordingly, objective methods for validating goals, outcome, and proposed interventions include studying normative or exemplary performance, comparing current performance with objective indices of effective performance, performing experimental analyses of the effects of alternative performances that are candidates for intervention, and conducting experimental analyses of alternative interventions themselves.

To the extent that what the consumer desires conflicts with a professional's (or agency's) estimation of what is needed for effective habilitation, this approach may seem to be at odds with a notion commonly expressed in TQM literature that it is consumers' "wishes," first and foremost, that must be met. Finding a balance between achieving consumer satisfaction and desired habilitation is the challenge that professionals and consumers must work collaboratively towards. If both the short- and long-term effects of an intervention, viewed in terms of costs and benefits to the consumer (which needs to be well understood by the practitioner planning or providing the intervention), are considered by both parties, there should be a high likelihood that the consumer will be satisfied. Thus, assessing and responding to consumer satisfaction indices, and coordinating those actions with the provision of effective habilitation stands as the critical challenge in OBM. We suggest that OBM practitioners and researchers involved in the development of quality improvement systems might benefit from using a more comprehensive and sophisticated approach to the social validation of organizational goals, outcomes, and interventions than is currently practiced in OBM and suggested by most TQM approaches. Such an approach would involve multiple data collection methods, e.g., repeated consumer surveys in addition to more objective methods such as those suggested by Hawkins (1991), and multiple informants, e.g., the full range of consumers, other professional experts, etc.

Assessing social validity for a large range of consumers within an organizational system, including employees, is apt to be an extremely complex task, particularly when one begins to consider the important ways in which changes in one performance domain can contrast in an undesirable manner with performance in another (perhaps unmeasured) domain. Stated differently, the ecological validity of quality improvement data collection systems in general must be evaluated. Schwartz and Baer (1991) suggest that behavior analysts attempt to identify social *invalidity*, e.g., when some consumers are discontented with some aspects of a program but perhaps do not report it. Moreover, Willems (1974) has challenged behavior analysts to consider the ecological effects, planned and unplanned, of interventions. Clearly, this will be a daunting, but very important, task for future research and practice.

## Teams, TQM, and Behavior Analysis

As noted earlier, the establishment and effective use of cross-functional teams is a central component of TQM. Effective teams appear to be ones in which team members are selected for: (a) the diverse skills they have and perspectives they would likely bring to bear on quality-related problems; and (b) their ability to work cooperatively to define, analyze, and ultimately solve these problems. Unfortunately, little empirical research has been conducted on the determinants of selecting members and promoting effective team performance in quality improvement systems. Because there is a particular lack of research on teams in the OBM literature, we turn first to the more general industrial/organizational psychology literature.

Most current psychological theories of organizational team effectiveness propose that performance is best understood in terms of variables that enter into an input-process-output model. Broad classes of variables identified in current models include organizational and environmental variables (Knerr, Berger, & Popelka, 1980), task and individual variables (Hackman, 1987), and team variables (Cannon-Bowers, Tannenbaum, Salas, & Volpe, 1995). From these broad classes, reward systems, education and training opportunities, and information management are examples of input variables, all hypothesized to influence team effectiveness. Task variables (e.g., task complexity, task interdependence) and team member interactions exemplify process variables. And finally, the primary output variable in all of the theories is team productivity. Based on Steiner (1966), team productivity is hypothesized to be a function of individual productivity minus any process losses associated with ineffective task communication and task coordination among members.

Limited research on team effectiveness suggests that the performance requirements of team members should be derived from an analysis and specification of behaviors or skills required for team success (Cannon-Bowers et al., 1995). Once accomplished, instructional techniques considered to be most effective for training the different behaviors or skills can be determined (Cannon-Bowers et al., 1995).

In a recently-completed OBM study conducted with four-member military teams (tank crews), it was found that effective team coordination behaviors could be identified and operationalized (Oliver, 1995) and subsequently increased, through the systematic application of a behavioral training and performance feedback package (Oliver & Fleming, in preparation). This study has implications for the use of behavioral training procedures with teams in a variety of work settings in which the effective performance of highly interdependent team tasks is required. Clearly, cross-functional teams, established as a component of TQM interventions, seem to be a prime candidate for such an approach. The steps of analyzing team task characteristics (e.g., the need to coordinate communications) prior to training, operationalizing the behaviors required of *individual* team members, and, finally, selecting and implementing effective training procedures (e.g., instructions, demonstrations, repeated practice, and feedback) appear critical to this process.

In summary, although there has been little research on team effectiveness in OBM and in general, behavior analytic methods appear well suited to the development of research and practice on teams. In line with the purpose of this paper, research is needed to guide the development and to determine the effectiveness of cross-functional teams in quality improvement efforts in developmental disabilities. There is a particular need to study complex clinical decision-making in human service teams. Additionally, research in the areas of organizational context and team reward structures would further advance more traditional models of team effectiveness. Last, repeated process and outcome measurement of individual team members' behavior is needed in order to determine the specific type of competencies required for effective team performance.

## Data Analysis

Control charts and related statistical judgement aids have as their purpose the assignment of variability in time series data to common (random) versus assignable (nonrandom) causes. For example, a chart showing data on tire width at a cutting machine will seem to vary from the random pattern in a way that can be recognized using a number of simple rules for interpreting control chart data (see Mainstone & Levi, 1987, and Pfadt et al., 1992, for further discussion). Then the worker must do something to modify the process, either directly or by alerting managers of the existence of a specific problem.

In manufacturing environments, control charts have provided much of the basis for the development of TQM. However, as the above discussion indicates, there is much more to TQM than the use of control charts, per se. In this section we question whether, given the nature of human services (which involves carefully managing complex patterns of social behavior, rather than human-machines interactions), and the success of OBM techniques previously used without SPC (e.g., as reviewed above), OBM practitioners in DD might be well advised to omit or adopt only very cautiously the use of control charts traditionally associated with SPC.

The use of control charts and related statistical data analysis techniques has been advocated in OBM in general (Mawhinney, 1987; Notz, Boschman, & Tax, 1987); and in applied behavior analysis treatment programs in developmental disabilities services (Pfadt et al., 1992; Pfadt & Wheeler, 1995; Hantula, 1995). Perhaps the strongest argument for including control charts in a quality improvement system would be that they would contribute to the accomplishment of important systems-level, organizational outcomes. Hantula (1995) suggested that in human services the effects of professional training and specialization in different disciplines may cause members of interdisciplinary teams to have difficulty collaborating in team decisions, such as might be needed in developing and using a data system. This author suggested that control charts could be very helpful in establishing a common basis for planning integrated efforts using repeated measures data. However, it isn't clear how important it would be to use statistical decision rules to create greater unity in decision making. Perhaps the process of learning, as a team, how to define and carefully measure some aspects of quality would establish a common ground for making decisions. For example, team-collected data reflecting average active treatment levels of only 19%, as was found in Parsons et al. (1989), the data might spur team members to decide that an intervention was needed to promote active treatment. Further, average levels in any area below this norm might prompt special attention to the particular area. The premise that control charts would constructively contribute to this process is an interesting, but untested idea.

Another question about control charts is whether they would help to focus attention in the right places in DD organizations. While control charts would permit teams to intervene only when changes in the data indicated something unusual had happened, close attention to other factors, such as clinical priorities and the actual behavior-environment interactions, in addition to changes in baseline or treatment data might be more helpful. Hopkins (1995) made this point in critically reviewing the use of control charts in clinical data presented by Pfadt et al. (1995) and the interested reader might compare the priorities and perspectives offered by these two authors.

Finally, we believe that a much more basic point should be asked about the potential meaning of statistical control in data measuring performance within human service environments. Do we wish to assume, and teach managers and key executives, that statistical control in repeated measures means that random variability is inherent in the current design of the process? That might be helpful in person-machine interactions where non-systematic variations in the materials, the machine performance, and operator behavior interact to produce variation that is difficult to eliminate without systems-level changes (e.g., working with the supplier on increasing the consistency of materials purchased). Or, is most of the variability in performance within human service settings controlled by weak social variables operating in the environment? In the case of the person-machine-material interface, OBM interventions using social contingencies might (or might not) be appropriate if the process is within statistical control. However, in the case of human interactions controlled by weak social contingencies operating in complex and apparently non-systematic ways, one of the first things to do is probably to consider whether, and how, it would be helpful to the consumer to intervene to create better staff interaction patterns. If it would, and we can, then an intervention to prompt and shape staff behavior using supervisory contingencies might be an appropriate place to start almost regardless of the momentary level of variability in the data.

## CONCLUDING COMMENTS

A growing yet relatively small number of large-scale OBM studies have improved quality in DD organizations over extended periods of time. These incremental efforts and a complete organizational transformation of at least one human service agency demonstrate that behavioral supervision of important performances can be highly effective in DD organizations. Indeed, the literature includes a number of systematic replications of effective interventions in these settings. However, both the small number of large-scale, long term studies and the relatively limited number of performances targeted by these studies, suggest that expanded use of OBM as a pervasive technology for improving quality in DD organizations has yet to occur.

TQM efforts provide an approach to organizational change at a systemic level using cross-functional teams to identify and solve important problems related to quality defined as the satisfaction of consumers on all of the relevant dimensions. In considering the OBM literature in DD organizations on four components of TQM approaches, this paper concludes that in most areas, integrating OBM and TQM in DD organizations may expand the scope and effectiveness of both approaches. In some areas (organizational systems analysis) OBM may gain from TQM's practical *emphasis* on generating systems-level action. In other arenas, (the measurement of consumer responses, team effectiveness) combining OBM with TQM offers great potential and will require considerable additional research. Finally, in the area of data analysis, we argue that, given some clear differences between manufacturing and human service environments combined with the previous success of OBM interventions in human services environments, efforts to integrate OBM and TQM may be most productive if behavior analysts emphasize the use of well established aspects of the technology of OBM over control charts.

## REFERENCES

Agnew, J.L., & Redmon, W.K. (1992). Contingency specifying stimuli: The role of rules in organizational behavior management. *Journal of Organizational Behavior Management, 12(2)*, 67-76.

Albin, J.M. (1992). *Quality improvement in employment and other human services: Managing for quality through change.* Paul H. Brooks: Baltimore.

American Society for Quality Control (1993). *1993 Award Criteria: Malcolm Baldrige National Quality Award.* United States Department of Commerce, Technology Administration, National Institute of Standards and Technology.

Babcock, R.A., Sulzer-Azaroff, B., Sanderson, M., & Scibak, J. (1992). Increasing nurses' use of feedback to promote infection-control practices in a head-injury treatment center. *Journal of Applied Behavior Analysis, 25*, 621-627.

Brethower, D.M., & Wittkopp, C.J. (1987). Performance engineering: SPC and the total performance system. *Journal of Organizational Behavior Management, 9*, 83-103.

Burg, M.M., Reid, D.H., & Lattimore, J. (1979). Use of a self-recording and supervision program to change institutional staff behavior. *Journal of Applied Behavior Analysis, 16*, 37-54.

Burgio, L.D., Whitman, T.L., & Reid D.H. (1983). A participative management approach for improving direct care staff performance in an institutional setting. *Journal of Applied Behavior Analysis, 16*, 37-54.

Cannon-Bowers, J.A., Tannenbaum, S.I., Salas, E., & Volpe, C.E. (1995). Defining team competencies: Implications for training requirements and strategies. In R. Guzzo & E. Salas (Eds.), *Team effectiveness and decision making in organizations* (pp. 22-78). New York: Frontier Series Publications.

Christian, W.P. (1983). A case study in the programming and maintenance of institutional change. *Journal of Organizational Behavior Management, 5(3/4)*, 99-153.

Coles, E., & Blunden, R. (1981). Maintaining new procedures using feedback to staff, a hierarchical reporting system, and a multidisciplinary management group. *Journal of Organizational Behavior Management, 3(2)*, 19-33.

Dyer, K,. Schwartz, I.S., & Luce, S.C. (1984). A supervision program for increasing functional activities for severely handicapped students in a residential setting. *Journal of Applied Behavior Analysis, 17*, 249-259.

Fawcett, S.B. (1991). Some values guiding community research and action. *Journal of Applied Behavior Analysis, 24*, 621-639.

Feigenbaum, A.V. (1991). *Total Quality Control*. New York: McGraw Hill, Inc.

Fixsen, D.L., & Blase, K.A. (1993). Creating new realities: Program development and dissemination. *Journal of Applied Behavior Analysis, 26*, 597-613.

Fleming, R.K., Oliver, J.R., & Bolton, D. (1996). Training supervisors to train staff. *Journal of Organizational Behavior Management, 16(1)*, 3-25.

Fleming, R.K., & Reile, P.A. (1993). A descriptive analysis of client outcomes associated with staff interventions in developmental disabilities. *Behavioral Residential Treatment, 8(1)*, 29-43.

Geller, E.S., (1991) Is applied behavior analysis technological to a fault? *Journal of Applied Behavior Analysis, 24*, 401-406.

Geller. E.S. (1991). Where's the validity in social validity? *Journal of Applied Behavior Analysis, 24*, 179-249.

Gillat, A., & Sulzer-Azaroff, B. (1994). Promoting principals' managerial involvement in instructional improvement. *Journal of Applied Behavior Analysis, 27*, 115-129.

Greene, B.F., Willis, B.S., Levy, R., & Bailey, J.S. (1978). Measuring client gains from staff-implemented programs. *Journal of Applied Behavior Analysis, 11*, 395-412.

Hackman, J.R. (1987). The design of work teams. In J. Lorsch (Ed.), *Handbook of Organizational Behavior* (pp. 315-324). Englewood Cliffs: Prentice-Hall.

Hantula (1995). Disciplined decision making in an interdisciplinary environment: Some implications for clinical applications of statistical process control. *Journal of Applied Behavior Analysis, 28*, 371-377.

Harchik, A.E., Sherman, J.A., Sheldon, J.B., & Strouse, M.C. (1992). Ongoing consultation as a method of improving performance of staff members of a group home. *Journal of Applied Behavior Analysis, 25*, 599-610.

Hawkins (1991). Is social validity what we are interested in? Argument for a functional approach. *Journal of Applied Behavior Analysis, 24*, 205-213.

Hopkins, B.L. (1995). Applied behavior analysis and statistical process control? *Journal of Applied Behavior Analysis, 28*, 379-386.

Ivancic, M.T., Reid, D.H., Iwata, B.A., Faw, G.D., & Page, T.J. (1981). Evaluating a supervision program for developing and maintaining therapeutic staff-resident interactions during institutional care routines. *Journal of Applied Behavior Analysis, 14*, 95-107.

Knerr, C.M., Berger, D.C., & Popelka, B.A. (1980). *Sustaining Team Performance: A Systems Model*. Springfield, VA: Mellonics Systems Development.

Luce, S.C., Christian, W.P., Anderson, S.R., Troy, P.J., & Larrson, E.V. (1992). Development of a continuum of services for children and adults with autism and other severe behavior disorders. *Research in Developmental Disabilities, 12*, 9-25.

Malott, R.W. (1992). A theory of rule-governed behavior and organizational behavior management. *Journal of Organizational Behavior Management, 12(2)*, 45-65.

Mainstone, L.E., & Levi, A.S. (1987). Fundamentals of statistical process control. *Journal of Organizational Behavior Management, 9*(1), 5-21.

Malagodi, E.F. (1986). On radicalizing behavior analysis: A call for cultural analysis. *The Behavior Analyst, 9*, 1-17.

Mawhinney, T.C. (1986). OBM, SPC, and Theory D: A brief introduction. *Journal of Organizational Behavior Management, 8*, 89-105.

Mawhinney, T.C. (1987). Introduction: Organizational behavior management and statistical process control: Theory, technology, and research. *Journal of Organizational Behavior Management, 9(1)*, 1-4.

Mawhinney, T.C. (1992). Total quality management and organizational behavior management: An integration for continual improvement. *Journal of Applied Behavior Analysis, 25(3)*, 525-543.

Mawhinney, T.C. (1992). Evolution of organizational cultures as selection by consequences: The Gaia Hypothesis, metacontingencies, and organizational ecology. *Journal of Organizational Behavior Management, 12(2)*, 1-26.

Notz, W.W., Boschman, I., & Tax, S.T. (1987). Reinforcing punishment and extinguishing reward: On the folly of OBM without SPC. *Journal of Organizational Behavior Management, 9(1)*, 33-46.

Oliver, J.R. (1995, May). *Crew Coordination Training: The Role of Needs Analysis.* Paper presented at the twenty-first Annual Convention of the Association for Behavior Analysis: International, Washington, D.C.

Oxford English Dictionary (1971), *The compact edition of the Oxford English Dictionary, 2*, 3213-3213. Oxford University Press, Oxford England.

Parsons, M.B. (1998). *Journal of Organizational Behavior Management.*

Parsons, M.B., Cash, V.B., & Reid, D.H. (1989). Improving residential treatment services: Implementation and norm-referenced evaluation of a comprehensive management system. *Journal of Applied Behavior Analysis, 22*, 143-156.

Parsons, M.B. & Reid, D.H. (1995). Training residential supervisors to provide feedback for maintaining staff teaching skills with people who have severe disabilities. *Journal of Applied Behavior Analysis, 28*, 317-322.

Parsons, M.B., Schepis, M., Reid, D.H., McCarn, J.E., & Green, C.W. (1987). Expanding the impact of behavioral staff management: A large-scale, long term application in schools serving severely handicapped students. *Journal of Applied Behavior Analysis, 20*, 139-150.

Pfadt, A., Cohen, I.L., Sudhalter, V., Romanczyk, R.G., & Wheeler, D.J. (1992). Applying statistical process control to clinical data: An illustration. *Journal of Applied Behavior Analysis, 25*, 551-560.

Pfadt, A., & Wheeler, D.J. (1995). Using statistical process control to make data-based clinical decisions. *Journal of Applied Behavior Analysis, 28*, 349-370.

Pollack, M.J., Fleming, R.K., & Sulzer-Azaroff, B. (1994). Enhancing professional performance through organizational change. *Behavioral Interventions, 9(1)*, 27-42.

Redmon, W.K. (1992). Opportunities for applied behavior analysis in the total quality movement. *Journal of Applied Behavior Analysis, 25*, 545-550.

Redmon, W.K., & Wilk, L.A. (1991). Organizational behavior management in the United States: Public sector organizations. In P.A. Lamal (Ed.), *Behavioral*

*Analysis of Societies and Cultural Practices.* New York: Hemisphere Publishing Corporation.

Redmon, W.K., & Dickinson, A.M. (1987). A comparative analysis of Statistical Process Control, Theory D, and behavior analytic approaches to quality control. *Journal of Organizational Behavior Management, 9(1)*, 47-65.

Reid, D.H., Parsons, M.B., & Green, C.W. (1989). *Staff management in human services.* Springfield, Illinois: Charles C. Thomas.

Reid, D.H., Parsons, M.B., McCarn, J.E., Green, C.W., Phillips, J.F., & Schepis, M.M. (1985). Providing a more appropriate education for severely handicapped persons: Increasing and validating functional classroom tasks. *Journal of Applied Behavior Analysis, 18*, 289-301.

Reid, D.H., Parsons, M.B., Green, C.W., & Shepis, M.M. (1991). Evaluation of components of residential treatment by Medicaid ICF-MR survey: A validity assessment. *Journal of Applied Behavior Analysis, 24*, 293-304.

Repp, A.C., & Barton, L.E. (1980). Naturalistic observations of institutionalized retarded persons: A comparison of licensure decisions and behavioral observations. *Journal of Applied Behavior Analysis, 13*, 333-341.

Richman, G.S., Riordan, M.R., Reiss, M.L., Pyles, D.A.M., & Bailey, J.S. (1988). The effects of self-monitoring and supervisor feedback on staff performance in a residential setting. *Journal of Applied Behavior Analysis, 21*, 401-409.

Riley, A.W., & Frederiksen, L.W. (1984). Organizational behavior management in human service settings: Problems and prospects. *Journal of Organizational Behavior Management, 6*, 3-16.

Saunders, R.R., & Saunders, J.L. (1994). W. Edwards Deming, quality analysis, and total behavior management. *The Behavior Analyst, 17(1)*, 115-125.

Schwartz, I.S., & Baer, D. M. (1991). Social validity assessments: Is current practice state of the art? *Journal of Applied Behavior Analysis, 24*, 189-204.

Selinske, J.E., Greer, D., R., & Seema, L. (1991) A functional analysis of the comprehensive application of behavior analysis to schooling. *Journal of Applied Behavior Analysis, 24*, 107-117.

Shore, B.A., Iwata, B.A., Vollmer, T.R., Lerman, D.C., & Zarcone, J.R. (1995). Pyramidal training in the extension of treatment for severe behavior disorders. *Journal of Applied Behavior Analysis, 28*, 323-332.

Steiner, I.D. (1966). Models for inferring relationships between group size and potential group productivity. *Behavioral Science, 11*, 273-283.

Sturmey, P. (1998). *Journal of Organizational Behavior Management.*

The Accreditation Council (1993). *Outcome based performance measures.* Landover, MD.

Willems (1974). Behavioral technology and behavioral ecology. *Journal of Applied Behavior Analysis, 7*, 151-165.

# SECTION 2:
# APPLICATIONS AND CONTRIBUTIONS OF ORGANIZATIONAL BEHAVIOR MANAGEMENT IN SPECIAL SUPPORT SETTINGS

## Organizational Behavior Management in Large Residential Organizations: Moving from Institutional to Client-Centered Care

Martin T. Ivancic
William J. Helsel

**SUMMARY.** This paper suggests larger residential organizations have a unique contribution to offer people with developmental dis-

Martin T. Ivancic is affiliated with Western Carolina Center, Morganton, NC. William J. Helsel is affiliated with Allegheny General Hospital, Department of Psychiatry, Pittsburgh, PA.

Correspondence concerning this article should be addressed to Martin T. Ivancic, Western Carolina Center, 300 Enola Road, Morganton, NC 28655 (INTERNET: martin@wcc.dhr.state.nc.us).

[Haworth co-indexing entry note]: "Organizational Behavior Management in Large Residential Organizations: Moving from Institutional to Client-Centered Care." Ivancic, Martin T., and William J. Helsel. Co-published simultaneously in *Journal of Organizational Behavior Management* (The Haworth Press, Inc.) Vol. 18, No. 2/3, 1998, pp. 61-82; and: *Organizational Behavior Management and Developmental Disabilities Services: Accomplishments and Future Directions* (ed: Dennis H. Reid) The Haworth Press, Inc., 1998, pp. 61-82. Single or multiple copies of this article are available for a fee from The Haworth Document Delivery Service [1-800-342-9678, 9:00 a.m. - 5:00 p.m. (EST). E-mail address: getinfo@haworthpressinc.com].

abilities who require managed environments or research solutions to their living needs. It claims no organization should be managed to be "institutional" regardless of its size, but that size alone is not the sole determinant of self-motivated service delivery. A move toward adoption of short-term goals geared to the immediate benefit of people with developmental disabilities and away from more traditional yearly developmental goals is cited as the key to keeping residential organizations focused on the consumers of their service. However, in order to utilize the unique advantages of larger organizations, these organizations will need to solve the problems created by having large groups of people living in close proximity and managed by multiple managers. A brief review of six general steps to organizational management is offered as the outline for effective management. An emphasis is placed on a need for immediate supervisors to have upper level administrator support to carry out these six managerial steps and to receive continuous feedback from consumers and staff on the acceptability of this service. In addition, because of their large size, history of abuses, and/or lack of consumer self-advocacy, larger residential organizations appear to have a special responsibility to show how they emphasize the concerns of their consumers over the institutional concerns of organizational survival. *[Article copies available for a fee from The Haworth Document Delivery Service: 1-800-342-9678. E-mail address: getinfo@haworthpressinc.com]*

Undertaking the task of suggesting applications and contributions of the field of Organizational Behavior Management (OBM) to institutions assumes there is something appropriate about caring for people with developmental disabilities in large residential organizations (i.e., 16 or more people). Many professionals believe institutions represent all that is wrong with residential care services for people with developmental disabilities (e.g., Bradley, Ashbaugh, & Blaney, 1994). Even the word "institutionalism" as defined by at least one dictionary indicates institutions emphasize their own organizational concerns at the expense of other factors (Webster's New Collegiate Dictionary, 1973). In the service for people with developmental disabilities there is a particular concern about a tendency toward organization-centered residential care because many persons with developmental disabilities are unable to redress compromised concerns themselves. In fact, lawsuits which required large residential facilities to downsize in order to correct abusive "warehousing" of people with developmental disabilities (e.g., *Wyatt v. Stickney,* 1972; *Halderman v. Pennhurst,* 1977) appeared to accurately represent the self-serving connotation of the word "institution." The effect of these lawsuits has been significant for reducing the emphasis large organizations place on their own concerns while increasing the emphasis on the concerns of the individuals they serve.

The court decisions against large residential organizations have resulted in implementation of regulatory monitoring (*New York State ARC v. Carey,* 1975; U.S. HEW, 1974) and a distribution of available residential monies away from large facilities into smaller community facilities (cf. Wagner, Long, Reynolds, & Taylor, 1995). Most importantly, there has been a general ideologic trend away from the concerns of the service organization and toward centering on the individual and the relatively immediate supports s/he needs for living the best life possible (Bradley et al., 1994). Even the definition of developmental disabilities has been challenged to describe the support an individual needs to live with the skills s/he now has rather than describing that individual in terms of the deficits s/he must overcome to be considered normal (Luckasson et al., 1992).

## A CONTINUING NEED FOR OBM RESEARCH IN LARGE RESIDENTIAL ORGANIZATIONS

### Client Research

More than two-thirds of the OBM research in developmental disabilities over the past 20 years was conducted in larger facilities and, generally, for individuals with severe or profound disabilities (Fleming & Reile, 1993). The reason so much of the research for people with developmental disabilities is conducted at larger facilities has not been explained. Given that larger, public residential facilities are not able to select the characteristics of their residents, a possible explanation for why so much research occurs in these organizations is that the problems their residents present require the careful analysis provided by OBM research. As downsizing into the community proceeds, people who remain in larger residential organizations are likely to present problems requiring even more research solutions. An additional problem shared by all human service agencies has to do with how to measure quality living environments (Jenks, 1995). In the future, institutions may be one of the few organizations with enough resources to identify life quality for an individual whose current preferred living conditions are unknown.

### Administrative Research

While larger facilities are refocusing on the individual resident, their large numbers have always demanded that service be provided in the most efficient, cost-effective manner possible (Jenks, 1995, p. 39). Previous research has focused on staff behaviors resulting in large expenditures of funds including absenteeism (Boudreau, Christian, & Thibadeau, 1993) and accidents/injuries (Alavosius & Sulzer-Azaroff, 1986, 1990). Recycling is also a management activity that has saved money for organizations (Austin, Hatfield, Grindle, & Bailey, 1993; Brothers, Krantz, & McClannahan, 1994).

## Research Alternatives

It is important to note that a call for problem solving research such as suggested in this article does not imply it is appropriate for organizations to wait for the research that solves their organizational problems. Many research careers could be made and gone without ever approximating the knowledge needed to successfully run a human service organization. Unfortunately, specific research answers are available for very few organizational problems. It is suggested that every organization identify practices with strong potential for effectiveness even though there is no specific knowledge available for how the proposed solution might remediate particular problems.

Although specific research solutions may never be available for all organizational problems, there are some ways of researching management practices that may be more efficient than others. One research technique suggested is to systematically replicate successful procedures by including some but not all of their relevant conditions and observing for similar results (Neef, 1995). If procedures can be successfully replicated with different types of population/staff, different numbers of population/staff, and/or decreased management effort, knowledge of procedure application can be extended without analyzing each of the components individually (cf. Sturmey, 1995). Achievement Place has attempted to replicate not just specific procedures, but a whole program of services by carefully describing the most relevant components and then systematically adding or deleting components as information from monitoring indicated success or failure in their overall mission (Wolf, Kirigin, Fixsen, Blase, & Braukman, 1995). As data are generated on more and less effective practices, successful programs can be maintained and unsuccessful programs can be efficiently identified and removed. With the OBM approach of documenting how the organization impacts on the behavior of an individual, OBM research is in a unique position for helping to determine whether procedures in larger organizations implemented on behalf of an individual with developmental disabilities actually serve to improve that person's welfare.

# A CRITICAL REFOCUS
## FOR LARGE RESIDENTIAL ORGANIZATIONS

Evaluating the effectiveness of an organization begins by identifying the goals of the organization. Changing the goals of large residential organizations to emphasize immediate client concerns means revising the yearly evaluation goals on which the current system is based (e.g., ICF-MR regulations). Yearly goals were generated from organizational missions that focused on maximizing developmental growth (Felce & Perry, 1995, p. 53). Coincidentally, it is likely that yearly goals fit into organizational plans which could be tracked more easily by administrators and regulatory agencies than goals requiring a more immediate response for people with developmental disabilities. In contrast, the move toward focusing on more short-term goals most likely began because focusing on yearly progress appeared to lack consumer responsiveness (Emerson, 1985). The evolution of habilitative focus from longer term goals to shorter term goals may create important questions for larger residential organizations to address such as: (a) can short-term goals be tracked so that service providers can be held accountable and, (b) are consumers satisfied with a system that targets their shorter term, more immediate concerns?

Many human service agencies now recognize the need for continuous routine feedback on goal progress from their consumers (Wolf et al., 1995) and staff (Reid & Whitman, 1983). This feedback appears to be essential not only to the survival of their programs (see Corrigan et al., 1995) but to the survival of their organizations as well (see Wolf et al.). Such reciprocal feedback systems assume a program is more likely to survive if unacceptable practices are revealed through solicited feedback. Solicited feedback can take the form of systematic monitoring and/or interviews prior to the discovery of problems rather than receiving unsolicited feedback in the form of consumer or staff problems and/or complaints.

There is currently little research providing direction for obtaining client feedback on program acceptability. The more disabled the individual the more difficult soliciting feedback is likely to be (Sigelman et al., 1981); it is these severely disabled individuals who represent the majority of people living in large residential organizations. Organizational systems may be able to proactively help management by identifying which client preferences are most related to client welfare (see Parsons & Reid, 1993, for a discussion) and which issues can be addressed most efficiently after they have been identified as problems through post-active systems such as suggestion boxes, hot lines, incident reports, etc. Careful selection of goals that consumers or their significant others prefer and prioritize should go a long way to avoiding unsolicited feedback that could threaten the survival of the organization.

## Goal Selection Issues in Large Residential Organizations

Moving to systems that address shorter term goals for more immediate concerns of people is not likely to be an easy change for organizations comfortable with addressing yearly goals of developmental progress. Some assessments are being developed that attempt to identify moments in the day when preference (i.e., choice of events or materials) may be an important consideration (Kearney, Durand, & Mindell, 1995). However, the challenge of providing for a quality life is compounded for individuals who cannot readily report their preferences (Green et al., 1988; Green, Reid, Canipe, & Gardner, 1991) or for individuals who prefer conditions that result in harm to others (Mace, Page, Ivancic, & O'Brien, 1986) or themselves (Iwata et al., 1994).

When an individual cannot reveal personal preferences or his/her preferences violate social standards, goals that follow general social norms are usually selected by others (Felce & Perry, 1995). Nevertheless, it is important for the organization to remain focused on the individual's indicated preference regardless of the normative standard. For example, there are individuals who show high rates of aggressive, self-injurious, or stereotypic behavior despite being in environments considered to be normal or ideal (Felce & Repp, 1992). Clearly, some individuals require specialized conditions to live without harm.

Although the specification of extensive, standardized guidelines and regulatory reviews to enforce these guidelines have likely spared many individuals with developmental disabilities from abusive and inhumane living conditions, concern remains that regulated and unregulated environments are not easily distinguishable and not necessarily enriching (Repp & Barton, 1980; Reid, Parsons, Green, & Schepis, 1991). Although by definition all people with developmental disabilities need support, most disabled people likely need only minimal help to live as they desire. An interesting proposition for the efficient provision of acceptable living conditions for individuals who are developmentally disabled has to do with providing support for the life they already have rather than attempting to "give" a person a life in a residential organization (Risley, 1995). When residential service is based on maintaining current living conditions instead of creating all new living conditions, organizations can expect less effort at meeting predetermined standards of residential care and more effort educating their consumers and their families about what they can do to enrich their immediate lives (Dunst, Trivette, & Deal, 1994). However, it is not clear in this supportive type of program what standards an agency would have to meet in order to receive funds.

Providing a life to an individual who is unable to indicate what s/he desires or who is unable to live safely or comfortably without a systematically designed life is likely to require personnel to provide specific support. Parsons, McCarn, and Reid (1993) found providing a choice procedure at mealtime for severely disabled individuals was clearly more difficult for the staff to accomplish than simply feeding a meal. Procedures such as these, which are used to provide preferred conditions for severely disabled individuals, will likely require extensive evaluation and management.

Large residential organizations should be designing environments for individuals who can experience increased quality in their lives only through formally managed environments. In order to produce these environments the goals chosen must focus on improving an individual's relatively immediate conditions rather than attempting to provide a standardized quality life to everyone in the same organization.

### The Most Difficult Case

An individual's ability to identify preferences is a tremendous help in determining that person's life quality. Although some individuals with profound multiple disabilities (Reid, Phillips, & Green, 1991) can express their preferences with some assistive technology (Reid & Hurlbut, 1977; Wacker, Berg, Wiggins, Muldoon, & Cavanaugh, 1985), others cannot identify their preferences (Ivancic & Bailey, 1996). A person who is unable to indicate preferences presents management problems to an organization which, heretofore, have not been addressed.

For people who show difficulty identifying their preferences, the only first hand information available is effortful preference assessments (e.g., Pace, Ivancic, Edwards, Iwata, & Page, 1985; Green et al., 1988) or "happiness" assessments (e.g., Green & Reid, 1996). Other indices may be important for these difficult-to-train individuals such as tracking behaviors which anticipate discomfort (Gunsett, Mulick, Fernald, & Martin, 1989; Peine et al., 1995), indicate readiness to learn (Green, Gardner, Canipe, & Reid, 1994) or relate to more biologically controlled states (Guess et al., 1990). Even after preferences have been identified for these individuals, no procedures have been offered that would help identify the most optimal schedule to offer opportunities to respond for these preferred conditions. Individuals with unknown preferences will likely receive programming resulting in contact of stimulation noncontingently with periodic opportunities to respond contingently or show preference for this stimulation.

Optimal schedules for the delivery of enriching stimulation for these individuals is not yet available because a specific description of how staff should provide opportunities for these difficult-to-serve individuals does not exist. However, it seems unlikely that people who do not reliably indicate their preferences should be left with no stimulation.

## Managing Shorter Term Goals in Large Residential Organizations

After a goal has been identified, an organization needs some way for its participants to achieve the objective. Reid, Parsons, and Schepis (1990) describe six general steps to effective organizational management including (1) specifying staff behaviors, (2) determining a structure (i.e., with whom, when, where, and with what) for the specified staff performance, (3) instructing staff on the first two steps, (4) monitoring that performance, (5) providing feedback or support for that performance, and (6) repeating steps 4 and 5 until proficiency occurs or a change is required. Research on these six steps has been reviewed with an emphasis on promoting procedure acceptability and on using the management of an immediate supervisor to carry out these critical steps (Reid, Parsons, & Green, 1989). The rest of this paper will selectively highlight the importance of each of these components for conducting the precise procedures necessary to effectively and efficiently manage treatments provided by staff in large residential organizations.

*Specification.* Here, it is assumed that an acceptable client goal has been described specifically enough to be objectively observed. The concern with specification in this section is whether or not the procedure is described in sufficient detail to achieve this goal (step 1). Procedures resulting in permanent products (e.g., Repp & Deitz, 1979) or procedures with obvious benefits for staff such as safety (e.g., Alavosius & Sulzer-Azaroff, 1990) appear to maintain with less supervision than some other resident activities such as academic or leisure programs (see Arco, 1993, p. 123 for a discussion). However, there may be very few client-centered goals for the severely disabled which produce permanent products or natural benefits for staff. It is likely that goals alone, no matter how well specified or accepted, will rarely be enough to provide effective management (Doerner, Miltenberger, & Bakken, 1989).

*Programming for structure.* Structure concerns the conditions under which the goal for the consumer should occur such as specifying which staff should do what activity with which clients, where, when, and with what materials (step 2). It is likely such structure could be enhanced by combining people with similar needs in these groups (e.g., high interaction vs. low interaction; high noise vs. low noise; high stimulation vs. low stimulation; high medical vs. low medical). For example, it is known that interaction goals for residents are generally more effectively addressed if provided by staff assigned to small groups (Harris, Veit, Allen, & Chinsky, 1974; Repp, Felce, & de Kock, 1987) in enclosed areas (Dalgleish & Matthews, 1980). There is no reason to believe the opposite conditions might be preferred by other people. Although within-room analysis has been recommended by several researchers (Sturmey & Crisp, 1989; Repp et al., 1987), there is little work showing what variables might be important and what individuals might be most appropriate to participate.

It is recognized that combining people in groups violates the suggestion of some who believe that total opportunity can only be accomplished by mainstreaming individuals into the normal settings (Sands & Kozleski, 1994). All residential organizations have a responsibility to offer age-appropriate, normal living conditions (Dyer, Schwartz, & Luce, 1984; Reid et al., 1985), but if an individual shows improved behavior under less common, more specialized conditions, arranging the latter conditions should be an important feature to the provision of quality living for that individual. It could be that some groups of individuals with developmental disabilities would prefer conditions that are generally different from their peers such as environments with multiple/intense or minimal sensory stimulation, interactions, spaces, people present, and/or demands.

*Providing structure.* There has been considerable research lately on how staff learn about the structure of the specific procedures for which they are responsible. Informing staff of the structure of their day amounts to providing staff with a schedule of where, when, and with what they are to provide service (step 3) (e.g., Burch, Reiss, & Bailey, 1987). One effective technique has been to let staff know what they are supposed to do by providing them with a daily written schedule of their duties (Richmond, Riordan, Reiss, Pyles, & Bailey, 1988). Such a process appears to allow staff to control their own behavior instead of being dependent on supervisor directives (Burg, Reid, & Lattimore, 1979). However, public posting of the schedule also gives a supervisor the opportunity to prompt and/or reinforce compliance with the goals of the organization. There is some evidence that publicly set goals are more effective than privately set goals (Hayes et al., 1985). In any case, strong leadership on setting staff goals appears to be an important characteristic of an effective organization.

*Effective supervision.* The staff leadership role most recognized in residential organizations is the position of the immediate supervisor. Recently, attempts have been made to identify the essential steps required for a supervisor to train their staff how to teach clients (Parsons & Reid, 1995). Characteristics and responsibilities of the immediate supervisor are being recognized as critical components in effective residential organizations

(Reid & Parsons, 1995, Chapter 8). This appears to be particularly true in larger residential organizations where there may be multiple persons of "authority" to influence staff behavior.

Favell and Phillips (1986) suggest that immediate supervisors require a single line of authority to manage client goals. In addition, they suggest that this supervisor be a person who has authority to orchestrate services for a manageable number of clients (e.g., 15) and who is held accountable for service quality to those clients. Creating a job with so many important job responsibilities could prove over-burdensome. It is important to recognize such a supervisor does not have to actually carry out every aspect of an individual's program. However, s/he or must have primary responsibility for all staff and work closely with those staff who directly provide service (Reid et al., 1989).

One method of relieving the training and management tasks of a supervisor is a procedure described as reciprocal peer management or pyramidal management. Pyramidal management efforts have effectively demonstrated that one person can learn a procedure and then teach another person who the supervisor would have had to teach (Demchak & Browder, 1990; Fleming & Sulzer-Azaroff, 1992; Shore, Iwata, Vollmer, Lerman, & Zarcone, 1995). However, the cost-effectiveness of the pyramidal management system has yet to be proven. The train-the-trainer model (Green & Reid, 1994) has been demonstrated to be an efficient way to keep staff proficient at caring for switch activated equipment, but it is unclear how long such a program could continue without a management procedure to maintain it. However, any procedure that reduces supervision responsibilities to allow more time for the immediate supervisor to be with staff in a residential organization may have significant benefits for all relevant participants.

While procedures to relieve the immediate supervisor of certain duties may be very important to encourage, supervisors who figure out how to spend considerable time with their staff are typically more effective than other supervisors (Komaki, 1986). Reid and Parsons (1995) suggest staff will be more motivated with an immediate supervisor who spends time every day helping out and intervening on their behalf. In addition, they suggest a reliable, daily occasion for supervisor presence likely generates a more rapid response to staff concerns and avoids problems leading to decreased morale. Avoiding staff "burn out" and increasing staff morale is an important challenge for every supervisor (Lawson & O'Brien, 1994).

*Monitoring.* Although the challenges of monitoring are cited as one of the major reasons why most management procedures are not more successful (Hyrdowy & Martin, 1994), no goal can be considered achieved unless there is some observation that the activity was completed (step 4). Most residential management programs now measure outcomes and behavioral engagement as their programmatic indicators (Fleming & Reile, 1993). Outcome measures are typically taken in lieu of measuring the processes that produced them. Measuring outcomes, as opposed to the procedures to produce those outcomes, is more efficient and more directly related to client concern. Nevertheless, if a terminal outcome is not achieved in a timely fashion and that outcome is a product of a precise procedure, periodic measurement of process will be an unavoidable task for an effective management system.

Although the numerous programs showing the measurement of individual program outcomes leave no doubt OBM behaviors can be reliably defined and measured (Reid et al., 1989), the information from individual programs is likely to represent only a small part of the measures that are needed to run a large organization effectively and efficiently. There has been significant attention to comprehensive monitoring of business organizations (Brethower, 1982; Mawhinney, 1992). However, there is a conspicuous absence of reports on comprehensive observation systems for care of persons with developmental disabilities.

Nevertheless, the only way to hold an organization responsible for its activities is to measure its procedures and their outcomes (i.e., quality assurance) so that decisions for future programming can be based on progress or lack of progress on these goals (i.e., program development).

Failure to meet business goals (i.e., profit) threatens the survival of the organization, but this does not appear to be the case in the management of most programs for the developmentally disabled. Particularly for programs following models designed to maximize developmental progress, if managers are unable to meet their goals they simply choose other goals that are also identified as deficits for the resident but more likely to show progress. The futility of this process is most clearly seen for individuals who year after year fail to meet their individualized goals designed to maximize their clients' potentials (cf. Bailey, 1981). It is also clear, but maybe not so easily seen, with a higher skilled individual who makes progress year after year on goals meeting developmental deficits but not necessarily contacting any significant improvements in their immediate quality of life. It is possible if goals chosen for organizations serving the developmentally delayed were made more immediate and consumer oriented that monitoring systems to assess progress on these objectives would become more meaningful.

Although accurate and reliable measurement systems can be produced without any relation to the importance of the goals for the residential consumer, even the most useful observation systems require some effort. As such, there will always be concern about reducing the effort of monitoring systems. Some organizations have moved to computerized scoring (Paggeot, Kvale, Mace, & Sharkey, 1988; Repp, Karsh, Van Acker, Felce, & Harman, 1989) and others to automated documents (Habilitative Software, Inc., 1995). In a recent attempt to eliminate the time and effort involved in graphing and charting, Hyrdowy and Martin (1994) successfully demonstrated a management procedure using a photocopied checklist which was used for feedback at the moment of observation.

There is not only concern over how much effort monitoring systems take, but also over the reactivity generated by having one person observe another person's behavior (Hagen, Craighead, & Paul, 1975; Methot, Williams, Cummings, & Bradshaw, 1996). Reactivity to being observed may realistically represent the single most problematic issue in staff managed performance because decisions made from observation data are generated from a condition (observers present) that is very different from the situation during which most work occurs (observers not present). For example, if monitoring from a yearly regulatory review reports a program to look good, it is possible that program looked good only once a year—when the reviewer was present. Surprise reviews have been mentioned as a method to enhance quality programs (Bible & Sneed, 1976). Although surprise reviews may increase an organization's motivation to regulate itself, particularly if the reviewer belongs to a regulatory agency, surprise reviews may still not address care that is given to residents when no observer is present. In addition, there is some indication unannounced observations may not necessarily improve services (Reid et al., 1991). Others have used covert monitoring to validate treatment delivery outside of direct observation (Ivancic, Reid, Iwata, Faw, & Page, 1981), but covert observation systems may generate distrust from staff and encourage staff to circumvent the observation process. Most researchers suggest reactivity from being monitored can be controlled by increasing the frequency of observations (Fleming & Sulzer-Azaroff, 1992) and a reliable, data observation system with similarities between supervisors and regulatory agency items (Reid et al., 1991).

No program should shy from systematic monitoring because of the potentially false reactions generated from staff. At the very least, reactive measures indicate that staff can produce the appropriate response under at least one condition (i.e., being observed). Another potential solution to the concern over what staff do when they are not being directly observed has received attention with investigation of self-management procedures (Burg et al., 1979). The self-management concept implies a staff person can formulate rules about how to respond and later follow those rules without requiring any external prompt or instruction. It is implied that future performance of behavior consistent with a rule is attributed to self-reinforcement (see Malott, 1992, for a theoretical description). The theory is attractive because it provides a reason for how so much staff behavior occurs outside of any formal supervision activity. Others have questioned whether self-negative rather than self-positive reinforcement is a better explanation for the self-management phenomena. Self-negative reinforcement for following a rule would occur when the motivation for the behavior is avoiding disapproval from others by following rules that are well publicized to co-workers (Hayes et al., 1985). Whatever the actual process is, the concept of staff self-management should be taken seriously because in such a system it would be possible for staff to formulate rules and self-support following rules that are not desired by the organization (Hastings & Remington, 1994).

There are methodological problems with getting information about the private events people tell themselves. In any case, the need for staff to know what they should do and whether or not doing it is correct will still require some agent from the organization to explicitly provide this information to staff (i.e., effectively managing steps 1 to 3).

*Feedback.* Feedback or support for management goals (step 5) is described as one of the most important components to any multifaceted management system (Reid et al., 1989, p. 93; Wilson, Reid, & Korabek-Pinkowski, 1991). Much has been written about the importance of feedback in institutions because the natural reinforcers of client progress for organizations serving the most disabled individuals are absent (Coles & Blunden, 1982). While some argue the only meaningful incentive for residential work is monetary (Arco, 1993) and graduated pay ladders in residential organizations have been described and implemented (Wagner, 1995; Wolf et al., 1995, p. 50), large public organizations may have problems providing contingent monetary increases due to restrictions imposed by union contracts or civil service related guidelines (Green & Reid, 1991). However, it is likely that day-to-day incentives for job behavior may increase when staff focus on shorter term goals with more immediate benefits to their clients.

*Recycling.* The quality of a program is likely determined by observing how well a program meets its goals. Changing procedures so that goals are met in a timely fashion (step 6) is how such a program develops. The final step to achieving effective management might be called "recycling" because it requires a manager to keep returning to steps 1 through 5 until the goal for an individual is achieved. It could be that one of the major problems in large residential organizations is that changes such as this cannot be made without significant effort on the part of the service agent who requires input at several different levels of the organization before the change can be made. If organizations are to be made effective, supervisors responsible for providing habilitation must have information showing the accountability of programs, the skill to read this information, the ability to decide when changes need to be made, and the authority to make those changes.

## *Why Effective OBM Procedures in Large Residential Organizations Have Not Been More Widely Adopted*

With some notable exceptions such as the Achievement Places, Father Flannagan's Boys' Home in Boys Town (Fixsen & Blase, 1993; Wolf et al., 1995), and Princeton Child Development Institute (McClannahan & Krantz, 1993), there are very few reported attempts to systematically improve the management of residential services utilizing OBM procedures on a large scale. There are no reported attempts using procedures with documented effectiveness to systematically run large-scale public residential organizations for people with developmental disabilities. In addition, there are only a few examples of single OBM programs with proven effectiveness being adopted throughout an organization (e.g., Parsons et al., 1993; Parsons, Schepis, Reid, McCarn & Green, 1987). Even though there is little doubt that large-scale applications would be any less effective than the numerous effective smaller-scale demonstration projects reported (see Reid et al., 1989, for examples), there is an obvious lack of large scale application (see Hopkins, 1995, for a discussion). Although the lack of large scale OBM applications in human service may discourage some interested practitioners, the notable success of the few large scale attempts available exemplifies the continued evolution rather than a failed application of this powerful approach to human service delivery.

One can only speculate regarding reasons for the lack of support for systematic management procedures in large residential organizations for people with developmental disabilities. It is possible systematic procedures have not been necessary in the past because large residential organizations have maintained their funding without them. With the adoption of shorter term goals in these organizations, program effectiveness may become a more important issue which could make the accountability provided in OBM procedures more attractive. In any case, management procedures in large organizations attempting more client-centered care for the most severely disabled individuals will likely remain very important because these people provide very little natural support (i.e., feedback) for identifying and determining the acceptability of their treatments. Hopefully, regulatory agencies will help administrators by requiring accountability for these shorter term goals.

Another view suggests there is no particular problem with the slow adoption of OBM procedures. Rather, there is evidence that evolution toward more systematic management continues to progress and simply has not yet gained wide-spread acceptance. Recently, OBM projects of increasingly large size have been reported. Parsons, Cash, and Reid (1989) implemented a systematic procedure to increase appropriate and normalized engagement for 20 residential units across four states. This procedure has been refined and replicated at least twice (Parsons & Reid, 1993; Sturmey, 1995). Methot et al. (1996) showed increases in appropriate behavior throughout levels of an organization (supervisors-to-staff; staff-to-clients; client behavior) after supervisor training which included their manager.

The most pessimistic view of the future of OBM in large residential organizations suggests that the practice of focusing on long-term developmental goals has shaped organizational behavior which interferes with providing more immediate consumer needs. Specifically, without the need to make relatively immediate progress, it is possible that institutional organizational behavior was shaped and strengthened to respond *about* their consumers (i.e., verbal behavior) to such an extent that they now cannot adapt to responding to the actual behavior of their consumers. Incidentally, there is no reason to believe that smaller, more community-based residential organizations which are not designed to address immediate consumer needs will be any more responsive to their consumers than organizations which have focused on long-term developmental goals. Upper level adminstrators in all residential agencies should be monitoring the progress toward the immediate concerns of their consumers and insuring the supervisors responsible for managing this progress are adequately supported.

## CONCLUSION

The change from organization-centered to client-centered services will not be efficiently completed without support for the management work of immediate supervisors (i.e., the six steps). Given most larger residential organizations are funded by public monies under a current state of fiscal conservatism, efficiency is something that will be expected of public service organizations. Fortunately for those practicing OBM, the procedures they offer are ideal for residential organizations to efficiently develop, evaluate, and provide the special conditions necessary to provide the best possible life for people. However, the most efficient, effective service may still require significant effort to provide. The OBM approach will likely be successful wherever it is implemented, but it will be of particular value in institutional residential agencies where the problems addressed are likely to be the most difficult to solve. Hopefully, successful solutions generated from institutional investigations will continue to be exportable to other living environments which promote the greatest possible normality and inclusion with other people.

## REFERENCES

Alavosius, M. P., & Sulzer-Azaroff, B. (1986). The effects of performance feedback on the safety of client lifting and transfer. *Journal of Applied Behavior Analysis, 19,* 261-267.

Alavosius, M. P., & Sulzer-Azaroff, B. (1990). Acquisition and maintenance of health-care routines as a function of feedback density. *Journal of Applied Behavior Analysis, 23,* 151-162.

Arco, L. (1993). A case for researching performance pay in human service management. *Journal of Organizational Behavior Management, 14,* 117-136.

Austin, J., Hatfield, D. B., Grindle, A. C., & Bailey, J. S. (1993). Increasing recycling in office environments: The effects of specific, informative cues. *Journal of Applied Behavior Analysis, 26,* 247-253.

Bailey, J. S. (1981). Wanted: A rational search for the limiting conditions of habilitation. *Analysis and Intervention in Developmental Disabilities, 1,* 45-52.

Bible, G. H., & Sneed, T. J. (1976). Some effects of an accreditation survey on program completion at a state institution. *Mental Retardation, 14,* 14-15.

Boudreau, C. A., Christian, W. P., & Thibadeau, S. F. (1993). Reducing absenteeism in a human service setting: A low cost alternative. *Journal of Organizational Behavior Management, 13* (2), 37-50.

Bradley, V. J., Ashbaugh, J. W., & Blaney, B. C. (1994). *Creating individual supports for people with developmental disabilities: A mandate for change at many levels.* Baltimore: Paul H. Brookes Publishing Company.

Brethower, D. M. (1982). Total performance systems. In R. M. O'Brien, A. M. Dickinson, & M. Rosow (Eds.). *Industrial behavior modification* (pp. 350-369). New York: Pergamon Press.

Brothers, K. J., Krantz, P. J., & McClannahan, L. E. (1994). Office recycling: A function of container proximity. *Journal of Applied Behavior Analysis, 27,* 153-160.

Burch, M. R., Reiss, M. L., & Bailey, J. S. (1987). A competency-based "hands-on" training package for direct care staff. *Journal of The Association for Persons with Severe Handicaps, 12,* 67-71.

Burg, M. M., Reid, D. H., & Lattimore, J. (1979). Use of a self-recording and supervision program to change institutional staff behavior. *Journal of Applied Behavior Analysis, 12,* 363-375.

Coles, E., & Blunden, R. (1982). Maintaining new procedures using feedback to staff, a hierarchical reporting system, and a multidisciplinary management group. *Journal of Organizational Behavior Management, 3,* 19-33.

Corrigan, P., Holmes, E. P., Luchins, D., Basit, A., Delaney, E., Gleason, W., Buican, B., & McCracken, S. (1995). The effects of interactive staff training on staff programming and patient aggression in a psychiatric inpatient ward. *Be-*

*havioral Interventions: Theory & Practice in Residential & Community-Based Programs, 10,* 17-32.

Dalgleish, M., & Matthews, R. (1980). Some effects of environmental design on the quality of day care for severely mentally handicapped adults. *British Journal of Mental Subnormality, 26,* 94-102.

Demchak, M., & Browder, D. M. (1990). An evaluation of the pyramid model of staff training in group homes for adults with severe handicaps. *Education and Training in Mental Retardation, 25,* 150-163.

Doerner, M., Miltenberger, R. G., & Bakken, J. (1989). The effects of staff self-management on positive social interactions in a group home setting. *Behavioral Residential Treatment, 4,* 313-330.

Dunst, C. J., Trivette, C. M., & Deal, A. G. (1994). *Supporting and strengthening families: Methods, strategies, and practices,* Volume 1. Cambridge, MA: Brookline.

Dyer, K., Schwartz, I. S., & Luce, S. C. (1984). A supervision program for increasing functional activities for severely handicapped students in a residential setting. *Journal of Applied Behavior Analysis, 17,* 249-259.

Emerson, E. B. (1985). Evaluating the impact of deinstitutionalization on the lives of mentally retarded people. *American Journal of Mental Deficiency, 90,* 277-288.

Favell, J.E., & Phillips, J. E. (1986). Behavior therapy in residential programs for retarded persons (pp. 260-279). In F. J. Fuoco & W. P. Christian (Eds.), *Behavior analysis and therapy in residential programs.* NY: Van Nostrand Reinhold Company.

Felce, D., & Perry, J. (1995). Quality of life: Its definition and measurement. *Research in Developmental Disabilities, 16,* 51-74.

Felce, D., & Repp, A. (1992). The behavioral and social ecology of community houses. *Research in Developmental Disabilities, 13,* 27-42.

Fixsen, D. L., & Blase, K. A. (1993). Creating new realities: Program development and dissemination. *Journal of Applied Behavior Analysis, 26,* 597-615.

Fleming, R. K., & Reile, P. A. (1993). A descriptive analysis of client outcomes associated with staff interventions in developmental disabilities. *Behavioral Residential Treatment, 8,* 29-43.

Fleming, R., & Sulzer-Azaroff, B. (1992). Reciprocal peer management: Improving staff instruction in a vocational training program. *Journal of Applied Behavior Analysis, 25,* 611-620.

Green, C. W., Gardner, S. M., Canipe, V. S., & Reid, D. H. (1994). Analyzing alertness among people with profound multiple disabilities: Implications for provision of training. *Journal of Applied Behavior Analysis, 27,* 519-531.

Green, C. W., & Reid, D. H. (1991). Reinforcing staff performance in residential facilities: A survey of common managerial practices. *Mental Retardation, 29,* 195-200.

Green, C. W., & Reid, D. H. (1994). A comprehensive evaluation of a train-the-trainers model for training education staff to assemble adaptive switches. *Journal of Developmental and Physical Disabilities, 6,* 219-238.

Green, C. W., & Reid, D. H. (1996). Defining, validating, and increasing indices of happiness among people with profound multiple disabilities. *Journal of Applied Behavior Analysis, 29,* 67-78.

Green, C. W., Reid, D. H., Canipe, V. S., & Gardner, S. M. (1991). A comprehensive evaluation of reinforcer identification processes for persons with profound multiple handicaps. *Journal of Applied Behavior Analysis, 24,* 537-552.

Green, C. W., Reid, D. H., White, L. K., Halford, R. C., Brittain, D. P., & Gardner, S. M. (1988). Identifying reinforcers for persons with profound handicaps: Staff opinion versus systematic assessment of preferences. *Journal of Applied Behavior, 21,* 31-43.

Guess, D., Siegel-Causey, E., Roberts, S., Rues, J., Thompson, B., & Siegel-Causey, D. (1990). Assessment and analysis of behavior state and related variables among students with profoundly handicapping conditions. *Journal of the Association for Persons with Severe Handicaps, 15,* 211-230.

Gunsett, R. P., Mulick, J. A., Fernald, W. B., & Martin, J. L. (1989). Brief report: Indications for medical screening prior to behavioral programming for severely and profoundly mentally retarded clients. *Journal of Autism and Developmental Disorders, 19,* 167-172.

Habilitative Software, Inc. (1995). Habilitative Documentation System (HDS), 204 N. Sterling Street, Morganton, NC 28655.

Hagen, R. L., Craighead, W. E., & Paul, G. L. (1975). Staff reactivity to evaluative behavioral observations. *Behavior Therapy, 6,* 201-205.

Halderman v. Pennhurst, 446 F. Supp. 1295 (E.D. Pa. 1977).

Harris, J. M., Veit, S. W., Allen, G. J., & Chinsky, J. M. (1974). Aide-resident ratio and ward population density as mediators of social interaction. *American Journal of Mental Deficiency, 79,* 320-326.

Hastings, R. P., & Remington, B. (1994). Rules of engagement: Toward an analysis of staff responses to challenging behavior. *Research In Developmental Disabilities, 15,* 279-298.

Hayes, S. C., Rosenfarb, I., Wulfert, E., Munt, E. D., Korn, Z., & Zettle, R. D. (1985). Self-reinforcement effects: An Artifact of social standard setting. *Journal of Applied Behavior Analysis, 18,* 201-214.

Hopkins, B. L. (1995). An introduction to developing, maintaining, and improving large-scale data-based programming. *Journal of Organizational Behavior Management, 15,* 7-10.

Hyrdowy, E. R., & Martin, G. L. (1994). A practical staff management package for use in a training program for persons with developmental disabilities. *Behavior Modification, 18,* 66-88.

Ivancic, M. T. & Bailey, J. S. (1996). Current limits to reinforcer identification for some persons with profound multiple disabilities. *Research In Developmental Disabilities, 17,* 77-92.

Ivancic, M. T., Reid, D. H., Iwata, B. A., Faw, G. D., & Page, T. J. (1981). Evaluating a supervision program for developing and maintaining therapeutic staff-resident interactions during institutional care routines. *Journal of Applied Behavior Analysis, 14,* 95-107.

Iwata, B. A., Pace, G. M., Dorsey, M. F., Zarcone, J. R., Vollmer, T. R., Smith, R. G., Rodgers, T. A., Lerman, D. C., Shore, B. A., Mazaleski, J. L., Goh, H.,

Cowdery, G. E., Kalsher, M. J., McCosh, K. C., & Willis, K. D. (1994). The functions of self-injurious behavior: An experimental-epidemiological analysis. *Journal of Applied Behavior Analysis, 27,* 215-240.

Jenks, S. F. (1995). Measuring quality of care under Medicare and Medicaid. *Health Care Financing Review, 16,* 39-54.

Kearney, C. A., Durand, J. M., & Mindell, J. A. (1995). Choice assessment in residential settings. *Journal of Developmental and Physical Disabilities, 7,* 203-213.

Komaki, J. L. (1986). Toward effective supervision: An operant analysis and comparison of managers at work. *Journal of Applied Psychology, 71,* 270-279.

Lawson, D. A., & O'Brien, R. M. (1994). Behavioral and self-report measures of staff burnout in developmental disabilities. *Journal of Organizational Behavior Management, 14,* 37-54.

Luckasson, R., Coulter, D. L., Poloway, E. A., Reiss, S., Schalock, R. L., Snell, M. E., Spitalnik, D. H., & Stark, J. A. (1992). *Mental retardation: Definition, classification, and systems of supports,* (9th ed.). Washington, DC: American Association on Mental Retardation.

Mace, C. F., Page, T. J., Ivancic, M. T., & O'Brien, S. (1986). Analysis of environmental determinants of aggression and disruption in mentally retarded children. *Applied Research in Mental Retardation, 7,* 203-221.

Malott, R. W. (1992). A theory of rule-governed behavior and organizational behavior management. *Journal of Organizational Behavior Management, 13,* 45-65.

Mawhinney, T. C. (1992). Total quality management and organizational behavior management: An integration for continued improvement. *Journal of Applied Behavior Analysis, 25,* 525-543.

McClannahan, L. E., & Krantz, P. J. (1993). On systems analysis in autism intervention programs. *Journal of Applied Behavior Analysis, 26,* 589-596.

Methot, L. L., Williams, W. L., Cummings, A., & Bradshaw, B. (1996). Measuring the effects of a manager-supervisor training program through the generalized performance of managers, supervisors, front-line staff and clients in a human service setting. *Journal of Organizational Behavior Management, 16,* 3-34.

Neef, N. A. (1995). Research on training trainers in program implementation: An introduction and future directions. *Journal of Applied Behavior Analysis, 28,* 297-299.

NY State ARC v. Carey, 393 F. Supp. 715, at 718-19 (E.D.N.Y. 1975).

Pace, G. M., Ivancic, M. T., Edwards, G. L., Iwata, B. A., & Page, T. J. (1985). Assessment of stimulus preference and reinforcement value with profoundly retarded individuals. *Journal of Applied Behavior Analysis, 18,* 249-255.

Paggeot, B., Kvale, S., Mace, F. C., & Sharkey, R. W. (1988). Some merits and limitations of hand-held computers for data collection. *Journal of Applied Behavior Analysis, 21,* 429.

Parsons, M. B., Cash, V. B., & Reid, D. H. (1989). Improving residential treatment services: Implementation and norm-referenced evaluation of a comprehensive management system. *Journal of Applied Behavior Analysis, 22,* 143-156.

Parsons, M. B., McCarn, J. E., & Reid, D. H. (1993). Evaluating and increasing meal-related choices throughout a service setting for people with severe disabilities. *Journal of The Association for Persons with Severe Handicaps, 18,* 253-260.

Parsons, M. B., & Reid, D. H. (1993). Evaluating and improving residential treatment during group leisure situations: A program replication and refinement. *Research In Developmental Disabilities, 14,* 67-85.

Parsons, M. B., & Reid, D. H. (1995). Training residential supervisors to provide feedback for maintaining staff teaching skills with people who have severe disabilities. *Journal of Applied Behavior Analysis, 28,* 317-322.

Parsons, M. B., Schepis, M. M., Reid, D. H., McCarn, J. E., & Green, C. W. (1987). Expanding the impact of behavioral staff management: A large-scale, long-term application in schools serving severely handicapped students. *Journal of Applied Behavior Analysis, 20,* 139-150.

Peine, H. A., Darvish, R., Adams, K., Blakelock, H., Jensen, W., & Osborne, J. G. (1995). Medical problems, maladaptive behaviors, and the developmentally disabled. *Behavioral Interventions: Theory & Practice in Residential & Community-Based Programs, 10,* 149-159.

Reid, D. H., & Hurlbut, B., (1977). Teaching nonvocal communication skills to multihandicapped retarded adults. *Journal of Applied Behavior Analysis, 10,* 591-603.

Reid, D. H., & Parsons, M. B. (1995). *Motivating human service staff: Supervisory strategies for maximizing work effort and work enjoyment.* Morganton, NC 28680: Habilitative Management Consultants, P.O. Box 2295.

Reid, D. H., Parsons, M. B., & Green, C. W. (1989). *Staff management in human services.* Springfield, IL: Charles C. Thomas.

Reid, D. H., Parsons, M. B., Green, C. W., & Schepis, M. M. (1991). Evaluation of components of residential treatment by Medicaid ICF-MR surveys: A validity assessment. *Journal of Applied Behavior Analysis, 24,* 293-304.

Reid, D. H., Parsons, M. B., McCarn, J. E., Green, C. W., Phillips, J. F., & Schepis, M. M. (1985). Providing more appropriate education for severely handicapped persons: Increasing and validating functional classroom tasks. *Journal of Applied Behavior Analysis, 18,* 289-301.

Reid, D. H., Parsons, M. B., & Schepis, M. M. (1990). Management practices that affect the relative utility of aversive and nonaversive procedures. In S. L. Harris & J. S. Handleman (Eds.) *Aversive and nonaversive interventions: Controlling life threatening behavior by the developmentally disabled* (pp. 144-162). New York: Springer Publishing.

Reid, D. H., Phillips, J. F., & Green, C. W. (1991). Teaching persons with profound multiple handicaps: A review of the effects of behavioral research. *Journal of Applied Behavior Analysis, 24,* 319-336.

Reid, D. H., & Whitman, T. L. (1983). Behavioral staff management in institutions: A critical review of effectiveness and acceptability. *Analysis and Intervention in Developmental Disabilities, 3,* 131-149.

Repp, A. C. & Barton, L. E. (1980). Naturalistic observations of institutionalized retarded persons: A comparison of licensure decisions and behavioral observations. *Journal of Applied Behavior Analysis, 13,* 333-341.

Repp, A. C., & Deitz, D. E. D. (1979). Improving administrative-related staff behaviors at a state institution. *Mental Retardation, 17*, 185-192.

Repp, A. C., Felce, D., & de Kock, U. (1987). Observational studies of staff working with mentally retarded persons: A review. *Research in Developmental Disabilities, 8*, 331-350.

Repp, A. C., Karsh, K. G., Van Acker, R., Felce, D., & Harman, M. (1989). A computer-based system for collecting and analyzing observational data. *Journal of Special Education Technology, 9*, 207-217.

Richman, G. S., Riordan, M. R., Reiss, M. L., Pyles, D.A. M., & Bailey, J. S. (1988). The effects of self-monitoring and supervisor feedback on staff performance in a residential setting. *Journal of Applied Behavior Analysis, 21*, 401-408.

Risley, T. (1995). Get a Life! Positive behavioral intervention for challenging behavior through life arrangement and life coaching. In L. K. Koegel, R. L. Koegel, & G. Dunlap (Eds.), *Community, school, family, and social inclusion through positive behavioral support.* Baltimore: Brookes Publishing Company.

Sands, D. J., & Kozleski, E. B. (1994). Quality of life difference between adults with and without disabilities. *Education and Training in Mental Retardation, 29*, 90-101.

Shore, B. A., Iwata, B. A., Vollmer, T. R., Lerman, D. C., & Zarcone, J. R. (1995). Pyramidal staff training in the extension of treatment for severe behavior disorders. *Journal of Applied Behavior Analysis, 28*, 323-332.

Sigelman, C. K., Schoenrock, C. J., Winer, J. L., Spanhel, C. L., Hromas, S. G., Martin, P. W., Budd, C., & Bensberg, G. J. (1981). Issues in interviewing mentally retarded persons: An empirical study. In R. H. Brunininks, C. E. Meyers, B. B. Sigford, & Lakin, K. C. (Eds.) *Deinstitutionalization and community adjustment of mentally retarded persons* (pp. 114-129). Washington, DC: American Association on Mental Deficiency.

Sturmey, P. (1995). Evaluating and improving residential treatment during group leisure situations: Independent replication. *Behavioral Interventions: Theory & Practice in Residential & Community-Based Programs, 10*, 59-67.

Sturmey, P., & Crisp, A. G. (1989). Organising staff to provide individual teaching in a group: A critical review of room management and related procedures. *Australia and New Zealand Journal of Developmental Disabilities, 15*, 172-142.

U. S. Department of Health, Education, & Welfare (1974). Standards for Intermediate Care Facilities in Institutions for the Mentally Retarded. *Federal Register, 39*, 2220.

Wagner, B. R., Long, D. F., Reynolds, M. L., & Taylor, J. R. (1995). Voluntary transformation from an institutionally-based to a community-based service system. *Mental Retardation, 33*, 312-321.

Wacker, D. P., Berg, W. K., Wiggins, B., Muldoon, M., & Cavanaugh, J. (1985). Evaluation of reinforcer preferences for profoundly handicapped students. *Journal of Applied Behavior Analysis, 18*, 173-178.

Wagner, B. R. (1995, August). *Evergreen Presbyterian Ministries Merit Pay Plan.*

Paper presentation at 8th Annual Conference of Developmental Disabilities Services Managers, Inc., Memphis, TN.

Webster's New Collegiate Dictionary. (1973). Springfield, MA: G. & C. Merriam Company.

Wilson, P. G., Reid, D. H., & Korabek-Pinkowski, C. A. (1991). Analysis of public verbal feedback as a staff management procedure. *Behavior Residential Treatment, 6*, 263-277.

Wolf, M. M., Kirigin, K. A., Fixsen, D. L., Blase, K. A., & Braukmann, C. J. (1995). The Teaching Family Model: A case study in data-based program development and refinement (and dragon wrestling). *Journal of Organizational Behavior Management, 15*, 11-68.

Wyatt v. Stickney, 344 F. Supp. 387, at 390 (M.D. Ala. 1972).

# Supporting People
## with Developmental Disabilities
## in Their Homes in the Community:
## The Role
## of Organizational Behavior Management

Alan E. Harchik
Arthur R. Campbell

**SUMMARY.** In this article, the authors review the current status of organizational behavior management research and application in community living settings for people with developmental disabilities. Ten studies were identified. Findings and limitations in the amount and breadth of research conducted to date were noted. Correlational and descriptive studies were also reviewed briefly. Suggestions for best practices and future research are provided. *[Article copies available for a fee from The Haworth Document Delivery Service: 1-800-342-9678. E-mail address: getinfo@haworthpressinc.com]*

Today, more people with developmental disabilities are living in the community than ever before while the number of individuals living in large

Alan E. Harchik and Arthur R. Campbell are both affiliated with The May Institute, Inc., West Springfield, MA.

Correspondence concerning this article should be addressed to Alan E. Harchik, The May Institute, Inc., 1111 Elm Street, #2, West Springfield, MA 01089.

The authors thank Walter P. Christian for comments on an earlier draft of this article.

[Haworth co-indexing entry note]: "Supporting People with Developmental Disabilities in Their Homes in the Community: The Role of Organizational Behavior Management." Harchik, Alan E., and Arthur R. Campbell. Co-published simultaneously in the *Journal of Organizational Behavior Management* (The Haworth Press, Inc.) Vol. 18, No. 2/3, 1998, pp. 83-101; and: *Organizational Behavior Management and Developmental Disabilities Services: Accomplishments and Future Diretcions* (ed: Dennis H. Reid) The Haworth Press, Inc., 1998, pp. 83-101. Single or multiple copies of this article are available for a fee from The Haworth Document Delivery Service [1-800-342-9678, 9:00 a.m. - 5:00 p.m. (EST). E-mail address: getinfo@haworthpressinc.com].

state institutions continues to decline (Lakin, Prouty, Smith, & Braddock, 1996). As of 1992, more than 180,000 individuals in the United States lived in community settings with 15 or less individuals and, in most cases, the settings were home to 6 or fewer individuals (Braddock, Hemp, Bachelder, & Fujiura, 1995).

The shift to smaller community residences has occurred in response to calls for improvement in the overall quality of life for individuals who resided in large institutions as well as those already residing in the community (e.g., Christian, Hannah, & Glahn, 1984). Consequently, the creation of conditions that foster the development and maintenance of successful community living settings is of great interest to individuals with disabilities and their family members, advocates, funding sources, and provider agencies. Further, an increasing number of people living in these types of settings means that individually-designed support services, supportive direct-care staff skills, and specific organizational activities are required if individuals with developmental disabilities are to live high quality lives in the community.

Organizational behavior management (OBM) provides one way of looking at both the design of organizations and the procedures that organizations use to teach and maintain the skills of staff members. The purposes of this article are to briefly describe community living settings for people with developmental disabilities, to describe and review research examining applications of OBM techniques in these types of settings, to review other related research and writings, to recommend best practices in the application of OBM techniques in community living settings, and to point to areas of future research and study.

## COMMUNITY LIVING SETTINGS

Throughout the late 1960s and early 1970s, community living settings were organized based on the idea that the type of setting required for an individual was solely a function of the severity of the individual's disability (Hitzing, 1987; Nisbet, Clark, & Covert, 1991; Taylor, 1988). Thus, individuals were restricted to a limited number of residential options, typically large group homes or independent apartments. By the mid 1980s, however, alternative approaches to supporting people with developmental disabilities in the community began to emerge. These approaches were based upon the notion that planning services around the personal characteristics of each individual was key to his or her success in the community (Racino & Knoll, 1986). Presently, this responsive and flexible approach, termed "non-facility based," "person-centered," or "separation of housing and support," is becoming more prevalent (Racino, Walker, O'Connor, & Taylor, 1993).

Today, people with developmental disabilities live in a variety of arrangements and settings in the community. These include large group homes (7-15 people), small group homes (6 or fewer people), supervised apartments with less than 24-hour supervision, and family-care situations where the individual with disabilities lives with his or her own family or with a care-providing family (Burchard, Hasazi, Gordon, & Yoe, 1991). Services and supports can be modified and adapted to each individual and might include health-care, nursing, psychiatry, psychology, physical and occupational therapies, and speech and language supports. In some cases, all services are provided in the home by the service provider agency, however, traditional ways of providing staff supervision can be adapted. For example, staff might provide "live-in" support as a paid or unpaid roommate, neighbors might be recruited to provide supervision at certain times to individuals who do not require 24-hour staff presence, and technology can be used to enhance independence (e.g., telephones, pagers). Further, variations on housing, such as shared housing, home ownership with agency supervision, collectives, and cooperatives are being explored (Nisbet et al., 1991; Racino et al., 1993).

Perhaps the most significant departure from the more traditional group home arrangement for individuals with developmental disabilities is the development of small living arrangements where persons with developmental disabilities live where they want, with whom they want, and for as long as they want with the on-going support needed to sustain the choices they have made (Bellamy & Horner, 1987). This approach to providing alternatives to group home arrangements also focuses on the needs and desires of the individual rather than on the availability of service models (Boles, Horner, & Bellamy, 1988).

Although community living arrangements are increasing throughout the country, there is scant research on their overall effects (Taylor, 1988; also see below), however, a number of benefits of living in the community have been identified. Most recently, Knobbe, Carey, Rhodes, and Horner (1995) reported that the number and variety of social contacts and the frequency of preferred activities increased for a group of individuals after they moved from an institution to the community. Still, there is little support for why some people are served in small community living settings while others are not (Conroy, 1996; Hill et al., 1989).

Successfully supporting small community living settings for individuals with developmental disabilities presents economic and organizational challenges for service providers (Campbell, 1995; Knobbe et al., 1995) due primarily to the individualization of services and because the settings are often located a considerable distance from one another. As a result, innovative management systems are needed, such as emergency response systems that rely on the immediate resources available within the community; high quality professional support services (such as those listed above) must be maintained; and innovative supervision and oversight mechanisms must be developed by organizations. As a result of these concerns, providing services to individuals with developmental disabilities in smaller, highly individualized community-based settings presents unique challenges to organizations.

## RESEARCH AND LITERATURE REVIEW

The professional literature on developmental disabilities is replete with examples of (a) outcome research examining the effects of OBM interventions upon direct-care and supervisory staff and residents in institutions and vocational settings, (b) correlational research examining the relationship of a variety of variables in community living settings, and (c) non-experimental descriptions of practices in community living settings. There is, however, a noticeable lack of empirical studies that examine the effects of OBM interventions within community living settings.

For example, Fleming and Reile (1993) reviewed 20 years of OBM research in developmental disabilities (1971-1990) published in 11 behavioral journals. They identified a total of 59 research articles of which only 5% (i.e., 3 studies) examined OBM procedures in community living settings. Moreover, our own review (described below) identified only 11 studies through publication year 1996.

### Review of OBM in Community Living Settings

*Method.* In order to identify published research studies, our review of the literature was conducted in the following way. First, we examined every issue of 10 relevant journals from publication year 1990 through publication year 1996 inclusive. The journals reviewed were *Journal of Organizational Behavior Management, Journal of Applied Behavior Analysis, Behavior Modification, Research in Developmental Disabilities, American Journal on Mental Retardation, Mental Retardation, Education and Training in Mental Retardation and Developmental Disabilities, Journal of the Association for Persons with Severe and Profound Handicaps, Psychosocial Rehabilitation Journal,* and *Administration and Policy in Mental Health.* Second, a computer search using PsychLit (citations through December 1996) was conducted. Third, library searches of relevant texts and journals were conducted. Keywords such as organizational, behavior, management, staff, training, community, residential, developmental, disability, and retardation were used in these computer and library searches. Finally, we reviewed any relevant references cited in any published studies found during the above search processes and/or that were cited in previously published reviews by Fleming and Reile (1993); Harchik, Sherman, Hopkins, Strouse, and Sheldon (1989); Demchak (1987); Repp, Felce, and de Kock, (1987); and Reid and Whitman (1983).

We included all studies that met the following criteria: (a) participants were persons with developmental disabilities or staff members who provided support to those individuals; (b) procedures were conducted in community living settings (as described above); (c) procedures were empirical and examined "an operant approach to organizational change" (Fleming & Reile, 1993, p. 30); that is, the studies included the collection of observable, reliable data and the studies examined an effect of application of an intervention; and (d) was published in a peer-refereed journal.

*Findings.* Our review identified only 11 studies that met the four criteria described above. These studies are briefly summarized in Table 1 and below.

Across the 11 studies, 6 were published since 1990, participants in all studies were staff members (i.e., house supervisors, direct-care staff), residents were adults (except some adolescent residents in Smith, Parker, Taubman, & Lovaas, 1992), and residents had mild to profound developmental disabilities. All of the studies took place in group homes for residents who received 24-hour supervision by staff (although they might have attended day programs during the week). Only one study (Demchak & Browder, 1990) took place in a group home with less than six residents. In the other studies, the number of residents in each home ranged from 6 to 20.

Typical dependent measures were house supervisors' supervisory skills (e.g., instructing staff), staff members' direct interactions with residents (e.g., use of teaching procedures, use of prompting, use of positive reinforcement), staff members' general and specific knowledge, and measures of resident behavior (e.g., skills, interactions, problem behaviors). Less frequently examined dependent measures were quality of house records and documentation, staff self-ratings of confidence, and staff turnover.

The most frequently examined intervention was a combination of direct observation and positive and corrective feedback conducted in the actual work setting (Demchak & Browder, 1990; Davis, McEachern, Christensen, & Voort, 1987; Fleming, Oliver, & Bolton, 1996; Harchik, Sherman, Sheldon, & Strouse, 1992). Four studies examined the effects of workshop training (Parsons, Reid, & Green, 1996; Rosen, Yerushalmi, & Walker,

TABLE 1. Summary of Studies Reviewed

| Authors | Setting | Participants | Dependent Measures | Procedures | Results |
|---|---|---|---|---|---|
| Parsons, Reid, & Green, 1996 | 2 group homes | (a) staff (b) residents with moderate or severe DD | staffs' instructional performance | taught teaching skills to staff in a special one-day training format; used didactic, role-play, and performance feedback at group home | performance improved for all staff who participated |
| Fleming, Oliver, & Bolton, 1996 | 2 group homes (8 and 10 persons) | (a) supervisors (b) staff | (a) supervisors' staff training performance (b) staffs' instructional performance | taught supervisors how to teach staff to instruct residents; used didactic, modeling, and role play procedures | increases in performance of most supervisors and staff in most areas; all participants reported satisfaction with procedures |
| Harchik, Sherman, Sheldon, & Strouse, 1992 | 1 group home (8 persons) | (a) staff (b) residents with severe to profound DD (c) supervisor | (a) staff positive interactions using token reinforcers (b) staff teaching interactions (c) resident engagement in activities | taught staff each of dependent measures; used didactic and role play procedures in 1:1 sessions, provided performance feedback and suggestions based upon direct observation | increases in all areas when specific feedback was provided, performance decreased when feedback was discontinued; successful use by supervisor; all participants reported satisfaction with procedures |
| Ducharme & Feldman, 1992 | 2 group homes in a 4-home complex (8 persons each) | (a) staff (b) residents with moderate to profound DD | staff instructional performance in generalized situations | taught staff how to teach self-care skills; compared written instructions, use of a single example, training with residents, and training based on general case examples | staff instructional performance generalized to new situations only after using general case examples |
| Smith, Parker, Taubman, & Lovaas, 1992 | 6-person group homes | (a) staff in training and control groups (b) residents with autism and DD | (a) teaching interactions, role playing, and, knowledge during workshop (b) staff and resident interactions, self-stimulatory behavior at home | taught staff how to do one-to-one instructing; used 5-day workshop including lecture, role play, analyzing videotapes, and practice with child at workshop site | staff receiving training increased interactions and role playing more than control group; no effects were observed at the homes |

| Authors | Setting | Participants | Dependent Measures | Procedures | Results |
|---|---|---|---|---|---|
| Demchak & Browder, 1990 | 3 group homes (2, 3, and 4 persons) | (a) supervisors (b) staff (c) residents with profound DD | (a) supervisors' staff training and instructional performance (b) staffs' instructional performance (c) resident performance on skills being taught | taught supervisors how to teach residents and how to teach staff to instruct residents; used didactic, role playing, and feedback procedures; prompted supervisors to instruct their staff | supervisors' instructional performance improved after training; staffs' instructional performance improved after supervisors were taught how to train and were prompted to provide training to staff; improvement of resident performance was noted |
| Doerner, Miltenberger, & Bakken, 1989 | 2 group homes (10 and 6 persons) | (a) staff (b) residents with mild to moderate DD | (a) staffs' interactions with residents (b) residents' interactions and problem behaviors | instructed staff to set personal goals for number of interactions, to self-monitor whether they met the goal, to provide self-evaluation, and to make self-praise statements | (a) no strong effects upon staff performance were found; no effects upon residents were found |
| Davis, McEachern, Christensen, & Voort, 1987 | 1 group home (11 persons) | (a) staff (b) supervisor | (a) staff and resident interactions (b) staff self-ratings of expertise and confidence | taught staff how to teach and interact with residents and use self-management; used didactic workshop, role play, readings, "homework" activities, and 1:1 in vivo sessions; taught supervisor to promote staff use of skills | some increase in positive interactions after training; staff rated selves as more expert and confident after training, but supervisors rated no change in staffs' expertise |
| Rosen, Yerushalmi, & Walker, 1986 | 6 group homes (7–15 persons) | staff in training and control groups | (a) staff knowledge (b) staff interactions with residents at home (c) resident records (d) turnover (e) resident behavior at home | taught staff teaching skills, behavioral principles, and home management; used didactic workshops, role plays, and "homework" assignments | staff receiving training showed greater improvements in interactions, resident behavior, and records than control group; no differences in staff knowledge and turnover |

## TABLE 1 (continued)

| Authors | Setting | Participants | Dependent Measures | Procedures | Results |
|---|---|---|---|---|---|
| Gage, Fredericks, Johnson-Dorn, & Lindley-Southard, 1982 | 1 group home (12 persons) | staff from 58 facilities | (a) staff performance during training in teaching, writing behavior and teaching plans, and documentation<br>(b) staff performance at actual work site (same areas) | taught general behavioral skills; used didactic workshops, role plays, and "homework" assignments | staff in training group had increases in knowledge and attitude, less decrease in job satisfaction, and more interactions with residents than staff in control group |
| Schinke & Wong, 1977 | 12 group homes (6-20 persons) | staff in training and control groups | (a) staff knowledge, attitude, and job satisfaction<br>(b) staff and resident interaction and behaviors | taught dependent measures luring one week training at a model demonstration site; used didactic, role play, and actual practice procedures | large increases in staff performance at training site after training; staff performance reported at high levels at homes after training |

1986; Schinke & Wong, 1977; Smith et al., 1992). One study examined the effects of designing staff training to promote generalization of staff member skills (Ducharme & Feldman, 1992), one study examined goal-setting and self-management (Doerner, Miltenberger, & Bakken, 1989), and one study examined a special training site (Gage, Fredericks, Johnson-Dorn, & Lindley-Southard, 1982).

The results are fairly consistent across studies: (a) OBM interventions can be implemented in community group homes, (b) ongoing direct observation and feedback in the actual work setting while the staff member is engaged in actual work activities is consistently effective in improving and maintaining those skills addressed by the observation and feedback, (c) workshops alone are ineffective in improving the skills of staff members in the actual work site, and (d) staff members can be taught skills in a way that promotes their generalized use of these skills. Thus, for direct-service staff to do their jobs well, they must be taught what to do, must have opportunities to practice in their actual work setting, and must receive some sort of ongoing on-the-job feedback about their performance. Other results of this set of studies are more equivocal and require more examination. This includes (a) training supervisors to train their staff and (b) goal setting and self-management.

*Discussion.* Our review of this literature pointed out a number of issues that warrant further discussion. First, the number of studies that have been conducted is extremely low. Thus, any conclusions we draw are based upon a very limited number of research studies. Clearly, there needs to be an increase in research activity in community living settings.

Second, all of the studies were conducted in community group homes and in all cases (except Demchak & Browder, 1990), six or more residents lived in each home. Thus, OBM techniques have been researched in only one type of community living setting–group homes and, for the most part, large group homes. Individuals with developmental disabilities, however, live in a variety of different types of community living settings (as noted above). Given the large numbers of individuals who live in other types of community settings, it is not surprising that authors such as Racino (1995) have noted that "neither the professional literature nor research to date is keeping pace with the state of the art in community living for adults with disabilities" (p. 300). Our review supports this: we found no research that examined OBM techniques in supervised apartments or in family care settings. Thus, not only is more OBM research required in community living settings, but the research needs to examine OBM techniques across a variety of community living settings.

Third, these studies addressed, primarily, staff performance during staff-resident interactions. To a lesser extent, effects upon the residents themselves were examined. Certainly, these types of outcomes are very important and should be part of any OBM technique. No studies, however, examined the manipulation of any other organizational variables that might be of interest to organizational behavior analysts, such as key elements of organizational design (see below) or the many variables that have been examined by correlational researchers and/or discussed by qualitative researchers (see below). Thus, although very important variables have been examined, the scope of dependent variables in the current research base is narrow. As noted by Christian (1984), staff training is one component of a total OBM approach. Similarly, Pollack, Fleming, and Sulzer-Azaroff (1994) called for examination of "macro-variables" (e.g., system variables), rather than solely examining microvariables (e.g., staff-resident interactions). Consequently, the examination of effects of OBM techniques upon a wider range of dependent variables presents another area for OBM researchers to pursue.

Fourth, this set of research studies provides a number of examples of the effective application of direct observation and feedback techniques. In addition, the research points to some techniques that may be very useful in successfully supporting community living settings, but require more examination. Community living settings are, by design, integrated within the general community, and apartments and homes are often "scattered" through a community. Therefore, staff members often work more independently and with less direct supervision than in more congregate settings. For instance, a staff member might work alone with two individuals who live in their own supervised apartment. Techniques that increase the likelihood that staff members in community settings perform their teaching and support tasks well while working alone will be very useful. For example, Ducharme and Feldman (1992) showed that staff training procedures can be designed to promote generalization of staff members' skills, thereby increasing staff members' ability to use their skills in new situations. Another area for study is the provision of support and supervision to staff members via "pyramidal" procedures (Demchak & Browder, 1990; Fleming et al., 1996). That is, services in community living settings can likely be improved if effective procedures can be validated for teaching and maintaining the skills of middle managers, including their ability to teach and maintain the skills of their direct-care staff members. Self-management (e.g., self-recording, goal setting) is another area requiring further investigation.

In addition, OBM research must maintain a high standard of quality of empirical procedures and comprehensiveness in the design of research studies. For example, studies should include a convincing research design, reliability of dependent variables, procedural reliability (e.g., Demchak &

Browder, 1990; Harchik et al., 1992), assessment of generalization and maintenance, social validity and satisfaction measures, and an assessment of whether the outcomes of the procedures provide overall beneficial outcomes for the organization (Mawhinney, 1992). Within this set of research studies, we observed a range of attention to these issues across studies.

Finally, researchers will need to attend to the practical dynamics involved in conducting research in community living settings. This includes reactivity effects of direct observation and reactivity effects when reliability is obtained with a second observer. In smaller community living settings (e.g., supervised apartments, family care), the presence of observers may strongly influence both the behavior of staff members as well as the behavior of residents and housemates.

Thus, in summary, we were encouraged to find some research that showed the successful application of OBM techniques in community living settings and we noted the high quality of some of the studies. We were, however, disappointed by the small number and restricted nature of the set of studies.

*Descriptions of OBM applications.* Although there is a dearth of well-conducted OBM research in community settings, there are many agencies and programs that routinely apply OBM techniques in community living settings for people with developmental disabilities. For example, Luce, Christian, Anderson, and Troy (1992) and Campbell (1995) delineated key elements in the organizational design of human services that are routinely applied in community living settings by The May Institute in Massachusetts. These elements include a strong central organization, appropriate funding, recruitment of competent staff, and training and ongoing support of staff members at all levels. In another example, at Community Living Opportunities in Kansas, Strouse, Sherman, and Sheldon (1995) described an innovative approach to reducing turnover of direct-care staff members by making work more rewarding in community group homes for people with profound developmental disabilities, physical disabilities, and serious health-care needs. The approach gave responsibility for the day-to-day management of support services to a group of three to four direct-care staff members rather than assigning a single administrator to one or two homes. In a third example, Newton, Ard, Horner, and Toews (1996) described their work in Oregon to successfully support improvement in the quality of life of individuals with developmental disabilities who lived in community homes. Much of their work focused upon training and supporting staff in a variety of activities, such as conducting assessments, scheduling activities, recording and summarizing data, using these data for subsequent planning, and emphasizing each individual's goals, preferences, and lifestyle.

## Other Relevant Research and Writings

*OBM in institutions and vocational programs and with other populations.* Reviews of OBM research in institutions and in vocational settings are examined in detail in other articles in this special volume (Ivancic & Helsel, this volume; Phillips, this volume). In general, the findings of our review represent extensions of the work conducted in these settings. That is, current research in community living settings indicates that effective change in staff behavior requires specification of behavior, direct observation, opportunities to practice, and frequent specific performance feedback (Parsons & Reid, 1995; Harchik et al., 1989).

As indicated above, however, the dynamics of community living settings are much different than larger congregate residential and work settings, especially regarding the number of individuals present in each setting. Therefore, we hypothesize that a parent-training model might have some relevance for staff members who work in these small home settings, not necessarily because staff members are in a parental role, but because, much like parents, staff members working in community living settings (especially supervised apartments and family care settings) are typically involved with only one or two individuals and are without the immediate support and presence of another individual. Thus, although beyond the scope of this review, consideration of procedures that have been effective in teaching parents might have some relevant application in community living settings (e.g., Baker, 1989; Neef, 1995). Similarly, procedures for effectively teaching needed skills to respite care workers (who usually work alone with only one or two individuals) have been developed and evaluated by Neef, Trachtenberg, Loeb, and Sterner (1991).

*Correlational research.* A number of correlational studies have looked at the relationship of a variety of variables in community living settings. These studies did not meet our criteria for inclusion in the above review, however, they provide useful information. Correlational research has examined organizational factors (e.g., wages, benefits, type of community living setting, number of staff in the setting, number of residents in the setting, ratio of managers to direct-care staff members, number of treatment goals, unionization, opportunity for advancement, perception of effectiveness, integration within service community), employee factors (e.g., burnout, turnover, education, intention to quit, satisfaction, age, work performance), and resident factors (e.g., behavior problems, adaptive skill, satisfaction, age, community activities, social networks, health and well-being).

Findings include a relationship between (a) turnover and low wages, few opportunities for advancement, and number of direct-care staff (Lakin &

Larson, 1992; Larson & Lakin, 1992; Mitchell & Braddock, 1994); (b) job satisfaction and employment history, satisfaction with supervision, and the job's agreement with one's own personal goals (Razza, 1993); and (c) perceptions of organization effectiveness and both the organization's integration within the service community and the tenure of senior management (Grusky, 1995).

Lawson and O'Brien (1994) examined the relationship of job-related variables, such as absenteeism and tardiness with both self-report measures of burnout and direct observation of work performance. They found that direct observation correlated better with these job-related variables than did self-report measures. Based upon their findings, the authors called for future correlational research to include direct observation of staff behavior because of the limited relationship between self-reports and staff performance in research on burnout. For individuals with developmental disabilities, the type of residence in which the individual lived was related to the type of life the individual lived. Specifically, lifestyles of individuals in supervised apartments were more similar to people without disabilities than were the lifestyles of people who lived in group homes or family care settings (Burchard et al., 1992).

Correlational research points OBM researchers to a variety of important factors that have not been examined by OBM researchers in community living settings. These factors could be examined as dependent or independent variables in future OBM intervention research.

*Descriptions of qualitative research.* Descriptive-qualitative studies of how a number of organizations provide community residential services to individuals with developmental disabilities have been published (Racino et al., 1993; Taylor, Bogdan, & Racino, 1991). Although OBM techniques were not specifically evaluated, the studies provided information about how some organizations are designed and how staff are trained and supported (e.g., modeling/mentoring by more experienced staff members, making one staff the primary support person for one individual, training specific to each resident, supervisor direct involvement in program operation, supporting staff members to stay in touch with one another via staff social events).

A focus on organizational characteristics can be helpful (as is correlational research) in pointing out areas that require further analyses, the kind of analyses that could be conducted by OBM researchers. Examples of characteristics noted in this literature include a focus on values, an adherence to principles, a commitment to the people served as the focus of decisions, an openness to change and new ideas, empowerment of staff, a team approach, committed caring leadership, and supporting staff members to be facilitators.

## BEST PRACTICE RECOMMENDATIONS

It may be premature to make best practice recommendations given the quantity of research that has been conducted to date. Nevertheless, practitioners, researchers, and individuals with developmental disabilities are likely to benefit from the most effective application of OBM techniques based upon the research and descriptions of programs that are currently available.

To do so, organizations must determine their mission and values. Then, these principles should be translated into a variety of activities or skills that are relevant and specific for every position at the organization. Each activity or skill should be defined by a set of observable behaviors and defined in a way that allows for flexibility in implementation as appropriate to the situation and individuals involved. The validity of the correspondence of these activities with the organization's mission can be evaluated both by staff members and by external consultants. Every staff member will need to receive training in each area and the best way to conduct this training is by using brief didactic procedures, modeling, role playing, and practice in the actual work site. Staff members should be included in the defining of principles and in the determination of how training procedures are done. This is an ongoing process, requiring continual review and modification.

Then, periodic, on-the-job, direct observation and feedback from one's supervisor should become part of the regular routine of managers. Feedback should be positive, include specific descriptions of correct staff performance, and include suggestions for improvement. We have found that staff members respond favorably to direct observation and feedback when it is positive and when suggestions for improvement are practical, result in improvements in lifestyle for residents, and allow staff members to make better use of their time. These activities and skills should be incorporated into job descriptions and staff members should receive feedback about each activity as part of their regular performance reviews.

At the organizational level, administrative and board support for the programmatic and financial implications of a commitment to implementation of OBM techniques is crucial if procedures are to occur and maintain. Moreover, the design of the organization must allow for OBM techniques to be implemented. For example, managers' work schedules must allow for time to directly observe staff members, and staff members' schedules must allow for time to participate in review and feedback sessions with their supervisors. The organization should also engage in those activities that set the stage for OBM techniques to be effective, including maintaining stable funding and financial operations, recruiting competent staff members, and ensuring that the general working conditions (e.g., settings, responsibilities, wages, benefits, opportunities for advancement, professional development, staff input in decision-making) support staff member satisfaction, tenure, and exceptional performance.

## FUTURE RESEARCH DIRECTIONS

We have made numerous suggestions for future research throughout this article. These future directions for OBM research in community living settings are summarized below. We look forward to an increase in well-conducted relevant research and the positive outcomes that are likely to result for people with developmental disabilities.

Thus, future research should demonstrate high quality research procedures that focus upon (a) replications and systematic replications, (b) a variety of different types of community living settings (e.g., supervised apartments), (c) issues in conducting research in these varied settings (e.g., reactivity, reliability), (d) an increase in the breadth of dependent variables examined, (e) specific OBM procedures (e.g., supervisory skills, pyramidal training, self-management, staff participation), (f) factors that are typically only examined with correlational procedures, and (g) those variables that have an impact upon the lifestyles of residents.

## REFERENCES

Baker, B.L., & Brightman, A.J. (1989). *Steps to independence: A skills training guide for parents and teachers of children with special needs.* Baltimore: Brookes.

Bellamy, G.T., & Horner, R.H. (1987). Beyond high school: Residential and employment options after graduation. In M. Snell (Ed.), *Systematic instruction of persons with severe handicaps* (pp. 491-510). Columbus, OH: Merrill.

Boles, S., Horner, R.H., & Bellamy, G.T. (1988). Implementing transitions: Programs for supported living. In B.L. Ludow, A.P. Turnbull, & R. Luckason (Eds.), *Transitions to adult life for people with mental retardation* (pp. 101-118). Baltimore: Brookes.

Braddock, D., Hemp, R., Bachelder, L., & Fujiura, G. (1995). *The state of the states in developmental disabilities.* Washington, DC: AAMR.

Burchard, S.N., Hasazi, J.S., Gordon, L.R., & Yoe, J. (1991). An examination of lifestyle and adjustment in three community residential alternatives. *Research in Developmental Disabilities, 12*, 177-142.

Burchard, S.N., Rosen, J.W., Gordon, L.R., Hasazi, J.E., Yoe, J.T., & Dietzel, L.C. (1992). A comparison of social support and satisfaction among adults with mental retardation living in three types of community residential alternatives.

In J.W. Jacobson, S.N. Burchard, & P.J. Carling (Eds.), *Community living for people with developmental and psychiatric disabilities* (pp. 137-154). Baltimore: Johns Hopkins University Press.

Campbell, A.R. (1995, May). The generalization and maintenance of organizational change at the May Institute. In A.E. Harchik (Chair), *How human service agencies can best support their employees*. Symposium conducted at the meeting of the Association for Behavior Analysis, Washington, DC.

Christian, W.P. (1984). A case study in the programming and maintenance of institutional change. *Journal of Organizational Behavior Management, 5*, 99-153.

Christian, W.P., Hannah, G.T., & Glahn, T.J. (1984). *Programming effective human services: Strategies for institutional change and client transition*. New York: Plenum.

Conroy, J.W. (1996). The small ICF/MR program: Dimensions of quality and cost. *Mental Retardation, 34*, 13-26.

Davis, J.R., McEachern, M.A., Christensen, J., & Voort, C.V. (1987). Behavioral skills workshop for staff and supervisor in a community residence for developmentally handicapped adults. *Behavioral Residential Treatment, 2*, 25-36.

Demchak, M.A. (1987). A review of behavioral staff training in special education settings. *Education and Training in Mental Retardation, 22*, 205-217.

Demchak, M., & Browder, D.M. (1990). An evaluation of the pyramidal model of staff training in group homes for adults with severe handicaps. *Education and Training in Mental Retardation and Developmental Disabilities, 25*, 150-163.

Doerner, M., Miltenberger, R.G., & Bakken, J. (1989). The effects of staff self-management on positive social interactions in a group home setting. *Behavioral Residential Treatment, 4*, 313-330.

Ducharme, J.M., & Feldman, M.A. (1992). Comparison of staff training strategies to promote generalized teaching skills. *Journal of Applied Behavior Analysis, 25*, 165-179.

Fleming, R.K., Oliver, J.R., & Bolton, D. (1996). Training supervisors to train staff: A study in a human service organization. *Journal of Organizational Behavior Management, 16*, 3-25.

Fleming, R.K., & Reile, P.A. (1993). A descriptive analysis of client outcomes associated with staff interventions in developmental disabilities. *Behavioral Residential Treatment, 8*, 29-43.

Gage, M.A., Fredericks, B., Johnson-Dorn, N., & Lindley-Southard, B. (1982). Inservice training for staffs of group homes and work activity centers serving developmentally disabled adults. *TASH Journal, 4*, 60-70.

Grusky, O. (1995). The organization and effectiveness of community mental health systems. *Administration and Policy in Mental Health, 22*, 361-388.

Harchik, A.E., Sherman, J.A., Hopkins, B.L., Strouse, M.C., & Sheldon, J.B. (1989). Use of behavioral techniques by paraprofessional staff: A review and proposal. *Behavioral Residential Treatment, 4*, 331-357.

Harchik, A.E., Sherman, J.A., Sheldon, J.B., & Strouse, M.C. (1992). Ongoing consultation as a method of improving performance of staff members in a group home. *Journal of Applied Behavior Analysis, 25*, 599-610.

Hill, B.K., Lakin, K.C., Bruininks, R.H., Amado, A.N., Anderson, D.J., & Copher, J.I. (1989). *Living in the community: A comparative study of foster homes and small group homes for people with mental retardation.* Minneapolis: University of Minnesota, Center for Residential and Community Services.

Hitzing, W. (1987). Community living alternatives for persons with autism and severe behavior problems. In D.J. Cohen & A. Donnellan (Eds.), *Handbook of autism and pervasive developmental disorders* (pp. 396-410). New York: John Wiley & Sons.

Ivancic, M., & Helsel, W. (this volume). *Journal of Organizational Behavior Management.*

Knobbe, C.A., Carey, S.P., Rhodes, L., & Horner, R.H. (1995). Benefit-cost analysis of community residential versus institutional services for adults with severe mental retardation and challenging behaviors. *American Journal on Mental Retardation, 99,* 533-541.

Lakin, K.C., & Larson, S.A. (1992). Satisfaction and stability of direct care personnel in community-based residential services. In J.W. Jacobson, S.N. Burchard, & P.J. Carling (Eds.), *Community living for people with developmental and psychiatric disabilities* (pp. 244-262). Baltimore: Johns Hopkins University Press.

Lakin, K.C., Prouty, B., Smith, G., & Braddock, D. (1996). Nixon goal surpassed–twofold. *Mental Retardation, 34,* 67.

Larson, S.A., & Lakin, K.C. (1992). Direct-care staff stability in a national sample of small group homes. *Mental Retardation, 30,* 13-22.

Lawson, D.A., & O'Brien, R.M. (1994). Behavioral and self-report measures of staff burnout in developmental disabilities. *Journal of Organizational Behavior Management, 14,* 37-54.

Luce, S.C., Christian, W.P., Anderson, S.R., & Troy, P.J. (1992). Development of a continuum of services for children and adults with autism and other severe behavior disorders. *Research in Developmental Disabilities, 13,* 9-25.

Mawhinney, T.C. (1992). Total quality management and organizational behavior management: An integration for continual improvement. *Journal of Applied Behavior Analysis, 25,* 525-543.

Mitchell, D., & Braddock, D. (1994). Compensation and turnover of direct-care staff in developmental disabilities residential facilities in the United States II: Turnover. *Mental Retardation, 32,* 34-42.

Neef, N.A. (1995). Pyramidal parent training by peers. *Journal of Applied Behavior Analysis, 25,* 333-337.

Neef, N.A., Trachtenberg, S., Loeb, J., & Sterner, K. (1991). Video-based training of respite care providers: An interactional analysis of presentation format. *Journal of Applied Behavior Analysis, 24,* 473-486.

Newton, J.S., Ard, W.R., Horner, R.H., & Toews, J.D. (1996). Focusing on values and lifestyle outcomes in an effort to improve the quality of residential services in Oregon. *Mental Retardation, 34,* 1-12.

Nisbet, J., Clark, M., & Covert, S. (1991). Living it up! An analysis of research on community living. In L.H. Meyer, C.A. Peck, & L. Brown (Eds.), *Critical issues in the lives of people with severe disabilities* (pp. 115-144). Baltimore: Brookes

Parsons, M.B., & Reid, D.H. (1995). Training residential supervisors to provide feedback for maintaining staff teaching skills with people who have severe disabilities. *Journal of Applied Behavior Analysis, 28*, 317-322.

Parsons, M.B., Reid, D.H., & Green, C.W. (1996). Training basic teaching skills to community and institutional support staff for people with severe disabilities: A one-day program. *Research in Developmental Disabilities, 17*, 467-485.

Phillips, J. (this volume). *Journal of Organizational Behavior Management.*

Pollack, M.J., Fleming, R.K., & Sulzer-Azaroff, B. (1994). Enhancing professional performance through organizational change. *Behavioral Interventions, 9*, 27-42.

Racino, J.A. (1995). Community living for adults with developmental disabilities: A housing and support approach. *Journal of the Association for Persons with Severe Handicaps, 20*, 300-310.

Racino, J.A., & Knoll, J. (1986). Life in the community: Developing non-facility based services. *TASH Newsletter, 12*, 6.

Racino, J.A., Walker, P., O'Connor, S., & Taylor, S.J. (1993). *Housing, support, and community: Choices and strategies for adults with disabilities.* Baltimore: Brookes.

Razza, N.J. (1993). Determinants of direct-care staff turnover in group homes for individuals with mental retardation. *Mental Retardation, 31*, 284-291.

Reid, D.H., & Whitman, T.L. (1983). Behavioral staff management in institutions: A critical review of effectiveness and acceptability. *Analysis and Intervention in Developmental Disabilities, 3*, 131-149.

Repp, A.C., Felce, D., & de Kock, U. (1987). Observational studies of staff working with mentally retarded persons: A review. *Research in Developmental Disabilities, 8*, 331-350.

Rosen, H.S., Yerushalmi, C.J., & Walker, J.C. (1986). Training community residential staff: Evaluation and follow-up. *Behavioral Residential Treatment, 1*, 15-38.

Schinke, S.P., & Wong, S.E. (1977). Evaluation of staff training in group homes for retarded persons. *American Journal on Mental Deficiency, 82*, 130-136.

Smith, T., Parker, T., Taubman, M., & Lovaas, O.I. (1992). Transfer of training from workshops to group homes: A failure to generalize. *Research in Developmental Disabilities, 13*, 57-71.

Strouse, M.C., Sherman, J.A., & Sheldon, J.B. (1995, May). Turning over turnover: Reducing turnover for direct service employees serving persons with developmental disabilities. In A.E. Harchik (Chair), *How human service agencies can best support their employees.* Symposium conducted at the meeting of the Association for Behavior Analysis, Washington, DC.

Taylor, S.J. (1988). Caught in the continuum: A critical analysis of the principle of the least restrictive environment. *Journal of the Association for Persons with Severe Handicaps, 13*, 45-53.

Taylor, S.J., Bogdan, R., & Racino, J.A. (1991). *Life in the community: Case studies of organizations supporting people with disabilities.* Baltimore: Brookes.

# Applications and Contributions of Organizational Behavior Management in Schools and Day Treatment Settings

## James F. Phillips

**SUMMARY.** Organizational behavior management (OBM) has been applied in school and day placement settings for approximately 35 years. During this time, OBM has made numerous and varied contributions in terms of improving quality supports and services through effective training and management of school and day placement staff. Previous reviews have summarized and critiqued the OBM literature through the 1980s. This review summarizes and describes the most recent findings, developments, and trends with respect to behavioral training and management of educational staff in classrooms and related settings. Nineteen studies are reviewed with respect to: intervention effectiveness, efficiency, effects on student performance, durability, acceptability, reactivity, generalization and comprehensiveness. While considerable knowledge has been acquired about various aspects of behavioral training and management of educational staff, much more information is needed in a variety of areas. Suggestions for future research include additional investigations of methods to: increase efficiency of OBM efforts through antecedent interventions, ensure durability of intervention efforts, increase generality of training and management efforts, and increase acceptance of OBM efforts. *[Article copies available for a fee from The Haworth Document Delivery Service: 1-800-342-9678. E-mail address: getinfo@haworthpressinc.com]*

James F. Phillips is affiliated with the Murdoch Center, Butner, NC.

[Haworth co-indexing entry note]: "Applications and Contributions of Organizational Behavior Management in Schools and Day Treatment Settings." Phillips, James F. Co-published simultaneously in *Journal of Organizational Behavior Management* (The Haworth Press, Inc.) Vol. 18, No. 2/3, 1998, pp. 103-129; and: *Organizational Behavior Management and Developmental Disabilities Services: Accomplishments and Future Directions* (ed: Dennis H. Reid) The Haworth Press, Inc., 1998, pp. 103-129. Single or multiple copies of this article are available for a fee from The Haworth Document Delivery Service [1-800-342-9678, 9:00 a.m. - 5:00 p.m. (EST). E-mail address: getinfo@haworthpress inc.com].

*103*

An early and critical development that prompted efforts by applied behavior analysts to train staff working in human service settings such as institutions and classrooms was the demonstration across a number of studies that contingent staff behavior affected client behavior in important and reliable ways. A key pioneering study in the area of staff training was undertaken by Ayllon and Michael (1959). Based on pretreatment analysis of various problem behaviors exhibited by patients living in a psychiatric hospital, staff were presented with a rationale for interventions for individual patients and specific instructions on how to behave in response to particular patient behaviors. It was determined in a series of case studies that direct care staff could have important effects on various behaviors of patients as a function of their own behavior. Contingent attention as well as extinction were identified as effective procedures in modifying seemingly intractable problem behaviors in patients.

In fact, inservice training for human service staff was generally nonexistent with respect to teaching skills beyond basic custodial skills until the mid 1960s (Ziarnik & Bernstein, 1982). Few institutions provided formal inservice training programs. Staff were typically recruited on the basis of personality characteristics rather than specific skills related to effective client interactions and treatment. Little consideration was given to training treatment-related skills such as ways to interact with or teach residents. Instead, care and custody were considered to be the primary functions of staff at the time.

Demonstrations that educational staff could increase or decrease rates of various student behaviors in their classrooms through contingent application of attention and extinction (e.g., Hall, Lund, & Jackson, 1968; Hall, Panyan, Rabon, & Broden, 1968) had an important and lasting effect with respect to work expectations and job responsibilities of teachers and aides. Typically, these classroom demonstration studies involved an experimenter instructing the teacher in ways to respond to specific student behaviors during brief observation sessions. The purpose of these studies was primarily to demonstrate the relation between teacher and student behavior. Hence, carefully designed staff training and management procedures were typically not implemented during these studies because comprehensive, generalized, or durable changes in teacher behavior was not the primary objective. Nevertheless these studies resulted in clear demonstrations that teachers could have a direct impact on student behavior in their classroom. Training educational staff to skillfully use applied behavior analysis procedures (e.g., contingent attention, recording responses, and responding to data from the classroom) soon became an important issue for researchers, professionals, and managers in educational settings (Reid, Parsons, & Green, 1989).

Generally, early efforts to train educational staff relied heavily on the use of the preservice or inservice model (Filler, Hecimovic, & Blue, 1978) in which information regarding key teaching skills was provided via lectures, discussions, slides, and videotapes. In the Filler et al. (1978) investigation, information and performance competencies of the teachers and aides were measured via pre- and post-test questions. The findings indicated that initially there was considerable variation among staff with respect to information and performance competencies. The lectures and discussion resulted in consistent improvement in terms of answering information recall questions. However, there was wide variability regarding correct responses to performance questions that required the staff to apply information obtained during the inservice. The investigators concluded that this traditional type of instructional model was successful in imparting verbal information but that some staff (particularly primary caregivers) had difficulty translating knowledge into performance.

In contrast to typical early studies (e.g., Filler et al., 1978), more recent investigations (e.g., Langone, Koorland, & Oseroff, 1987) have evaluated the effectiveness of inservice training for teachers by measuring teacher behavior during actual classroom observations. In the Langone et al. (1987) study, teacher behavior (e.g., correct use of verbal instructions, modeling, physical prompts, guidance and consequences) was measured before and after one-to-one inservice sessions. Ten-minute observations were conducted in the classroom during which desired changes were observed across most behaviors for all teachers.

In addition, researchers were beginning to acquire information from a series of investigations indicating that antecedent interventions including the use of workshops and instructions of various kinds were generally ineffective in obtaining durable behavior change on the part of staff in human service settings (Quilitch, 1975). This was an important finding given that early investigations frequently incorporated a didactic model.

In the early to mid 1970s, investigations of effective ways to ensure the skillful delivery of educational services to students with various backgrounds and needs began to emerge. Researchers began developing training programs for staff that were effective, efficient and acceptable to staff. In addition, procedures that increased the likelihood of obtaining training results that were generalizable to the classroom, durable, beneficial for clients and comprehensive across teaching skill domains began to be investigated.

## PURPOSE, FOCUS AND FORMAT OF REVIEW

The purpose of this review is to summarize and describe recent findings, developments and trends with respect to behavioral training and management of educational staff in classroom and related settings such as vocational training programs. Previous reviews of behavioral training and management (i.e., Organizational Behavior Management) of teacher performance in classroom settings have summarized and critiqued studies published through 1987 (Demchak, 1987; Reid et al., 1989, Chap. 9). Therefore, this review will focus on applied literature pertaining to behavioral training and management of educational staff published since 1987, although results from several studies published prior to 1987 will be incorporated into the discussion where relevant. Also, pertinent findings from previous reviews will be included in this review. In all, 19 studies were reviewed for this paper. These 19 studies are a sample of the most recent available literature; hence, this review should not be considered exhaustive.

The format of this review will include a summary and discussion of the 19 studies with respect to: intervention effectiveness, efficiency, effects on student performance, durability, acceptability, reactivity, generalization and comprehensiveness. This review will include critiques of the sample studies and suggestions for future research directions. The term educational staff used in this review is defined to include all staff responsible for implementation of training programs for students in classroom and vocational settings. Included are principals, teachers, teacher aides, undergraduate and graduate students of education, and direct care staff assigned to implement programs in these settings.

## EFFECTIVENESS OF INTERVENTIONS

Previous reviews of behavioral training and management literature have shown that there have been successful interventions (at a minimum, short term changes in behavior) in educational settings using antecedent procedures such as instructions and modeling, consequence procedures such as feedback and positive reinforcement, and multifaceted procedures using both antecedent and consequence procedures (Demchak, 1987; Reid et al., 1989). One conclusion of these reviews is that there have been relatively few studies implemented in educational settings when compared to the number of studies completed in other settings such as institutions (Demchak, 1987). Thus the generality of the findings is limited. In addition a number of methodological problems in several studies have made conclusions regarding effectiveness difficult (Demchak, 1987).

### Antecedent Interventions

A review of the current sample of investigations with educational staff indicates that six investigations analyzed the effectiveness of antecedent interventions on various types of teacher behavior. Of these, two investigations looked at the effectiveness of training on staff *skill acquisition only.* Four additional studies analyzed the effects of antecedent interventions on *skill acquisition and generalization of skills* to the classroom.

With respect to the two investigations that analyzed *skill acquisition,* both used multiple training components such as written and vocal instructions, skill practice, and feedback (Green & Reid, 1994; Inge & Snell, 1985). These investigations demonstrated that behavioral training procedures helped teachers acquire various skills including switch assembly and client positioning and handling techniques. All participants improved their skills. Neither of these studies conducted an analysis of the effects of individual components of inservice.

With respect to *generalization of skills* to the classroom, four investigations employing antecedent interventions are pertinent. Reinoehl and Halle (1994) investigated the effects of multiple antecedent interventions to increase the use of incidental teaching interactions by teacher aides. Inservice training (multiple components) plus self-regulated implementation of training and data collection procedures resulted in infrequent and inconsistent teacher responses. The addition of incidental modeling by one of the investigators resulted in a similar level of performance. However, delivering partially completed self-recording data cards to the educational staff resulted in more frequent and consistent responses.

Haring, Neetz, Lovinger, Peck, and Semmel (1987) developed an intervention that was designed to increase the use of four incidental teaching procedures by teachers. The teachers were provided with a self-instruction manual and daily planning sheets to plan their teaching strategies. Results indicated improvement in the use of three of four incidental teaching techniques. The teachers varied in the degree of reliance on the pre-planning procedure.

Sasso et al. (1992) taught two teachers via inservice training to effectively conduct systematic analyses of severe problem behaviors and to implement interventions based on the analyses. Nakano, Kageyama and Kinoshita (1993) apparently used inservice procedures alone to teach direct instruction skills to two teachers, with improvements in performance of instructional skills observed with both teachers. No indication of specific consequence procedures was included in this study.

The outcomes of the investigations just summarized replicate and extend the findings of previous behavioral training literature (Reid et al., 1989) that indicate antecedent interventions can be effective in improving skill performance, although mixed results have been observed when staff performance was measured in the classroom setting in the absence of additional management procedures (e.g., Haring et al., 1987). In addition, the outcomes of these studies extend the literature in that a broader array of skills were targeted (Green & Reid, 1994; Inge & Snell, 1985). Overall however, the number of studies investigating the effects of antecedent interventions remains small.

### Consequence Interventions

Two studies focused primarily on the use of consequence procedures to effect changes in educational staff behavior. O'Reilly et al. (1992) compared the effects of immediate versus delayed feedback with results indicating that immediate feedback was more effective with two student teachers and delayed feedback was more effective with the remaining student teacher. Both students were enrolled in a practicum as part of their teacher training program. No indication of specific antecedent procedures was included in this study.

One investigation employed the use of a *multicomponent inservice as well as goal setting* to increase positive interactions between staff and clients in a vocational setting (Suda & Miltenberger, 1993). This antecedent approach did not increase staff positive interactions to an acceptable level. The addition of self-management (instructions plus goal setting, self-monitoring, self-evaluation and self-praise) resulted in improved performance for all six staff. However, two staff required feedback to maintain their rate of positive interactions.

Both studies add to the body of evidence that demonstrates the critical role of consequence procedures in effecting change in staff behavior. Studies which employ consequence procedures alone are rare given the necessity of certain antecedent procedures (e.g., instructions) in providing staff with knowledge that is critical for correct implementation of their duties.

### Multifaceted Interventions

The majority of the investigations reviewed used a combination of antecedent procedures (e.g., inservice) with some form of consequence such as feedback or feedback and praise. Three investigations focused on increasing the use of age-appropriate/functional activities and materials by students residing in residential facilities (Dyer, Schwartz, & Luce, 1984; Green, Canipe, Way, & Reid, 1986; Reid et al., 1985). All three studies used multiple component inservices to teach educational staff how to increase the opportunities for students to access functional materials and activities. One study incorporated the use of participatory management during the inservice in which the educational staff had the opportunity to provide input regarding materials and activities (Reid et al., 1985). All three studies used feedback in various forms including vocal and written (Dyer et al., 1984) and vocal positive and corrective feedback (Green et al., 1986; Reid et al., 1985). Dyer et al. (1984) used an external monitor to provide feedback while the in-house supervisors implemented the feedback in the other two investigations.

Gillat and Sulzer-Azaroff (1994) used inservice training, feedback and praise to improve the performance of two school principals with respect to scheduling their time and using goal setting, feedback, and praise with students. In a second experiment (Gillat & Sulzer-Azaroff, 1994) a principal used modelling, instructions and feedback to successfully encourage a teacher to increase goal setting, feedback, and praise to students.

One study analyzed the effects of immediacy of feedback with undergraduate students in education (Duker, Hensgens, & Venderbosch, 1995). Duker et al. found that delayed feedback which focused on errors during sessions was effective in improving teaching skills.

Northup et al. (1994) determined that classroom teachers could complete assessments of severe behavior disorders and implement treatment procedures effectively such that students showed improvements in educational settings. The investigators used inservice procedures along with on-site consultation and collaboration.

Fleming and Sulzer-Azaroff (1992) used peer feedback with six staff employed in a vocational program. Pairs of staff were trained to monitor peer teaching, record and graph data, provide feedback, and set goals with the peer. While improvements were noted for four of the six participants, there were inconsistencies in the magnitude and durability of the increases.

Several additional studies resulted in increased teacher performance using a combined inservice and feedback approach (Ingham & Greer, 1992; Schwartz, Anderson, & Halle, 1989). In addition, Schwartz et al. (1989) used a cash bonus as an incentive. Several investigators looked comprehensively at teacher behavior change over long periods of time (Gage, Fredericks, Johnson-Dorn, & Lindley-Southard, 1982; Selinske, Greer, & Lodhi, 1991) and across large numbers of staff (Gage et al., 1982).

These studies make important contributions to the behavioral training and management literature in several ways. Primarily, these investigations add to the findings of previous studies that show that consequence procedures, particularly feedback, are critical components with respect to ensuring generalization of skills to the work setting.

Additional evidence from several investigations demonstrates that on-site supervisors can be effective in ensuring that skills acquired by educational staff during training in fact generalize to the work setting. Evidence is beginning to appear with respect to procedures for assisting managers in their attempts to provide training and supervisory support for educational staff (Gillat & Sulzer-Azaroff, 1994).

As Reid et al. (1989) indicated, analysis of the effectiveness of individual management components is not generally observed. However, the outcomes of various management efforts are typically positive.

## EFFICIENCY OF INTERVENTIONS

A critical aspect of both training and management of educational staff pertains to the efficiency of these efforts for those responsible for conducting training and supervision as well as for educational staff who are recipients of training and supervision (Reid et al., 1989, Chap. 1; Green & Reid, 1994). Indeed efforts have been made by some investigators to incorporate time saving aspects into behavioral training and management efforts to increase the likelihood that the procedures will be used by trainers (Green & Reid, 1994) and supervisors (Gillat & Sulzer-Azaroff, 1994), as well as minimize time away from the classroom and related settings for educational staff (Reid et al., 1989).

Some investigators have indicated that their behavioral training and management efforts while effective could have been designed differently for increased efficiency. For example, Langone et al. (1987) investigated the effects of one-to-one inservice instruction on teacher classroom behaviors. The two-hour inservice for each teacher was correlated with desirable changes in classroom skills. However, the investigators pointed out that one-to-one inservice training is not always possible or cost efficient. They suggested that future research analyze a pyramid training model. Selinske et al. (1991) investigated a comprehensive training program for supervisors and teachers to increase applied behavior analysis skills. Although teachers were trained in groups, and the skills taught were numerous across several skill areas, the investigators were unsure about the functionality of various training components (e.g., completion of quizzes by teachers, administrative tasks completed by supervisors). The investigators stated that some components for both supervisors and teachers required substantial work and intense effort. They acknowledged the need for testing components for possible streamlining.

Although many investigators acknowledge the need for efficiency for educational supervisors and staff, in fact very few studies include a thorough analysis of the efficiency of the intervention. Descriptions of training for teachers that specify time parameters indicate that inservice training can last from less than 30 minutes (Schwartz et al., 1989) to 5 days (Gage et al., 1982). A small number of the sample studies indicated specific durations for inservice training. Some investigators indicated that "brief" inservices were provided (e.g., Dyer et al., 1984) while several investigators provided no indication of duration of training.

There are some factors that might lessen the desirability for collecting efficiency measures. For example, requesting that a principal self-record data (e.g., on time spent observing staff or giving feedback) could increase the effort of the entire task resulting in negative outcomes such as noncompliance. Also, completing an accurate comparison of efficiency outcomes across studies can be difficult given the vast number of variables that are a part of interventions and that vary across interventions (e.g., number of skills taught, complexity of skills, number of students observed, duration of interventions).

A small number of investigators have provided information regarding the amount of time required to complete various management components. For example, observations of educational staff can last 5 minutes, review meetings can last 15 minutes (Fleming & Sulzer-Azaroff, 1992), and feedback can take less than 5 minutes to provide (Reid et al., 1985).

Several investigators have incorporated a number of approaches into their behavioral training and management efforts in an attempt to increase efficiency. One approach to training educational staff efficiently is to include only those components in behavioral training packages that have been repeatedly demonstrated to be effective (and efficient). Such a training approach has been described in Reid et al., 1989 (Chap. 3) and has been demonstrated to be useful across skills (Green et al., 1986; Green & Reid, 1994; Parsons et al., 1987). This approach to training can in fact be brief (Green & Reid, 1994) and effective. In conjunction with behavioral supervision this training approach can also produce durable effects across large numbers of staff (Reid et al., 1989). This approach is consistent with recommendations by other investigators (e.g., Fleming & Sulzer-Azaroff, 1992) to streamline intervention packages when possible to increase efficiency.

Another approach to increasing training efficiency is to train staff in groups (McKeown, Adams, & Forehand, 1975). With regard to managing the training demands placed on supervisors (e.g., principals) for ensuring that large numbers of educational staff are trained in various skills, a procedure that has been investigated is the pyramid training or train-the-trainers model (Jones, Fremouw, & Carples, 1977; Dyer et al., 1984; Green & Reid, 1994). In order to help supervisors manage difficult training demands that can be inherent in a large staff, when there is a shortage of training staff, or if time requirements preclude the use of traditional training models, a train-the-trainers model can be helpful in training a variety of skills across different populations of teachers. With this model, staff who are trained in specific skills in turn train other staff thus reducing administrative time needed to conduct training.

A related approach to pyramidal training has been investigated by Fleming and Sulzer-Azaroff (1992) in which staff performance in a vocational setting was improved via reciprocal peer management. Briefly, staff were divided into pairs with both members of each pair trained to monitor peer teaching, record and graph data, provide feedback, and set goals with each peer. In this particular study, outcomes were mixed although some positive results indicate that this approach could potentially be useful.

A unique approach to increasing efficiency in behavioral management interventions is to teach specific skills to individuals to help them use their time effectively and efficiently. Gillat and Sulzer-Azaroff (1994) trained principals several techniques to use in order to manage their time. Specifically, they were taught how to: set achievable goals by dividing tasks into components that could be accomplished in brief periods of time, develop daily schedules, assign tasks into time blocks, and record completion of tasks. The purpose of this training was to help the principals set aside time to complete important tasks such as visiting classrooms and training teachers.

A final approach to decreasing the training demands of staff trainers is to incorporate a self-instruction component into the training program for teachers (e.g., Haring et al., 1987). An additional feature of this investigation is that teachers were provided with forms and instructions to guide them in planning specific interventions with students, eliminating the need for supervisors to complete these planning tasks.

Reid et al. (1989) have indicated that additional research in antecedent intervention procedures is warranted given the effectiveness of these procedures with specific staff (e.g., teachers who have a history of education and practicum experience), and the efficiency that is inherent in antecedent procedures which prove to be effective. In some cases, elaborate labor intensive managerial efforts to affect behavior change can be relied upon less, to the extent that antecedent procedures are used effectively.

## EFFECTS OF INTERVENTIONS ON STUDENT PERFORMANCE

Greene, Willis, Levy, and Bailey (1978) reviewed the research with regard to staff implementation of programs in institutional settings and found that most of the research focused exclusively on the behavior of staff. However, they maintained that the behavior of clients is the most relevant unit of analysis for determining the effectiveness of staff training and management techniques and recommended the inclusion of this measure in future investigations. Their study was among the first to measure the impact of staff implemented training programs on client behavior.

Reid et al. (1989) reviewed the literature with respect to student gains as a function of behavioral teacher training and management procedures. Approximately 65% of these studies included measures of student performance. Reid et al. also indicated that student performance was the ultimate test of the social significance of teacher performance.

Of the 19 sample studies in the current review, 13 (68%) included measures of student performance. Student behaviors that were measured included: being on task, responses to academic tasks such as quizzes, multiplication problems, and pages read, appropriate social behavior such as compliance and social interactions, use of words, signs and other communication responses, work skills including pieces completed in a vocational setting, and inappropriate behavior such as self-injury, aggression and inappropriate language.

All of the sample investigations that incorporated measures of generalization of teacher performance to the classroom reported at least some degree of improved student performance following the implementation of behavioral teaching and management procedures. Nakano et al. (1993) reported that the poorest performing students benefitted the most from the training their teachers received in direct instruction.

## ASSESSMENT OF DURABILITY

The purpose of assessing the durability of intervention effects with educational staff is to determine whether improvements in staff and student behavior maintain after intervention procedures are removed (Demchak, 1987). However, maintenance of educational staff behavior usually indicates the presence of some type of maintaining consequences such as intermittent feedback from supervisory staff, feedback from peers, or ongoing positive reinforcement from students. Some recent investigations have included follow-up data that were obtained under conditions in which some aspect of the original intervention was in place [e.g., reduced but on-going schedule of feedback from an external monitor (Dyer et al., 1984)]. Although the importance of assessing durability of intervention effects has been acknowledged, Reid et al. (1989) indicated that less than one-third of the studies reviewed reported any follow-up data. Nonetheless, reports that included follow-up data were said to be encouraging with respect to maintenance of behavior change in teachers.

Often variables that maintain changes in staff behavior when intervention contingencies are withdrawn are difficult to isolate. Occasionally investigators speculate about possible maintaining variables that might account for durable results. For example, Alavosius and Sulzer-Azaroff

(1986) reported on the effects of performance feedback on increasing appropriate lifting and transferring techniques by direct care staff. After the intervention was concluded, follow-up probes (no feedback provided) indicated that the various skills were maintained. The investigators speculated that one possible maintaining variable was that participants reported that safer transfer techniques required less effort.

In a similar study by Alavosius and Sulzer-Azaroff (1990) the maintenance of health-care routines during a 7-month follow-up period (no feedback) was noted to be atypical of findings from other studies using feedback. Alavosius and Sulzer-Azaroff (1990) noted that a number of investigators have found that improved performance typically does not maintain in the absence of consequence procedures, including feedback. The investigators considered several possible maintaining variables (in the absence of feedback) including natural reinforcers associated with the tasks in the form of less effort, stimuli present during both training and follow-up, and peer support in the form of feedback from other employees.

Within the classroom setting, it has been determined that under some conditions student behavior change can have an effect on teacher behavior (Sherman & Cormier, 1974). Sherman and Cormier found that student behavior change (decrease in disruptive behavior) had an effect on subsequent teacher behavior. For example, when a student's appropriate behavior increased, the teacher's response to appropriate behavior also increased. Likewise, when a student's appropriate behavior decreased, so did the percentage of teacher responses to appropriate behavior. The investigators speculated that having students train teachers might be more cost effective than using inservices. However, in a classroom setting in which students are relatively unresponsive (e.g., students who have profound multiple handicaps) frequent positive reinforcement from students is unlikely (e.g., Ivancic, Reid, Iwata, Faw, & Page, 1981).

In additional classroom-based investigations, two principals maintained their increased rates of visits to classrooms (during withdrawal phase and follow-up) possibly due to naturally reinforcing events such as student progress or positive social reactions to the visits (Gillat & Sulzer-Azaroff, 1994). Anecdotal reports indicated an increased rate of visits being maintained for up to a few years after the conclusion of the study. Other investigators have noted the durability of intervention outcomes. In an investigation by Parsons et al. (1987), behavior change in multiple classrooms up to a period of two years was hypothesized to be maintained by continued prompts and feedback provided by staff supervisors who conducted the initial inservice and supervision.

A review of the 19 sample studies indicated that: 37% reported no follow-up data, 26% reported follow-up data obtained while some aspect of the intervention continued to be in place, and 37% reported follow-up data under conditions of fully discontinued intervention. Investigations in which follow-up data were reported while some aspect of the original intervention was in place indicated that 1-11 months of data were obtained. Investigations in which follow-up data were reported under conditions of discontinued intervention indicated that one week to two months of data were obtained.

While follow-up data have been reported under conditions in which the intervention (supervision) has been discontinued (e.g., Gillat & Sulzar-Azaroff, 1994) some investigators have continued to implement supervision during follow-up probes (although less frequently than during the initial intervention). An example of follow-up data obtained within the context of reduced supervision is an investigation by Dyer et al. (1984) in which feedback continued to be provided on a monthly basis while follow-up data were collected. Even though the frequency of supervisory contacts was greatly reduced, staff performance was maintained. Dyer et al. (1984) noted that following the reduction of observations, several staff members requested that frequent observations be reinstated. Several staff indicated they appreciated the observations and feedback. Nonetheless, there are potent factors that mitigate against the continuation of ongoing intervention components. For example, many administrators have too many key responsibilities that prevent a rich schedule of observations and feedback. While follow-up observations and consequences are typically warranted, strategies for reducing supervisory contacts while maintaining staff performance are probably essential in most cases.

Several diverse strategies have been used by a number of investigators to ensure durable results. One strategy involves systematically and slowly fading the schedule of feedback (Alovosius & Sulzer-Azaroff, 1990; Gross et al., 1983). Another approach that has taken multiple forms has been to create a model of supervision in which existing supervisors learn appropriate supervisory skills (e.g., observation, training, scheduling, providing prompts, feedback), and apply those skills, sometimes with training and additional support from an administrator or external monitor (e.g., Dyer et al., 1984; Gillat & Sulzer-Azaroff, 1994; Green et al., 1986; Parsons et al., 1987). Finally, some investigators have found a pyramid model of training (Jones et al., 1977) to be effective in building a structure to ensure quality control and maintenance of behavior change while reliance on outside experts or consultants decreases.

## ACCEPTABILITY OF INTERVENTIONS

Educational staff acceptance of training and management procedures has been identified as an important but often overlooked aspect of investigations (Demchak, 1987; Reid et al., 1989). It has been noted that while particular procedures may be effective in improving the performance of educational staff, if the procedures are unacceptable to either supervisors or staff, the procedures are less likely to be adopted or maintained. For example, supervisors are less likely to use procedures that are overly time consuming or that result in other negative or unpleasant outcomes. Similarly, teachers and aides are less likely to participate in a program that results in negative or uncomfortable outcomes for them.

Indeed investigators have reported on a variety of ways that supervisors and staff indicate their displeasure with specific aspects of investigations. Suda and Miltenberger (1993) reported that two vocational program staff withdrew their participation from the investigation prior to the implementation of self-management procedures. In addition, the vocational supervisor refused to complete his duties which included providing instructions and feedback to his staff.

In another study which took place in a vocational setting (Fleming & Sulzer-Azaroff, 1992), two staff withdrew prior to the implementation of peer management procedures indicating that they felt "threatened" by the responsibility of giving evaluative feedback to one another. Other investigators indicated that participants in their studies were uncomfortable with assessment procedures (e.g., video taping, observers in the classroom, use of data collected by teachers themselves) to such an extent that the assessment procedures were abbreviated, or replaced with other procedures (Inge & Snell, 1985; Ingham & Greer, 1992).

Not all responses by educational staff to assessment and/or intervention procedures are negative, however. Gillat and Sulzer-Azaroff (1994) reported that both of the principals maintained an increased rate of classroom visits, delivery of consequences and goal setting as well as other performance management skills acquired during the studies, and both indicated positive responses regarding their new skills.

Some investigators have attempted to systematically determine the responses of the participants to training procedures, goals, and outcomes. For example, Green and Reid (1994) presented teachers and teacher assistants with a 5-point Likert scale to assess their opinions about various aspects of the training program including how effective or useful the training was, and how beneficial their newly acquired skills would be for assisting their students. Interestingly, teachers and assistants differed in their opinions regarding most effective/useful training components.

Although not typically done, systematic analysis of opinions by educational staff regarding usefulness of, and preferences for training procedures reportedly can be helpful for practitioners and future investigators in designing intervention goals and procedures (Reid et al., 1989). Investigators have found that when provided with the opportunity staff will indicate nonpreferences for assessment and training strategies (e.g., Inge & Snell, 1985) as well as topics (Morgan, Ames, Loosli, Feng, & Taylor, 1995). An additional effort made by a small number of investigators has been to involve the participating educational staff in the design of the training goals (Inge & Snell, 1985), and procedures (Green & Reid, 1994). Inge and Snell (1985) had two teachers who were learning positioning and handling techniques determine, along with their instructor, objectives to include in training. In addition the participants developed a contract specifying trainer and teacher responsibilities during the inservice.

Reid et al. (1985) incorporated a participative management approach based on an earlier study by Burgio, Whitman and Reid (1983) in which educational staff were encouraged by the principal to determine how to increase functional activities and materials in their classrooms using a handout that included examples of functional and nonfunctional activities and materials as a guide. The purpose was to encourage staff to generate ideas for intervention and become more active participants in the planning process.

One possible outcome of using a participative management approach is to increase the likelihood that the training would be acceptable to the participating staff. There is evidence that such an approach leads to greater acceptability. Whyte, Van Houten, and Hunter (1983), through the use of a questionnaire, determined that there was a high percentage of high school teachers (47%) who indicated "resentment" regarding how the study that they participated in was presented to them, and about not being informed beforehand of the study. However, more direct evidence that specific participatory management results in greater implementation compliance is needed (Peck, Killen, & Baumgart, 1989).

## REACTIVITY

Several investigators have discussed concerns that behavior change observed in educational staff may have occurred at least partly in response to the presence of observers, experimenters, and supervisors rather than as a function of procedures specific to each study (Reid et al., 1989). When participating educational staff perform differentially in the presence or absence of observers or recording equipment (e.g., Haring et al., 1987) rather than as a function of procedures specific to the study, it is difficult to determine the effectiveness of the intervention.

While the possibility exists that participants change their behavior to meet the expectations of the experimenters in the presence of discriminative stimuli such as observers, data suggest that this situation may be less likely or pervasive than is feared (Reinoehl & Halle, 1994). Reinoehl and Halle (1994) partially analyzed the effects of supervisor presence by manipulating a supervisor's presence and absence across experimental conditions. Results indicated that the antecedent procedure designed to prompt educational staff performance was a crucial variable affecting the staff's level of performance. The supervisor's presence alone did not appear to be a functional variable with respect to staff performance. The investigators indicated however, that their analysis of reactivity was incomplete because analysis of the intervention in the absence of the supervisor was not conducted. This investigation indicates that participant reactivity to observations should be considered and addressed but that the extent and pervasiveness of the problem may be less serious than feared.

Other investigators have implemented observation procedures to minimize the potential for participant reactivity (Reid et al., 1989, Chap. 2). For example, Fleming and Sulzer-Azaroff (1992) acknowledged that the use of a microphone to record staff behavior and predictable observation schedules may have prompted increased teaching interactions. However, it was also suggested that extended baselines, and the participant's history of being videotaped while working may have limited reactivity during this study. The use of randomly scheduled observations throughout the day or frequent unannounced momentary time samples was recommended by Fleming and Sulzer-Azaroff. In fact, several investigators have incorporated procedures designed to limit reactivity including the use of unannounced observations (Green et al., 1986; Parsons et al., 1987) and the use of additional observers not associated with the investigation during post-training observation (O'Reilly et al., 1992).

## GENERALIZATION OF TEACHING SKILLS

It is clear that given appropriate training and supervision, educational staff typically generalize skills learned during inservice or other antecedent conditions to the situations that are specified during training (e.g., to time periods specified by the supervisor). Frequently what has not been demonstrated are other types of generalization (e.g., generalized implementation of skills to other instructional times not specified by the supervisor or trainer).

Some investigators have stated the importance of assessing the generality of educational staff behavior change across the school day (Fleming & Sulzer-Azaroff, 1992). While Fleming and Sulzer-Azaroff did not assess generalization of teaching skills to non-targeted times, the need for this measure in future research was indicated.

Only a few of the 19 sample studies measured generalization of staff performance across the day. Suda and Miltenberger (1993) completed observations of staff behavior at different times throughout the day when staff were unaware that the observer was associated with the study and that staff behavior was being recorded. The purpose was to measure how well staff behavior changes had generalized beyond the experimental session time, when staff knew they were being observed. Instructions and goal setting did not increase frequency of positive interactions during generalization probes; however, during the self-management phase, improvements were observed for three staff, and for a fourth staff member positive interactions improved after a subsequent feedback phase.

Reid et al. (1985) observed classrooms with respect to effects of inservice and supervisory prompts and feedback on increases in the use of functional educational tasks in classrooms serving students with severe handicaps during targeted and non-targeted (generalization) time periods. During generalization time periods no feedback or prompts were presented with respect to the targeted outcomes. Increases in functional educational tasks occurred during target and generalization periods and were maintained throughout follow-up observations. In addition, generalization results for students were similar to those observed during target periods.

Ingham and Greer (1992) also analyzed data collected by the teacher throughout the day for all instruction sessions, in addition to the data collected on individual students during the scheduled observation and feedback procedure. No feedback regarding these generalization data were provided at any point in the study. The results suggested that performance skills acquired during training were generalized to training sessions conducted with all students throughout the day following the implementation of observation procedures by supervisors. Teachers conducted more trials, collected more data, and obtained more correct responses from their students, including during generalization periods.

## COMPREHENSIVENESS OF INTERVENTIONS

A recurring concern about behavioral training and management interventions is that in many respects the focus of the majority of investigations has been limited. Criticisms regarding the limited focus of behavioral investigations have been made with respect to the breadth of educational staff and student needs and skills addressed, the number of participants involved in the investigation, the proportion of the educational system affected by the intervention, and the duration of the intervention particularly with respect to follow-up (Parsons et al., 1987). Critical reviews from within and outside of the field of applied behavior analysis indicate that too many investigations can be characterized as demonstration projects. Although demonstration projects certainly have a place in the research literature (e.g., prompting additional research pertinent to a question that has yet to be addressed), once a research question has been addressed initially, it then becomes important to address a broader array of issues related to the original question. For example, several early investigations focused on whether teachers could learn to use positive reinforcement and extinction to improve student skills such as on-task and academic performance, while decreasing problem behaviors (Hall et al., 1968). Although these important studies targeted a small set of teacher and student skills, included a small number of participants, and focused on brief parts of the school day for a limited duration, they nevertheless provided greatly needed information regarding useful classroom management procedures. However, the generality of the outcomes was limited by the demonstration-type focus of the interventions. These early studies laid the groundwork for large scale studies including those that looked at a greater number and variety of student behaviors (e.g., Parsonson, Baer, & Baer, 1974). Additional studies have also analyzed the effects of interventions that have incorporated a larger set of teachers, student populations presenting unique challenges, analyses of generalization across new behaviors and children, and measures of durability for extended periods of time (Koegel, Russo, & Rincover, 1977).

Some more recent interventions demonstrate attempts to improve broad sets of skills in both educational personnel and students, across an increased portion of educational settings (e.g., multiple classrooms), for longer parts of the day and over extended periods of time. Dyer et al. (1984) provided an example of a comprehensive investigation in which the purpose was to increase the amount of time severely handicapped students living in a residential facility engaged in age-appropriate and functional activities. The intervention included brief instructions to supervisors, and feedback to staff including those responsible for vocational-type training. This project included all students (37) and staff (43) at the facility. Observations occurred across multiple settings at the facility (residences, simulated vocational training workshop, and the entire grounds of the facility including pool, dining room, gym, and playground). Functionality and age-appropriateness of materials and tasks were measured across four domains (recreation/leisure, domestic, self-help and vocational). Socially inappropriate behavior was also measured. Observations occurred from 3-9 pm school days and 7 am-9 pm weekends for up to 26 weeks with an additional five-month follow-up period.

An additional example of a comprehensive investigation actually involves a series of related investigations (Green et al., 1986; Parsons et al.,

1987; Reid et al., 1985) which evaluated staff management programs designed to improve the functional utility of educational services for persons with severe handicaps. The interventions incorporated the use of a brief inservice followed by prompts and feedback from supervisors. The most comprehensive of the three studies (Parsons et al., 1987) included four schools located in a facility which included 39 educational staff providing services for 152 students. The students had a wide array of disabilities. Observations could occur throughout the day and intervention and maintenance occurred up to 24 months.

Some additional recent studies were comprehensive with respect to number of educational staff and students involved, behaviors targeted for change, and duration of the investigations (e.g., Gage et al., 1982; Green et al., 1986; Reid et al., 1985; Selinski et al., 1991). However, in general, investigations continue to include a limited number of participants in a limited number of settings with observations conducted over a brief duration of time.

## GENERALITY OF FINDINGS: STUDENT POPULATIONS

Two investigations took place in classrooms serving elementary, middle, and high school students. The remaining investigations took place in classrooms and related settings serving students with a variety of disabilities (e.g., severe behavior problems, autism, mental retardation, physical handicaps, multiple disabilities). The latter investigations were conducted in both congregate-care and community-based educational settings. Previous reviewers (Demchak, 1987) have pointed out the need to evaluate the effectiveness of techniques in different settings with different populations. Also, in order to determine the external validity of procedures, replications of training procedures with other staff in other settings is necessary.

## GENERALITY OF STUDIES: TARGETED SKILLS OF EDUCATIONAL STAFF

An additional criticism of behavioral training and management interventions is that historically, investigations have focused primarily on improving behavior modification skills of teachers and sometimes supervisors (Green & Reid, 1994). Thus, an argument can be made that the generality of training and management interventions is limited due to the restricted focus of skills taught in most investigations. Indeed Morgan et al. (1995) completed a survey of educational staff (supervisors and teachers) and found that while client reinforcement and management techniques were important topics for inservice training, a variety of other work-related tasks were also important, if not more important.

Of the sample studies, a majority (eight) focused on classroom teaching and management interactions although three of the 10 studies trained other behaviors as well (e.g., consultation skills, goal setting, program writing, data analysis). Four studies dealt with skills associated with arranging environments to increase availability of functional materials and activities. Two studies dealt with teaching skills related to assessment and treatment of severe behavior problems. Three investigations focused on teaching appropriate communication training skills (e.g., incidental teaching). One investigation targeted transfer and positioning skills, one study focused on training direct instruction techniques, and one study focused on switch assembly skills.

## EFFECTS OF BEHAVIORAL TRAINING AND MANAGEMENT ON ADDITIONAL SKILLS PERFORMED BY EDUCATIONAL STAFF

Several investigations focused on performance skills of various educational staff that were a part of their job description but that did not involve specific teaching interactions with students. As members of interdisciplinary teams and professional departments, educational staff are responsible for completing various tasks accurately, thoroughly, consistently and in a timely manner. Given performance decrements in each of these areas, investigators have analyzed the effects of various antecedents and consequences on the performance of a variety of tasks by educational staff.

Two investigations addressed quality of writing skills by educational staff. Hundert (1982) targeted several skills pertinent to writing and implementing behavior modification programs by 2 special education teachers. A training package which included written and verbal instructions, corrective tutoring, practice, feedback and praise resulted in improved writing and implementation skills for both teachers.

Horner, Thompsen, and Storey (1990) investigated the effects of feedback from case managers on the quality of individual habilitation plan (IHP) objectives developed by program staff providing residential and vocational services. Feedback from the case manager resulted in improvements in the quality of objectives with maintenance of effects observed for 18 months.

One study addressed the issue of timeliness by various professional staff including educational staff. Feldstein and Feldstein (1990) improved timely submission of evaluation reports through the use of positive reinforcement (poster and candy).

Two studies focused on completion of routine duties. Hutchison, Jarman and Bailey (1980) used publicly posted feedback to increase attendance at team meetings and number of agenda items completed during the meetings by multidisciplinary team members (including teachers at a mental retardation facility). Whyte et al. (1983) increased the percentage of teaching staff at a regular school setting carrying out assigned student supervision duties via publicly posted feedback.

## SUMMARY AND FUTURE DIRECTIONS

As this and previous reviews (Demchak, 1987; Reid et al., 1989) indicate, while considerable knowledge has been acquired about various aspects of behavioral training and management of educational staff over the past 35 years, much more information is needed in a variety of areas. All of the topics for future research indicated in previous overviews (Demchak, 1987; Reid et al., 1989) remain current.

With respect to antecedent interventions (instructions, prompts, cues, etc.), it has been pointed out that this general approach warrants further investigation because of its effectiveness with some educational staff, and the potential for greater efficiency (Reid et al., 1994). Given the limited time that most supervisors have to provide training for staff, more research into the effectiveness of self-instruction and train-the-trainers approaches is needed. In addition, the usefulness of training models with demonstrated effectiveness with some skills (e.g., Green & Reid, 1994) needs to be tested across a broader range of skills, and with educational staff working in a greater variety of educational settings. Also, ways to effectively teach a greater variety of comprehensive sets of skills is needed.

The use of consequence procedures as an integral part of behavioral training and management efforts that are effective has been described in this and previous reviews (Demchak, 1987; Reid et al., 1989). While consequence procedures are rarely used in the absence of other procedures, future research is warranted to determine the effectiveness of consequence procedures on staff behavior. Perhaps of greater importance is the need for additional research that investigates other outcomes of consequence procedures. For example, peer feedback as a consequence may be an effective and efficient procedure for improving staff performance. Various consequence procedures probably have advantages (and disadvantages) that warrant further study.

Efficiency of antecedent and consequence procedures will remain a critical issue with regard to usefulness and acceptance of these procedures. Future studies will be more beneficial to the extent that efficiency is incorporated and analyzed. Supervisors and other consumers are more likely to adopt procedures that require less time to implement while remaining effective. Additional analysis of a train-the-trainers approach is recommended across educational settings. A self-instruction and planning approach to improving staff performance has been studied very little, yet could yield desirable outcomes with respect to efficiency and acceptability.

Gillat and Sulzer-Azaroff's (1994) training package for principals in the areas of time management and scheduling is a creative approach to a most difficult problem, namely getting supervisors more involved in behavioral training and management functions. Indeed the simultaneous need for involvement by managers along with the lack of (durable) participation in active training and supervisory duties by managers continues to be an issue that requires careful analysis (Hopkins, 1987).

Continued investigation into behavioral staff training and management procedures that ensure improved student performance remains a critical issue. Previous reviewers' suggestions that student performance be incorporated into the investigation should be a fundamental part of every investigation (e.g., Demchak, 1987).

Ways to ensure durable effects of all levels of educational staff (and student) performances should continue to be investigated. In particular, procedures that maintain durable responding and that are a part of the organizational structure (e.g., use of principals, peers as sources of feedback and positive reinforcement) should be investigated. Several investigators (e.g., Alavosius & Sulzer-Azaroff, 1986) have suggested that natural consequences can play an important role in maintaining staff behavior. It might be beneficial for investigators to take the effort to isolate and incorporate naturally occurring consequences whenever possible.

Acceptability of various procedures to educational staff is clearly an important area of research. Because staff have been observed to respond differentially to various observation, training and management procedures, one potentially useful area of research would be in the area of providing staff with opportunities to select preferred topics, objectives, and modes of training (e.g., Inge & Snell, 1985). Continued efforts to incorporate staff input into training and management outcomes (e.g., Reid et al., 1985) may be a useful approach.

Very little research into generality of training and management efforts has been completed. While generality of staff skills across the school day has sometimes been analyzed (e.g., Suda & Miltenberger, 1993), other measures could be useful as well (e.g., generalization of effects across non-targeted students and skills).

As other investigators (e.g., Hopkins, 1987) have indicated, a major criticism of behavior training and management research has been the generally limited scope of many investigations. Comprehensive investigations (e.g., Parsons et al., 1987) have been the exception rather than the rule with the result being that the outcomes of behavioral training and management efforts have been often ignored. It has been suggested that outcomes which are comprehensive as well as effective, efficient, durable, etc., will be needed to prompt potential consumers to adopt this approach (Hopkins, 1987).

Several investigators have raised the issue of how to obtain supervisory support for behavioral training and management techniques. Gillat and Sulzer-Azaroff (1994) were successful in recruiting two principals to participate in training and management duties with maintenance of their involvement after the investigation was concluded. The investigators discussed potential antecedents and consequences that might have been responsible for the principals' involvement (e.g., professional relationship with one of the investigators). However, given the unique characteristics of the two principals who participated, the generality of the findings to other managers may be limited.

Given the importance of administrative acceptance of, support for, and involvement in training and management efforts, many questions remain regarding ways to increase the usefulness and acceptance of these procedures. Some investigators (Dyer et al., 1984) have speculated that administrative support may have contributed to the positive outcomes of their staff training and management interventions. Several investigators have noted the importance of obtaining the support of administrators and other staff throughout the course of a particular intervention whether small or large scale (Liberman, 1983). Failure to planfully and carefully obtain support from administrators and other staff can certainly result in the demise of a behavioral program regardless of the quality of the program. Even high quality programs are terminated in part due to lack of administrative support (Liberman, 1983). Many issues related to recruitment of individuals who are crucial to the initiation and maintenance of behavioral training and management efforts remain to be addressed by researchers in OBM.

## REFERENCES

Alavosius, M. P., & Sulzer-Azaroff, B. (1986). The effects of performance feedback on the safety of client lifting and transfer. *Journal of Applied Behavior Analysis, 19,* 261-267.

Alavosius, M. P., & Sulzer-Azaroff, B. (1990). Acquisition and maintenance of health-care routines as a function of feedback density. *Journal of Applied Behavior Analysis, 23*, 151-162.

Ayllon, T., & Michael, J. (1959). The psychiatric nurse as a behavioral engineer. *Journal of the Experimental Analysis of Behavior, 2*, 323-334.

Burgio, L. D., Whitman, T. L., & Reid, D. H. (1983). A participative management approach for improving direct-care staff performance in an institutional setting. *Journal of Applied Behavior Analysis, 16*, 37-53.

Demchak, M. A. (1987). A review of behavioral staff training in special education settings. *Education and Training in Mental Retardation, 22*, 205-217.

Duker, P. C., Hensgens, Y., & Venderbosch, S. (1995). Effectiveness of delayed feedback on the accuracy of teaching communicative gestures to individuals with severe mental retardation. *Research in Developmental Disabilities, 16*, 479-488.

Dyer, K., Schwartz, I. S., & Luce, S. C. (1984). A supervision program for increasing functional activities for severely handicapped students in a residential setting. *Journal of Applied Behavior Analysis, 17*, 249-259.

Feldstein, S., & Feldstein, J. H. (1990). Positive reinforcement for submission of timely reports by professional staff in a residential facility. *Education and Training in Mental Retardation, 25*, 188-192.

Filler, J., Hecimovic, A., & Blue, S. (1978). An analysis of the effectiveness of a preservice workshop for educators of severely handicapped young students. *AAESPH Review, 3*, 173-177.

Fleming, R., & Sulzer-Azaroff, B. (1992). Reciprocal peer management: Improving staff instruction in a vocational training program. *Journal of Applied Behavior Analysis, 25*, 611-620.

Gage, M. A., Fredericks, H. D. B., Johnson-Dorn, N., & Lindley-Southard, B. (1982). Inservice training for staffs of group homes and work activity centers serving developmentally disabled adults. *The Journal of the Association for Persons with Severe Handicaps, 7*, 60-70.

Gillat, A., & Sulzer-Azaroff, B. (1994). Promoting principals' managerial involvement in instructional improvement. *Journal of Applied Behavior Analysis, 27*, 115-129.

Green, C. W., Canipe, V. C., Way, P. J., & Reid, D. H. (1986). Improving the functional utility and effectiveness of classroom services for students with profound multiple handicaps. *The Journal of the Association for Persons with Severe Handicaps, 11*, 162-170.

Green, C. W., & Reid, D. H. (1994). A comprehensive evaluation of a train-the-trainers model for training education staff to assemble adaptive switches. *Journal of Mental and Physical Disabilities, 6*, 219-238.

Greene, B. F., Willis, B. S., Levy, R., & Bailey, J. S. (1978). Measuring client gains from staff-implemented programs. *Journal of Applied Behavior Analysis, 11*, 395-412.

Gross, A. M., & Ekstrand, M. (1983). Increasing and maintaining rates of teacher praise: A study using public posting and feedback fading. *Behavior Modification, 7*, 126-135.

Hall, R. V., Lund, D., & Jackson, D. (1968). Effects of teacher attention on study behavior. *Journal of Applied Behavior Analysis, 1*, 1-12.

Hall, R. V., Panyan, M., Rabon, D., & Broden, M. (1968). Instructing beginning teachers in reinforcement procedures which improve classroom control. *Journal of Applied Behavior Analysis, 1*, 315-322.

Haring, T. G., Neetz, J. A., Lovinger, L., Peck, C., & Semmel, M. I. (1987). Effects of four modified incidental teaching procedures to create opportunities for communication. *The Journal of the Association for Persons with Severe Handicaps, 12*, 218-226.

Hopkins, B. L. (1987). Comments on the future of applied behavior analysis. *Journal of Applied Behavior Analysis, 20*, 339-346.

Horner, R. H., Thompsen, L. S., & Storey, K. (1990). Effects of case manager feedback on the quality of individual habilitation plan objectives. *Mental Retardation, 28*, 227-231.

Hundert, J. (1982). Training teachers in generalized writing of behavior modification programs for multihandicapped deaf children. *Journal of Applied Behavior Analysis, 15*, 111-122.

Hutchison, J. M., Jarman, P. H., & Bailey, J. S. (1980). Public posting with a habilitation team: Effects on attendance and performance. *Behavior Modification, 4*, 57-70.

Inge, K. J., & Snell, M. E. (1985). Teaching positioning and handling techniques to public school personnel through inservice training. *The Journal of the Association for Persons with Severe Handicaps, 10*, 105-110.

Ingham, P., & Greer, R. D. (1992). Changes in student and teacher responses in observed and generalized settings as a function of supervisor observations. *Journal of Applied Behavior Analysis, 25*, 153-164.

Ivancic, M. T., Reid, D. H., Iwata, B. A., Faw, G. D., & Page, T. J. (1981). Evaluating a supervision program for developing and maintaining therapeutic staff-resident interactions during institutional care routines. *Journal of Applied Behavior Analysis, 14*, 95-107.

Jones, F. H., Fremouw, W., & Carples, S. (1977). Pyramid training of elementary school teachers to use a classroom management "skill package." *Journal of Applied Behavior Analysis, 10*, 239-253.

Koegel, R. L., Russo, D. C., & Rincover, A. (1977). Assessing and training teachers in the generalized use of behavior modification with autistic children. *Journal of Applied Behavior Analysis, 10*, 197-205.

Langone, J., Koorland, M., & Oseroff, A. (1987). Producing changes in the instructional behavior of teachers of the mentally handicapped through inservice education. *Education and Treatment of Children, 10*, 146-164.

Liberman, R. P. (Ed.). (1983). Sociopolitics of behavioral programs in institutions and community agencies. [Special Issue]. *Analysis and Intervention in Developmental Disabilities, 3*(2/3).

McKeown, Jr., D., Adams, H. E., & Forehand, R. (1975). Generalization to the classroom of principles of behavior modification taught to teachers. *Behavior Research & Therapy, 13*, 85-92.

Morgan, R. L., Ames, H. N., Loosli, T. S., Feng, J., & Taylor, M. J. (1995).

Training for supported employment specialists and their supervisors: Identifying important training topics. *Education and Training in Mental Retardation and Developmental Disabilities, 30,* 299-307.

Nakano, Y., Kageyama, M., & Kinoshita, S. (1993). Using direct instruction to improve teacher performance, academic achievement, and classroom behavior in a Japanese public junior high school. *Education and Treatment of Children, 16,* 326-343.

Northup, J., Wacker, D. P., Berg, W. K., Kelly, L., Sasso, G., & DeRaad, A. (1994). The treatment of severe behavior problems in school settings using a technical assistance model. *Journal of Applied Behavior Analysis, 27,* 33-47.

O'Reilly, M. F., Renzaglia, A., Hutchins, M., Koterba-Buss, L., Clayton, M., Halle, J. W., & Izen, C. (1992). Teaching systematic instruction competencies to special education student teachers: An applied behavioral supervision model. *Journal of the Association for Persons with Severe Handicaps, 17,* 104-111.

Parsons, M. B., Schepis, M. M., Reid, D. H., McCarn, J. E., & Green, C. W. (1987). Expanding the impact of behavioral staff management: A large-scale, long-term application in schools serving severely handicapped students. *Journal of Applied Behavior Analysis, 20,* 139-150.

Parsonson, B. S., Baer, A. M., & Baer, D. M. (1974). The application of generalized correct social contingencies: An evaluation of a training program. *Journal of Applied Behavior Analysis, 7,* 427-437.

Peck, C. A., Killen, C. C., & Baumgart, D. (1989). Increasing implementation of special education instruction in mainstream preschools: Direct and generalized effects of nondirective consultation. *Journal of Applied Behavior Analysis, 22,* 197-210.

Quilitch, H. R. (1975). A comparison of three staff-management procedures. *Journal of Applied Behavior Analysis, 8,* 59-66.

Reid, D. H., Parsons, M. B., & Green, C. W. (1989). *Staff management in human services: Behavioral research and application.* Springfield, IL: Charles C. Thomas.

Reid, D. H., Parsons, M. B., McCarn, J. E., Green, C. W., Phillips, J. F., & Schepis, M. M. (1985). Providing a more appropriate education for severely handicapped persons: Increasing and validating functional classroom tasks. *Journal of Applied Behavior Analysis, 18,* 289-301.

Reinoehl, R. B., & Halle, J. W. (1994). Increasing the assessment probe performance of teacher aides through written prompts. *Journal of the Association for Persons with Severe Handicaps, 19,* 32-42.

Sasso, G. M., Reimers, T. M., Cooper, L. M., Wacker, D., Berg, W., Steege, M., Kelly, L., & Allaire, A. (1992). Use of descriptive and experimental analysis to identify the functional properties of aberrant behavior in school settings. *Journal of Applied Behavior Analysis, 25,* 809-821.

Schwartz, I. S., Anderson, S. R., & Halle, J. W. (1989). Training teachers to use naturalistic time delay: Effects on teacher behavior and on the language use of students. *The Journal of The Association for Persons with Severe Handicaps, 14,* 48-57.

Selinske, J. E., Greer, R. D., & Lodhi, S. (1991). A functional analysis of the comprehensive application of behavior analysis to schooling. *Journal of Applied Behavior Analysis, 24,* 107-117.

Sherman, T. M., & Cormier, W. H. (1974). An investigation of the influence of student behavior on teacher behavior. *Journal of Applied Behavior Analysis, 7,* 11-21.

Suda, K. T., & Miltenberger, R. G. (1993). Evaluation of staff management strategies to increase positive interactions in a vocational setting. *Behavioral Residential Treatment, 8,* 69-88.

Whyte, R. A., Van Houten, R., & Hunter, W. (1983). The effects of public posting on teachers' performance of supervision duties. *Education and Treatment of Children, 6,* 21-28.

Ziarnik, J. P., & Bernstein, C. S. (1982). A critical examination of the effect of inservice training on staff performance. *Mental Retardation, 20,* 109-114.

# Organizational Behavior Management in Early Intervention: Status and Implications for Research and Development

Robert Crow
Patricia Snyder

**SUMMARY.** The term "early intervention" has been applied to a variety of services and supports offered to young children with disabilities, or those children at-risk for disabilities, and their families (Bailey & Wolery, 1992). Children from birth to 8 years of age might be considered appropriate for early intervention based on the rapidity and types of human development occurring in these years. In this paper, we include descriptions of early intervention (EI) principles and practices and a review of the status of OBM in early intervention. Related literature is reviewed for implications affecting the adoption of OBM practices in EI. We devote final sections to descriptions of opportunities for research and challenges to applying OBM practices in early intervention services. *[Article copies available for a fee from The Haworth Document Delivery Service: 1-800-342-9678. E-mail address: getinfo@haworthpressinc.com]*

## OVERVIEW OF EARLY INTERVENTION

Early intervention is a specialized category of human services that is unique in the characteristics of individuals served and distinctive in the

Robert Crow and Patricia Snyder are affiliated with the Louisiana State University Medical Center.

[Haworth co-indexing entry note]: "Organizational Behavior Management in Early Intervention: Status and Implications for Research and Development." Crow, Robert, and Patricia Snyder. Co-published simultaneously in *Journal of Organizational Behavior Management* (The Haworth Press, Inc.) Vol. 18, No. 2/3, 1998, pp. 131-156; and: *Organizational Behavior Management and Developmental Disabilities Services: Accomplishments and Future Directions* (ed: Dennis H. Reid) The Haworth Press, Inc., 1998, pp. 131-156. Single or multiple copies of this article are available for a fee from The Haworth Document Delivery Service [1-800-342-9678, 9:00 a.m. - 5:00 p.m. (EST). E-mail address: getinfo@haworthpressinc.com].

nature of the service paradigm. The population of children is very young and interventions commonly involve close interactions with family members in home- and community-based settings. Service activities are designed to promote child and family well-being through interventions targeted at the child, family, or community level.

Some early intervention services are instructional or therapeutic in nature. These services, like physical, occupational, or speech therapy, involve direct interventions provided or guided by professionals to promote child development. Other services or supports may be more family-directed, including provision of information, referral to community resources, and coordination of services delivered to the child and family. Unique features of early intervention include the central role of the family in developing plans for how services or supports will be designed and delivered to the child or family, and the functional and integrative nature of these services or supports.

In recent years, the goals and methods of early intervention have expanded and diversified due in part to federal mandates or incentives for programs for young children with disabilities. Other forces shaping early intervention practices include maxims and norms recognized widely by practitioners and families involved in early intervention, and accumulated research findings (see Bailey & Wolery, 1992, for a concise presentation of major principles, maxims, and norms of early intervention). Briefly, the primary postulates related to services for children call for interventions that involve physical and social qualities, stress child-initiated learning in context, and teach to the child's strengths according to known or assumed developmental sequences. These activities typically are accomplished by interdisciplinary teams who focus on supporting parental priorities in settings that are least restrictive and naturally occurring for the child and family.

The emphasis on interdisciplinary design of interventions and attention to promoting functional skill development are features of high quality human services in all venues. Distinctive features of early intervention include the continuing reference to age- and individually-appropriate developmental progressions for guiding interventions and the influences of family priorities and other ecological factors on the design and delivery of services or supports (Shonkoff, & Meisles, 1990). For example, practitioners need to learn about a child's current developmental status, home routines, and the extent to which the family desires child participation in these routines, before working with parents to establish an intervention plan. These features must be applied by early intervention professionals in a wide range of home and community settings. Professionals are challenged to use skills of observation and communication to determine relevant child, family, and ecological variables related to service design and delivery.

Early interventionists share with practitioners in other human service fields an emphasis on fostering individual skill acquisition in the context of daily routines and activities. The requirement for simultaneously involving other adult caregivers as partners in services for very young children and intervening with the children themselves is unique. Early interventionists work with children to engage them in naturally occurring childhood activities. These activities may be engineered so logical cues and consequences promote development across interrelated domains, for example, muscle usage, communication, and social interaction (Bricker, 1989). An illustration would be an eating routine where a child could be provided with opportunities to lift an adapted cup to drink, and to request more liquid when the cup is empty. The integration of environmental and behavioral engineering to foster multi-faceted, but child-specific skill acquisition is both challenging and rewarding for interventionists.

Several features of early intervention are similar to other areas of human service, including the stimulation of working with interdisciplinary teams, implementation of intervention plans, and evaluation of client progress. Yet, early intervention also has features not commonly encountered in other areas of human service.

Despite decades of using applied behavior analysis in the design and delivery of child- and family-level interventions (Strain, McConnell, Carta, Fowler, Neisworth, & Wolery, 1992), there is little evidence that the principles and practices associated with organizational behavior management (OBM) have been adopted in early intervention. We have heard testimonies from a number of administrators in early intervention programs that staff are "professionals" who do not need to be managed (e.g., Crow & Stewart, December, 1993). Yet, early intervention is struggling with a number of quality assurance issues, for example, ensuring that delivered services and supports reflect practices identified as "family-centered" (Sexton, Snyder, Lobman, Kimbrough, & Matthews, 1997). We believe that the practices of OBM found effective in other areas of human endeavor could be useful for advancing the use of recommended intervention practices in early intervention.

## *Conceptual Framework of Early Intervention*

An appreciation for the status of OBM practices in EI and opportunities for expanding their use in the field requires some fluency with the major conceptual paradigms guiding EI researchers and practitioners. These include perspectives from developmental, behavioral, ecological, and systems frameworks. The influence of these frameworks can be seen in the ways EI personnel conduct their activities with children, families, and one another. The integration of these perspectives is pragmatic by equipping interventionists with conceptual tools for observing, analyzing, developing, and implementing services and supports for children and families. By reviewing these frameworks those interested in OBM are better prepared to identify commonalities that can facilitate expanded use of validated OBM practices in EI. Further, OBM specialists might benefit from the stimulation provided by differences in the conceptual frameworks of EI and OBM by gaining new notions about variables for application and examination in both fields.

*The developmental perspective.* The premise that children grow and develop over time is well supported by empirical data (Capute & Accardo, 1996). Children are born with physical and performance potential and limitations which underlie changes due to maturational factors. Child development is seen from the developmental perspective as sequential and an outcome of maturation.

*The behavioral perspective.* This perspective maintains that children are born with the capacity to learn and learning occurs as a function of the child's history involving antecedents, behaviors, and consequences. Essentially, the behaviors of children are selected by their environments so repertoires are developed and maintained. The behavioral perspective in early intervention is relatively established and pervasive (e.g., Bijou & Baer, 1961a; Bijou & Baer, 1961b; see Strain, McConnell, Carta, Fowler, Neisworth, & Wolery,1992, for an eloquent discussion of "Behaviorism in Early Intervention").

*The ecological and systems perspective.* In the field of early intervention, there is widespread belief that the development of children is influenced by a complex of proximal and distal environmental variables (Brinker, 1985). These variables include interactions between children and other persons. It is assumed that interactions are transactional, that is, involve reciprocal impacts on the children and the people they contact (Sameroff & Friese, 1990). At another level, children are viewed as part of a family system that is embedded in broader systems of extended family and community (Bronfenbrenner, 1979). From these perspectives, an understanding of child and family development requires attention to how environments impact children as well as the nature and dynamics of these environments.

A degree of parsimony is provided to the conceptual landscape by the combined behavioral-ecological approach to early intervention in which child development is seen as involving multiple sources of influence and being interpretable in behavioral principles (Vincent, Salisbury, Strain,

McCormick, & Tessier, 1990). From this view "intervention targets are selected from an ecological or interactional perspective . . . trained in meaningful (natural) contexts . . . (and) incorporated more easily into diverse family perspectives" (Vincent et al., 1990, p. 190).

## RELATIONSHIPS AMONG OBM AND EI PRINCIPLES AND PRACTICES

The brief review of perspectives that guide EI is intended as a foundation to permit comparisons between the basic tenets of EI and OBM. These comparisons may be useful for identifying similarities and deriving opportunities to promote and advance OBM in EI. The reader is advised to see Crowell and Anderson (1982a) and Mawhinney (1984) for descriptions of OBM principles and practices. For the purposes of this paper we note that both OBM and EI involve applying behavior analytic strategies to human performance analyses and problems (cf. Bijou & Baer, 1961; Crowell & Anderson, 1982; Mawhinney, 1992; Strain et al. 1992; Vincent et al., 1990). Currently in EI, behavior analyses are primarily used with children who have special needs, that is, with children who require health or developmental services or supports. Seldom are behavior analytic techniques applied to family members or service personnel. The latter almost always includes early childhood educators, therapists, and paraprofessionals in roles that range from direct therapy to service coordination or consultation.

Environmental analyses in EI are similar to actions common in OBM for identifying functional roles and performances of people in organizations (Malott, Vunovich, Boettcher, & Groeger, 1995). Another similarity is that targeted personnel know and effectively perform activities related to achieving the objectives of the organization. Primary features of differentiation between EI practices and those required to be present in OBM literature include the nature of "productivity" and the factors involved in "cost-benefit analysis" (Mawhinney, 1984; p. 11). Furthermore, what is meant by "organization" in OBM in comparison to how people functionally relate to each other in EI might be a point of departure.

Salient features of organizations might include being a discernable entity with a recognizable mission, staff, and process and product variables that are defined and enforced by lines of authority, responsibility, employment, decision-making, and accountability. Viewed this way, EI services would be found confusing or challenging in several respects. First, the organizing aspects of EI are individual children along with their family and the systems in which they are embedded. In fundamental ways, decision-making authority in EI rests with family members to a greater extent than generally experienced in other human service contexts or private enterprise. This shift in decision-making authority results from the principles and practices adopted in response to family-centered requirements of law and recommended practices in EI. Once families and professionals decide what performances are desired, OBM practices would be applicable.

A second organizational challenge is the dynamic nature of EI services that makes services hard to locate and define. Settings in which EI practitioners work from day to day include homes, schools, day care classrooms, and offices where children receive medical, educational, and social services that are related to needs of the child and family. The work duties of EI staff vary according to the changing needs and priorities of the child and family (Bernheimer & Keogh, 1995; Brinker, 1985). Setting and intervention variables are affected by considerations of interagency roles, funding and monitoring requirements, personnel availability, and variations in the service models practiced by agencies who provide services and supports to the family.

These features of EI suggest that the definition of "organization" might be unfamiliar or elusive for purposes of delimiting where OBM practices might occur. In this paper, we define an EI organization as an ad hoc entity consisting of at least one EI practitioner performing intervention activities in any setting with a child, family, or other caregiver. This definition and other factors related to accomplishing OBM practices in EI circumstances are amplified below.

## LITERATURE REVIEWS REGARDING STATUS OF OBM IN EI

Reviews of two periodicals devoted to publishing in topics of OBM (i.e., *Journal of Organizational Behavior Management* and *Journal of Applied Behavior Analysis*) and four major journals in EI (see below) disclosed very little articulation across these fields. That is, very few papers were located in which the work performance of early interventionists was a dependent variable while systematic manipulations of their work environment were accomplished. This void in the literature is partially attributable to the specificity of the topic. Our definition of early intervention involved children with disabilities aged birth through 5 years, therefore, several papers concerned with OBM applications in other educational settings were excluded. The utility of holding to this criterion is based on the service paradigm differences found across age groups. In examining OBM-type activities in both literatures, we were searching for practices with credibility in both fields. From the perspective of OBM, this meant that the report was behavioral and included definition, manipulation, and measurement of work performance. For the EI perspective, we observed for age and presence of disability in the children affected by work performance and included all papers without regard to quality of interventions. We sought all articles meeting both EI and OBM criteria to determine the nature and extent of involvement of OBM in EI.

## ORGANIZATIONAL BEHAVIOR MANAGEMENT IN EARLY INTERVENTION

The extent of activity in EI literature related to OBM was examined by Crow and Stewart (December, 1993). These authors reviewed four major EI journals publishing studies in early intervention for articles with content related to managing staff behavior in the conduct of their duties. Crow and Stewart examined all articles appearing in recent volumes (i.e., 1988-1992) of *Infants and Young Children, Infant-Toddler Intervention, The Journal of Early Intervention,* and *Topics in Early Childhood Special Education* for content related to management. Management content was defined as textual or graphic display of (a) definition(s) of staff performance, (b) monitoring of performance in the work setting, (c) differential actions related to performance in the work setting, and (d) evaluation of performance(s) being defined, monitored or differentially acted upon. Overall, 565 articles appeared in these journals in the 5-year period and 14 (i.e., 2.5%) had content in two or more of the four categories of management being observed. Of these, only two articles (i.e., 0.35%) had content in all four features of management. The two papers were Bruder and Nikitas (1992), "Changing the Professional Practices of Early Interventionists: An Inservice Model to Meet the Service Needs of Public Law 99-457," and Venn and Wolery (1992), "Increasing Day Care Staff Members' Interactions During Caregiving Routines." These two studies are described in detail here to give readers information about current practices of staff development methods for obtaining the use of skills in the work site in EI. The methods, subsequently, are discussed relative to OBM practices.

The report by Bruder and Nikitas (1992) was focused on describing a rationale and overall approach for conducting staff development (specifically inservice training) to support early intervention service delivery. The training model was based on "some universally accepted assumptions about the adult as a learner," for example, adults have a need to know, a psychological need to be self directed, and will learn things that bring them greater satisfaction or success (p. 174). These authors cited Bailey (1989) as they defined inservice training as "the process by which practicing professionals participate in experiences designed to improve or change professionals practice" (p. 174). According to Bruder and Nikitas, the intended outcome of inservice training is trainees "will internalize new knowledge, applying it to their specific professional needs" (p. 174).

Training objectives, activities, and evaluation criteria were developed for each trainee based on a written needs assessment and an interview. Instruction included attending 4 to 10 weeks of half-day workshop sessions, completing a set of tasks, and participating in follow up activities. The latter activities involved meetings and observations by the trainer followed by consultations or feedback. Completed tasks were collected and discussed. Evaluation of the impacts of training included pre/post measures of knowledge, a skills checklist, consumer satisfaction questionnaire, and "competency-based program tasks" (p. 178). No outcome data were presented, but results were described as "positive changes within the trainees" on all effectiveness measures (p. 179).

This study demonstrated direct reference to recommended service practices in EI and attempts to establish transfer of new skills from the training session to the work place. Training activities were varied and included both skill practice and feedback. The authors also examined differential outcomes related to observed performance in the work site. These training activities coupled with relevant evaluation procedures marked this as an OBM study according to the four features defined by Crow and Stewart (December, 1993). The fact that the trainees provided services in EI settings to eligible children and families qualifies the Bruder and Nikitas (1992) paper as describing the use of OBM in EI.

As indicated previously, the second involving OBM activities in EI was reported by Venn and Wolery (1992). These authors conducted a staff development activity to increase skills and use of skills by staff in an infant day care program which included children with disabilities. Three of four direct care (paraprofessional) staff who served 16 infants in one room participated. Included in the study sample were three infants with identified disabilities and two who were at risk for developmental delay.

This study focused on modifying staff behavior in the diaper changing area while measuring staff performance in both the diaper changing and feeding areas. The targeted staff performance was staff interaction with children. Activities at these locations were videotaped and scored primarily for "game playing" while "looking, vocalizing, and touching were considered secondary dependent measures" (p. 306). These activities by staff were selected due to their relationship to the development by infants of play, language, and attending skills.

Videotaping occurred throughout the day and continued from a pre-training baseline through training and post-intervention conditions. Staff training targeted performance in the diaper changing area and included lectures, *in vivo* demonstration and practice with feedback, and interaction coaching. The latter involved the staff and instructor viewing and discussing a previously taped interaction. Scoring of interactions in the diaper changing and feeding areas allowed for evaluation of changes due to training or generalization.

The three staff showed increases in dependent measures in the diaper changing area after training, but no generalization to the feeding area was shown. The effectiveness and cost-feasibility of the training procedures were noted. Furthermore, the authors suggested the training format "could be delivered by persons indigenous to programs such as directors or coordinators" (p. 316).

A third paper illustrating OBM in EI appeared after the Crow and Stewart review described above was completed. This example was provided by Hendrickson, Gardner, Kaiser, and Riley (1993). These authors identified social interaction as a primary target for integrated early educational experiences of children with and without disabilities. Three teachers who had preschool children with disabilities enrolled in their classrooms participated. These teachers were taught a "peer coaching" protocol that (generally) involved the classroom teachers observing and providing feedback to one another about how they supported social interaction among the children in their classroom (pp. 217-218). Data showed greatly increased "support behaviors" by teachers after the implementation of coaching (p. 220). Concomitantly, child interactions increased and maintained at levels far above baseline. The authors discussed the coaching strategy as an in-context approach showing beneficial changes in teacher and child behaviors under these defined circumstances and suggested these procedures might be appropriate for wider adoption. These authors noted "teachers initially had difficulty thinking of ways to promote interaction" and "developing ideas and feedback" helped them identify and select interventions (p. 223). Finally, Hendrickson et al. noted the practical advantages of low cost and ease of implementation of their methods, but questioned the generality of these procedures without further research.

These studies display creditable attention to practices supported in both the EI and OBM literatures. That is, the performances of staff were identifiable as recommended in EI literature (e.g., Peters & Heron, 1993) and the management actions were within bounds described for OBM (e.g., Crowell & Anderson, 1983). While these papers contribute good illustrations of the compatibility of OBM and EI practices, they also stimulate questions about why there is so little OBM-type activity in EI. Certainly, this meager literature indicates little influence of occasional encouragement for increased attention to supervision and management by authors in early intervention (e.g., Johnson, Kilgo, Cook, Hammitte, Beauchamp, & Finn, 1992;

Lay-Dopyera, & Dopyera, 1985; Madle, 1982; Wimpelberg, Abroms, & Catardi, 1985).

## Other Relevant Literature

To clarify the need for expanded efforts of OBM in EI, we reviewed a published bibliography (Reid & Parsons, 1995), examined the contents of recent issues of journals publishing studies related to OBM and EI (i.e., *Journal of Applied Behavior Analysis* and *Journal of Organizational Behavior Management* plus issues of *The Journal of Early Intervention, Infants and Young Children, Topics in Early Childhood Special Education,* and *Infants-Toddlers* which were not contained in the Crow and Stewart review), and searched earlier publications in EI and related fields for studies which appeared to be representative of aspects of OBM and EI at the time of their publication. We expanded our inclusion criteria so reports involving children over age five and without disabilities were reviewed. This adjustment allowed examination of several more papers than when we required the subjects be five years old or younger and with disabilities. These publications were examined for information pertaining to establishing or altering the actions of staff in settings related to early intervention.

One of the earliest studies dealing with modification of staff skills and performance in an educational setting for children with disabilities was reported by Davison (1965). He trained undergraduate students to use behavioral procedures in a "day care center for autistic children" (p. 146). The author used a case study approach and discussions of assigned readings to teach four undergraduate psychology students how to use behavior modification methods with children who were autistic. Skills taught included differential positive reinforcement, imitation, and ignoring. After a month of simulated training, the author formed the students into two teams and conducted further training with the children themselves.

Daily sessions were completed by each team working with an individual 10-year old child. Data consisted of a written "behavioral report" submitted daily by each student that contained descriptions of the interventions and effects on child behaviors. These reports "enabled the author to monitor the treatment" and make "changes in the programmed behavior of the therapists" (p. 147). Direct observation of the college students as they intervened occurred at the end of the project. These observations indicated that intervention performance was "satisfactory." The behavior of children was found to evidence "striking increase in commands obeyed . . . from pre to postmeasurement" (p. 148).

This early paper is remarkable in showing many of the features desired of OBM and educational studies. Namely, behaviors sought of interventionists and the children were defined, trained, measured, and set the occasion for differential outcomes for the staff. The educational approach used with the children is far from the more naturalistic and functional practices recommended in the literature of today, but perfectly reasonable for the time. Furthermore, the design of the project makes it an early forerunner of those appearing in the OBM literature.

An early study of a preschool environment by LeLaurin and Risely (1972) looked at some major features of the work and supervisory environment of a (regular) day care setting. These authors varied whether the teacher moved with groups of children (aged 3-5 yrs.) when they rotated from area to area (i.e., "man-to-man") or each teacher remained in an area and children moved from and to them (i.e., "zone"). The dependent variable was "time children were engaged" in each classroom subsetting. They found the zone arrangement resulted in more children doing more of what the subsetting was supposed to engender in their behavior. The authors suggested engagement as a dependent measure of utility for early childhood and, in addition to individual child variables, certain environmental considerations should enter into comprehensive childcare technology; points well-taken for current EI approaches.

Pommer and Streedbeck (1974) manipulated antecedent and reinforcement operations applied to nine direct care staff to assess effects on their completion of assigned jobs and work duties. Completion of specific jobs (e.g., fix the toaster) was checked weekly. Performance of expected procedures, including giving medications or teaching hand-washing, were directly observed on a randomized basis. Overall, the treatment program was intended to be run "like a house" to include "activities that preschoolers engage in" (p. 218).

Results showed that "public notice resulted in immediate improvements" in staff performance, but these effects "decreased consistently" (p. 219). Addition of token reinforcement for work accomplishments was followed by slight improvements which continued on "an upward trend" (p. 219). The combined use of notices and reinforcement "increased staff performance to its highest levels" (p. 219-220). The authors discussed the relative contributions of publicly posted work assignments and token reinforcement on staff behavior. No data regarding child behavior or satisfaction of participants were presented.

The emphasis of the study by Pommer and Streedbeck was on documenting the impact of antecedent and consequent operations on staff performance. Because it was conducted in a preschool setting, these findings bear on the present review. Outstanding aspects of this paper include the simplicity of interventions and clarity of results. Readers should have no trouble concluding that posting assignments and applying token reinforcement could result in child care or EI personnel performing increased amounts of desired behaviors. This seems to be a powerful message that might be appreciated in present-day EI, but it appeared long ago and in a journal that is probably not high on the EI reading list. Possibly a systematic replication in an EI setting, using modern staff performances and appropriate reinforcers, would be well received.

A set of six studies reported by Twardosz, Cataldo, and Risley (1974) examined the effects of environmental arrangements on measures of staff and child performances. The setting was a child care center serving infants to walking age children, none of whom showed disabilities. Center activities occurred in one large room which was divided into areas according to function, for example, play and sleeping areas. The independent variable was room arrangement, which was altered by the addition or removal of movable partitions. Dependent measures included the amount of time a child could not be seen, distance staff must move to see children, ability of supervisors to see staff, and behaviors of children, for example, time sleeping or crying, and "pre-academic" activities.

These authors found the presence of partitions reduced visibility and increased efforts required to observe children and staff. These studies remain among the clearest demonstrations of how environmental arrangements affect the behavior of staff and children. In discussing their findings, the authors noted that in the open environment (i.e., barriers absent) "children were almost continuously visible to the staff and the staff were almost continuously visible to the supervisor" (p. 544). Furthermore, the sleep and pre-academic behaviors of the children were not adversely affected, therefore, "day care definitely can and should be accomplished in an open environment" (p. 544).

Twardosz et al. described the design and findings of their studies as appropriate for documenting the use of open environments to promote safety for the children by making them more observable. The truth of the authors' conclusion that children who are observed are safer, assumes that staff would perform appropriately based on their observations of children. Furthermore, the reference to staff being viewable by supervisors implies that supervisors would act differentially based on what they saw staff do. Of course, this relationship of staff doing what is expected and supervisors monitoring and consequating performance requirements is the heart of OBM and, in our opinion, something appropriate for widespread application in EI. Twardosz, Cataldo, and Risely (1974) add to understanding the contributions of environmental variables to staff, supervisor, and child behaviors.

Almost a decade later, Kunz et al. (1982) cited a "relative lack of research on staff management in infant centers" as they introduced their study. Their research involved the four components of basic OBM practices, that is, defining staff performance in measurable terms, observing staff behaviors in the work setting, providing differential outcomes based on the observed performances, and evaluating the effects of the intervention.

In two experiments Kunz et al. (1982) examined strategies to improve caregiver performance in an infant care facility. None of the seven infants had "any physical or developmental disabilities" (p. 525). Their two interventions consisted of posting charts for staff to see what performances (diapering and playing with the children) were expected and how often they had been done. This set of simple antecedent operations plus posted feedback resulted in increased and sustained high rates of desired performance. These results contrasted to the failure of "lectures, films, presentations, and numerous supervisory and administrative requests" to obtain improved performance (p. 530). The authors suggested that the use of antecedent and feedback activities to alter staff behaviors "provides a technology for maintaining . . . duties without daily instruction and costly training programs" (p. 530).

Goncalves, Iwata, and Chiang (1983) examined methods to improve the provision of feedback by supervisors to staff working with children and adults who were severely disabled. These authors tape recorded daily sessions involving supervisors and direct care staff discussing recent performance of the staff. These recordings were scored for the categories and number of evaluative comments, and the use of technical terms by number of different terms used, total number, and accuracy of use. These measures were used to assess the effect of weekly "illustrative case" interviews where the experimenter discussed with each supervisor portions of a scored tape recording. Data reflected "consistent improvements" following implementation of discussion sessions with supervisors. The authors concluded that the methods used in this study were a "very cost-effective means for both assessing and maintaining interaction between relatively large numbers of supervisors and staff" (p. 18).

The design and conclusions of the Goncalves et al. study are closely related to practices in OBM, but no efforts were directed to assessing staff-child interactions or effects of experimental variables on children. The results are instructive partly by demonstrating malleability of supervisory behaviors even when subjected to infrequent, brief, and apparently low intensity intervention. While previously reviewed studies examined staff performance as the primary variable, the focus on supervisory behavior by Goncalves et al. (1983) serves to demonstrate methods and underline the need to establish effective skills in supervisors of early intervention settings.

Shreve, Twardosz, and Weddle (1983) applied and evaluated procedures to encourage day care teachers to be affectionate with children. Eight teachers in two day care centers serving children 3 to 6 years of age participated; none were described as disabled. Affectionate behaviors were defined as smiling, using affectionate words, and affectionate contact. Intervention consisted of instructions and practice of affection behaviors in context (i.e., "Activities" condition) followed by supplying teachers with prompt cards located near work areas (i.e., "Activities and cards" condition). In addition, graphic feedback was provided each teacher showing her total behavior and "praise or encouragement" was provided (p. 709). Follow-up observations occurred in one day care center (Center 1) four months after intervention. Data for the Activities condition showed a decrease (Center 1) or little increase (Center 2) in affectionate behaviors over baseline. With Activities and Cards plus graphic feedback in effect, rates of affectionate behaviors increased to about twice baseline. The follow-up observation of Center 1 found continuation of increased rates of affectionate behaviors. No measures of child behaviors were reported. The authors discussed that affectionate behaviors can be increased, but changes they brought about were small and the components of their intervention were not analyzed.

The absence of children with disabilities precludes the Twardosz et al. (1983) study being an EI demonstration, per se, but it does demonstrate the effects of antecedent and consequent operations on staff behaviors in categories of performance relevant for quality early intervention. Furthermore, the use of a lead teacher to maintain the more effective condition may be an important strategy for use in the organization of center-based programs.

Supervisor training and its effects on teachers and preschool children was reported by Hundert and Hopkins (1992). They used role playing, coaching, and feedback to prepare supervisors who subsequently worked with classroom and consultant teachers to alter child-centered interventions. The supervisors met with teachers to encourage them to work together to increase social interaction among children with and without disabilities. Subsequently, the teachers' plans were reviewed, discussed, and observed in practice. Classroom teachers received feedback, but no specific suggestions, based on the supervisor's observations. Data showed all teachers increased their behavior toward children with disabilities and decreased contact with children without disabilities in both the training and generalization settings. Except for one classroom, all children showed increases in social interaction in the training and generalization settings. These results demonstrate the effectiveness of supporting supervisors to obtain teacher performance and achieve child change.

Several features of this study mark it as an outstanding example of OBM in EI. First, the rationale for the dependent variable was selected, at least in part, based on literature and recommended practices in EI. Second, the training of extant supervisors to alter classroom practices is an important demonstration for EI practitioners. Finally, to some extent the study involved an interdisciplinary approach to sharing technology in that behavior analysts provided instructional supports to early intervention personnel who used them to implement (approximations to) recommended practices in EI. This model of functionality and collaboration in developing OBM applications to support improvements in EI is appropriate for replication and dissemination; we suggest, to the betterment of both OBM and EI by adding new perspectives to each field.

The literature introduced above constitutes all the articles located in the major publications that show OBM in EI through December 1995 and selected papers that demonstrate prominent aspects of OBM in childhood settings. For the period 1992 through 1995, this review was a direct examination of literature and intended to be exhaustive. We relied on secondary sources for earlier publication dates and a broad base of periodicals. The methodological models and discussion points offered by these papers suggest issues appropriate for attention by either OBM or EI practitioners. However, a major impact of this review could be the realization of the dearth of OBM activity (cf. Kunz et al., 1982) in what is an important and stimulating area of human service.

## Summative View of EI and OBM Considerations in the Literature

The cumulative view of literature presented above suggests at least the following conclusions: (a) very little literature is available in which both OBM and EI quality practices are present, but (b) the relevance of OBM interventions in EI settings is indicated, and (c) reports of approximations to OBM applications in EI offer models that could stimulate interest and guide the design of future research projects.

The literature in OBM demonstrates the power and generalizability of behavioral application to obtain desired staff performance (cf. Crowell & Anderson, 1982b; Mawhinney, 1984). Concurrently, the EI literature contains indications of what might be expected of staff in quality EI service settings (Bailey & Wolery, 1992; Bricker, 1989; DEC Task Force on Recommended Practices (Eds.), 1993) including reliance on behavioral methods (Strain et al., 1992) and an ecological-behavioral approach to the EI environment (Rogers-Warren, 1982; Vincent et al., 1990). It seems reasonable that the pragmatic concern and behavioral roots of EI and OBM should serve as a foundation for bringing together practitioners from both fields for collaborative research and development.

## CHALLENGES AND OPPORTUNITIES
## FOR CONSTRUCTIVE RELATIONS BETWEEN OBM AND EI

Federal and state laws in the United States demonstrate that our country is committed to programs for young children and their families. These programs include early intervention services, child care programs, Head Start, and related programs. Public policy, budgetary commitments, and extensive systems of personnel preparation, research, and services are directed to improving outcomes for children and families. There can be little doubt that the field of EI should feel pressure to develop and provide services that are marked by top quality practices and outcomes for children and families. Our knowledge of EI and OBM leads us to conclude that constructive relations among early interventionists and those who practice OBM could result in improvements in quality and efficiency in activities of EI.

The field of OBM has an impressive data base that attests to the utility of behavioral applications for achieving improved performance of work duties in a wide array of settings. Practitioners of OBM are familiar with challenges associated with entering a work site, determining desired performances within certain environmental contexts, arranging observational and incentive procedures, and evaluating their effects. Early intervention is an appropriate, or even a high priority, area of human endeavor in which OBM should take a much more active role in developing top quality performance. We endorse this possibility and offer the following considerations regarding challenges and opportunities to facilitate the development of productive relations among practitioners of EI and OBM.

### Accommodating Intervention Frameworks

Similar to the OBM community of practitioners, those involved in EI see their work as important, well-conceived, and credible. The perspectives contained in developmental, behavioral, ecological, and systems literatures are seen by EI personnel as fundamental and deserving of the continuing influence these perspectives exert on the field. The prominence and complexity of these forces in EI could be seen as daunting or inhibiting of collaborative efforts among practitioners of EI and OBM. On the other hand, the relatively narrow focus of OBM on behavioral practices could be interpreted as too circumscribed to be of significant utility in supporting the complex interventions found in EI.

In fact, the power of OBM methods is evident in the accumulated literature of this field, particularly noticeable in more than a decade of articles appearing in the *Journal of Organizational Behavior Management*. The foundation for the success of OBM rests with its adherence to the basic principles of behavior analysis and practices of applied behavior analysis (cf. Mawhinney, 1982; Mawhinney, 1984). We have seen that this same set of principles and similar practices are prominent forces in EI, therefore, opportunities for methodological agreement between OBM and EI could be nurtured to spawn collaborative studies in EI issues.

More challenging might be identifying the research outcomes appropriate for OBM ventures in EI. The history of OBM in other venues of human service offers many demonstrations of success with modifying the performances of staff in professional, paraprofessional, and supervisory roles (see Reid & Parsons, 1995 for a bibliography). However, the "vast majority of training reports in OBM in human services have focused on training staff to use behavior modification techniques" (Green & Reid, 1994; p. 220). As indicated earlier, in EI little regard is directed to behavior modification *per se* while major attention is focused on features of family- and child-centered service practices (see Brinker, 1985, for an introduction to theoretical and curricular considerations). For OBM applications in EI to be most appropriate and productive, the variables of study must be attentive to the frameworks and features of intervention described previously, for example, how to ensure that staff embed opportunities for learning within naturally occurring routines in the child's environment.

It might be helpful for those designing OBM applications in EI to be alert to particular differences between intervention activities found in human services provided to older children or adults, and those expected to be seen with young children. First, interventions with children occur within the context of typical routines and activities where logically occurring cues and consequences are present (Bricker, 1989; Bricker & Cripe, 1992). While the particulars of adult services may be more a function of team decision-making, activities with younger children are guided by the notion that children are more likely to remain engaged in activities they initiate. This maxim essentially removes the use of standardized instructions or tasks commonly found in special education or adult services and replaces them with planful environmental engineering and spontaneous behavioral engineering (e.g., incidental teaching) as skills to be used by intervention personnel.

A second emphasis of EI that should affect the targets of OBM designs is the source of definitions of behavioral objectives for intervention. In services for adults the skills taught might be related to the clients' level of adaptive behavior relative to their life circumstances. Services may be aimed at establishing community living or recreational skills determined to be needed by observing a discrepancy between the client's skills and those skills required to be successful, for example, shopping for groceries or using the bus system. In EI, objectives for the child are based on developing generative, functional, and adaptive response repertoires. Similar to the absence of prescribed instructional packages for EI, this maxim reduces the presence of decontextualized discrete trial training. Also, it implies a challenge for OBM methods to assess observed interventions for the extent of congruence between what is appropriate for a specific child and what activities of intervention actually occur. This issue of appropriateness might be a key point of regard for OBM applications in EI.

Another conceptual challenge to the use of OBM methods in EI is the requirement that OBM "should focus on some aspect of organizational productivity and include a cost-benefit analysis" (Mawhinney, 1984; p. 11). It might be argued that the "product" of EI is as much the *process* as it is the outcome of early services. A review of the theoretical foundations of EI discloses repeated and emphatic support for the role of engaging environments on child development. Even as EI service activities work toward selected and measurable outcomes, the overall developmental well being of children should be an appreciated dimension of EI despite how elusive it might be for measurement. The challenge of developing cost-benefit analyses to account for the value of process variables as well as outcomes of EI is noticeable. But, each of the points raised above should be amenable to the "combination of methods of theoretical, technological, and practical strategies" found in OBM literature (Wolf et al., 1995; p. 41). The invitation for increased OBM activity in EI can be seen in comments by EI authors. For example, Kunz et al. (1982) noted that "management of staff duties is important," but there is a "paucity of research" in this area (p. 521). A more vigorous call for attention to effective management in EI was provided by Madle (1985) as he introduced behavioral supervision as a promising topic in which the field of early intervention should engage. The present condition of deficiency in attention to management of staff performances in EI could benefit from constructive efforts by practitioners of OBM.

### Overcoming Operational Barriers

Challenges related to identifying what is the "organization" for OBM in EI may be spurious or genuine, depending on the questions being answered. For example, OBM methods might be used to clarify the impact of alternative service models (e.g., home-based or center-based) on staff performance. That is, the organizational factors could be independent variables while measures of work activities are dependent measures. This sort of investigation might be productive of ideas about alternative ways to structure services, but OBM activities focused on management actions to support recommended practices in EI seem appropriate for a high priority.

A significant challenge to implementing OBM practices in early childhood services stems from their idiosyncratic nature. Major variables determining what performances are seen from EI staff include factors of the child, family, community, and service resources which interact and impact the design, delivery, and adjustment of services and supports available to the family. These dynamics require that the definition of desired staff performances be responsive to the specific circumstances under which the work is shown. From an OBM perspective, decisions about performance accuracy and what is appropriate feedback and differential consequences could be quite complicated and require fluency with principles of both EI and OBM.

Another prominent barrier to implementing the usual practices of OBM in EI services involves the locations and personal circumstances of interventions. Services often are provided in homes or other community locations where individual interventionists visit on a prearranged basis. Direct observations of staff performance would require large amounts of time and travel. Furthermore, these field-based services usually involve sensitive interactions with the child and a parent in their home or with a staff member at their provider agency, therefore, making the presence of an observer difficult or impossible to accommodate.

Challenges to the use of OBM practices in EI will include how staff performances are to be defined, observed, and consequated in an appropriate, timely, and cost-feasible way. Overcoming these challenges will not be a simple matter, but examples of successful collaborative strategies are available and should be pursued.

## Meeting Technical Challenges to Installing OBM Practices in EI Service Settings

After a common ground of shared interest in the outcomes to be reached by using OBM in EI is established, technical challenges to implementation can be faced. These include developing performance definitions and observation methods, identifying reinforcing operations, and establishing data handling procedures. Detailed descriptions and discussion of the development of OBM programs is provided by Crowell and Anderson (1982b) and are well suited to establishing procedures for use in EI.

As for any organizational setting, this set of technology must be validated before being implemented beyond initial development. Extending, studying, and interpreting OBM practices within EI settings would benefit from employing an interdisciplinary team approach. A functional and productive team to develop and validate OBM practices in EI may include EI staff and leadership, parents of children in EI services, and experts in OBM and EI who are experienced in research and development. This collection of perspectives, experiences, and expertise should be actively involved in every step of developing, applying, evaluating, and disseminating OBM practices in EI (cf. Winton, McWilliam, Harrison, Owens, & Bailey, 1992; Sexton, Snyder, Lobman, Kimbrough, & Matthews, 1997). A team-based approach, where members of various groups are involved within a behavioral framework, could accomplish idea-generation and selection that is appropriate, efficient, and creditable for both EI and OBM audiences. In turn, this could serve to promote interest and advancement of practices in both fields.

## DISCUSSION

The field of early intervention is an area of interesting and constructive endeavor. Young children with special needs and families enduring unusual stresses are approached with service activities and supports characterized as family- and child-centered (e.g., Andrews & Andrews, 1995; Bailey & Wolery, 1992). Interventionists are expected to work with families to develop and implement activities for the child and family in ways that are functional, integrative, and collaborative (e.g., Bricker, 1989). Instruction in the skills required for staff to perform effectively in EI is accomplished somewhat in college course work and more frequently through field-based staff development efforts (Bruder & Nikitas, 1992; Snyder & Wolf, 1997; Winton & McCollum, 1997). In the literature related to staff training in EI, the use of feedback based on observed skill use is promoted, but reports of performance feedback as part of the work setting are virtually absent (Crow & Stewart, December, 1993).

The field of EI shows a high level of staff development activities aimed at establishing skills required to deliver services according to recommended practices. A review of the content and methods of inservice training used in EI likely would support the conclusion that this training is adequate and probably effective at transmitting information. However, Madle (1982) concluded that training in EI "has shown little positive impact" (p. 75). Despite this observation, Green and Reid (1994) remind us that inservice training remains a "common means of attempting to incorporate technological advances into routine educational services . . . " (p. 220). We seem be to enmeshed in a cycle of identifying desired practices, trying to establish their use via one-shot training events, and lamenting that skills do not transfer to the work place.

Possibly the great interest for skill usage evidenced by widespread training efforts combined with concerns about obtaining the use of skills during work could be translated into interest in developing OBM within

EI. A general outcome appropriate for initial demonstrations of OBM in EI might be to increase the benefits of inservice training or other staff development activities. That is, develop and evaluate methods useful for EI leadership personnel to bring about the accurate and appropriate use of skills attempted to be established during training. This would be responsive to concerns about training not having impacts and be an attractive topic for collaboration by OBM and EI experts.

In discussing starting points for OBM-EI projects we are reminded by Green and Reid (1994) that much attention has gone to "train the trainers," but "despite the success of organizational behavior management . . . this approach to staff training is not fully developed . . . " (p. 220). These authors are constructive in directing attention to improving training practices, including using OBM to establish skill use, but their comments continue to focus on training staff or "trainers" as the primary issue. We suggest that conceptual adjustments regarding training could direct attention to including supervisors and other leadership personnel as primary targets in training events. Their role in causing accurate and continued use of skills could be recognized and supported by training them in OBM methods appropriate for use with the skills trained to direct service staff. This adjustment redirects attention from training of "trainers" to training of managers, an emphasis which appears congruent with concerns in OBM for systems change and cost effectiveness (cf. Mawhinney, 1984).

We suggest that developing appropriate management practices in EI should be approached integratively and pragmatically. Integration should come at the levels of theoretical context and operational practices. This general view was expressed by Malott, Vunovich, Boettcher, and Groeger (1995) as they offered direction to the field of applied behavior analysis to be more effective at accomplishing widespread improvements in "the well being of humanity" (p. 345). Their advice for improving behavioral applications, including those in educational organizations, emphasized use of behavioral systems engineering involving activities of analysis and specification followed by design, evaluation, and refinement for systems development. The stepwise approach Malott et al. (1995) advance appears relevant to how OBM experts could proceed in EI to be effective agents for change.

At the level of analysis and specification, OBM efforts in EI might benefit from adopting a larger theoretical and conceptual view. The pragmatic concern of EI has led practitioners to draw on theories of learning, systems, and human development for ideas and direction. The analysis of behavior is a prominent force in EI, but it is not generally recognized as accounting for the attractive aspects of the other perspectives in this field. That is, behavioral explanations and interventions have not been established for many aspects of EI, therefore, analyzing systems in EI necessitates appreciating divergent frameworks. Holding to a single, behavioral system by OBM practitioners is appropriate, but to be most effective in EI a functional regard for other perspectives must be present.

We are not advocating that OBM and EI experts join in conducting non-behavioral research. We are attempting to alert those who might conduct OBM efforts in EI to the special features of this field so they can choose to apply OBM effectively and appropriately. For example, current EI leadership may be less interested in obtaining the charting of diaper changes, but very interested in seeing that during diapering the staff encourages child communicative behaviors, prompts muscle use, assures correct positioning, prompts child behaviors, and engineers the environment to reward different levels of participation by the child in the diaper-changing routine. The former performance is relatively simple and using OBM methods to establish it is valuable only as a starting point. The second set of staff performance requires that the staff have skills for simultaneously shaping multiple child behaviors by antecedent and consequent actions, observing and responding to opportunities for engineering the child's environment to promote developmental learning, deciding if the child's physical posture needs to be adjusted to allow participation in their environment, as well as changing (and recording) the diaper. This is the sort of complex, multi-faceted staff performance that EI is struggling to define objectively, determine competencies, establish skills, and obtain staff performance. Importantly, these types of complex behaviors are topics OBM practitioners have dealt with (Reid & Parsons, 1995; Reid, Parsons, & Green, 1989), but the vast majority of these studies involved subject populations other than EI. We encourage the application of OBM methodology to complex performances in EI. We believe that OBM studies of this type in EI could make significant contributions, but prior understanding of EI systems and practices is required for optimal success.

The appropriate accomplishment of systems analysis and expression of fluency in behavioral concepts to EI systems requires a functional command of variables acting in and on the EI setting. These forces were described earlier as including conceptual frameworks and principles, maxims, and norms. We reiterate our call for effective actions by those who would attempt OBM in EI to ensure that these efforts are characterized by conceptualizations and practices credible in both the fields of EI and OBM. The accomplishment of such integrated activities should result in advancements in both fields as well as contribute to the well being of the professionals who work in these settings and the children and families with whom these individuals have the privilege of interacting.

# REFERENCES

Andrews, J.R., & Andrews, M.A. (1995). Solution-focused assumptions that support family-centered early intervention. *Infants and Young Children, 8,* 1, 60-67.

Bailey, D.B. (1989). Issues and directions in preparing professionals to work with young handicapped children and their families. In J. Gallagher, P. Tronhanis, & R. Clifford (Eds.), *Policy Implementation and P. L. 99-457: Planning for Young Children with Special Needs* (pp. 97-132). Baltimore, MD: Paul H. Brookes Publishing Co.

Bailey, D.B, & Wolery, M. (1992). *Teaching Infants and Preschoolers with Disabilities* (2nd Ed.). New York: Macmillan.

Bernheimer, L.P., & Keogh, B.K. (1995). Weaving interventions into the fabric of everyday life: An approach to family assessment. *Topics in Early Childhood Special Education, 15,* 4, 415-433.

Bijou, S.W., & Baer, D.M. (1961a). *Child Development, Volume One: A Systematic and Empirical Theory.* New York: Appleton-Century-Crofts.

Bijou, S.W., & Baer, D.M. (1961b). *Child Development, Volume Two: Universal Stage of Infancy.* New York: Appleton-Century-Crofts.

Bricker, D.D. (1989). *At-Risk and Handicapped Infants, Toddlers, and Preschool Children* (2nd Ed.). Palo Alto, CA: Vort Corp.

Bricker, D., & Cripe, J.J. (1992). *An activity-based approach to early intervention.* Baltimore: Brookes.

Brinker, R.P. (1985). Curricula without recipes: A challenge to teachers and a promise to severely mentally retarded students. In Bricker, D., & Filler, J. (Eds.), *Severe Mental Retardation: From Theory To Practice.* Reston, VA: Council for Exceptional Children.

Bronfenbrenner, U. (1979). *The ecology of human development: Experiments by nature and design.* Cambridge: Harvard University Press.

Bruder, M.B., & Nikitas, T. (1992). Changing the professional practices of early interventionists: An inservice model to meet the service needs of Public Law 99-457. *Journal of Early Intervention, 16,* 2, 173-180.

Capute, A., & Accardo, P. (1996). *Developmental Disabilities in Infancy and Childhood (Second Ed.) Volume I.* Baltimore: Paul H. Brookes.

Crow, R., & Stewart, W. (December, 1993). Directions and needs for research in management practices for early intervention services. Poster presentation to the annual meeting of DEC, San Diego, CA.

Crowell, C.R., & Anderson, D.C. (1982a). The scientific and methodological basis of a systematic approach to human behavior management. *Journal of Organizational Behavior Management, 4(1/2),* 1-31.

Crowell, C.R., & Anderson, D.C. (1982b). Systematic behavior management: General program considerations. *Journal of Organizational Behavior Management, 4,*1/2, 129-163.

Davison, G.C. (1965). The training of undergraduates as social reinforcers for autistic children. In Ullman, L.P., & Krasner, L. (Eds.), *Case Studies in Behavior Modification.* New York: Holt, Rinehart and Winston.

DEC Task Force on Recommended Practices. (1993). *DEC Recommended Practices: Indicators of Quality in Programs for Infants and Young Children with Special Needs and Their Families.* Reston, VA: Council for Exceptional Children, 15212.

Goncalves, S.J., Iwata, B.A., & Chiang, S.J. (1983). Assessment and training of supervisors' evaluative feedback to their staff in a operant learning program for handicapped children. *Education and Treatment of Children, 6,* 1, 11-20.

Green, C.W., & Reid, D.H. (1994). A comprehensive evaluation of a train-the-trainers model for training education staff to assemble adaptive switches. *Journal of Developmental and Physical Disabilities, 6,* 3, 219-238.

Hendrickson, J.M., Gardner, N., Kaiser, A., & Riley, A. (1993). Evaluation of a social interaction coaching program in an integrated day-care setting. *Journal of Applied Behavior Analysis, 26,* 2, 213-225.

Hundert, J., & Hopkins, B. (1992). Training supervisors in a collaborative team approach to promote peer interaction of children with disabilities in integrated preschools. *Journal of Applied Behavior Analysis, 25,* 385-400.

Kunz, G. G. R., Lutzker, J. R., Cuvo, A. J., Eddleman, J., Lutzker, S. Z., Megson, D., & Gulley, B. (1982). Evaluating strategies to improve careprovider performance on health and developmental tasks in an infant care facility. *Journal of Applied Behavior Analysis, 15,* 521-531.

Lay-Dopyera, M., & Dopyera, J. E. (1985). Administrative leadership: Styles, competencies, repertoire. *Topics in Early Childhood Special Education, 5,* 1, 15-23.

Lelaurin, K., & Risely, T. R. (1972). Organization of day care environments: "Zone" versus "Man-to-Man" staff assignments. *Journal of Applied Behavior Analysis, 5,* 225-232.

Madle, R.A. (1982). Behaviorally-based staff performance management. *Topics in Early Childhood Special Education, 2,* 1, 73-83.

Malott, R.W., Vunovich, P.L., Boettcher, W., & Groeger, C. (1995). Saving the world by teaching behavior analysis: A behavioral systems approach. *The Behavior Analyst, 18,* 2, 341-354.

Mawhinney, T.C. (1984). Philosophical and ethical aspects of organizational behavior management: Some evaluative feedback. *Journal of Organizational Behavior Management, 6,* 1, 5-31.

Mawhinney, T.C. (1992). Total quality management and organizational behavior management: An integration for continual improvement. *Journal of Applied Behavior Analysis, 25,* 525-543.

Peters, M.T., & Heron, T.E. (1993). When the best is not good enough: An examination of best practice. *The Journal of Special Education, 26,* 4, 371-385.

Pommer, D.A., & Streedbeck, D. (1974). Motivating staff performance in a operant learning program for children. *Journal of Applied Behavior Analysis, 7,* 217-221.

Reid, D.H., & Parsons, M.B. (1995). *Staff Training and Management: Bibliography of Organizational Behavior Management Reports in Developmental Disabilities and Related Human Services.* Morganton, NC: Developmental Disabilities Services Managers, Inc.

Reid, D.H., Parsons, M.B., & Green, C.W. (1989). *Staff Management in Human Services*. Springfield, IL: Charles C. Thomas.

Rogers-Warren, A.K. (1982). Behavioral ecology in classrooms for young, handicapped children. *Topics in Early Childhood Special Education, 2*, 1, 21-32.

Sameroff, A.J., & Friese, B.H. (1990). Transactional regulation and early intervention. In Meisels, S., & Shnonkoff, J. (Eds.) *Handbook of early childhood intervention*. New York: Cambridge University Press.

Sexton, D., Snyder, P., Lobman, M., Kimbrough, P., & Matthews, K. (1997). A team-based model to improve early intervention programs: Linking preservice and inservice. In Winton, P., McCollum, J., & Catlett, C. (Eds.), *Reforming Personnel Preparation in Early Intervention* (pp. 495-526). Baltimore: Paul H. Brookes.

Shreve, C., Twardosz, S., & Weddle, K. (1983). Development and evaluation of procedures to encourage teacher affectionate behavior in day care centers. *Behavior Therapy, 14*, 706-713.

Shonkoff, J.P., & Meisles, S.J. (1990). Early childhood intervention: The evolution of a concept. In Meisles, S., & Shonkoff, J. (Eds.), *Handbook of Early Childhood Intervention*. New York: Cambridge University Press.

Snyder, P., & Wolf, B. (1997). Needs assessment and evaluation in early intervention personnel preparation: Opportunities and challenges. In Winton, P, McCollum, J, & Catlett, C. (Eds.), *Reforming Personnel Preparation in Early Intervention* (pp. 127-171). Baltimore: Paul H. Brookes.

Stewart, B., & Vargas, J.S. (1990). *Teaching Behavior to Infants and Toddlers: A Manual for Caregivers and Parents*. Springfield, IL: Charles C. Thomas.

Strain, P.S., McConnell, S.R., Carta, J.J., Fowler, S.A., Neisworht, J.T., & Wolery, M. (1992). Behaviorism in early intervention. *Topics in Early Childhood Special Education, 12*, 1, 121-141.

Twardosz, S., Cataldo, M.F., & Risely, T.R. (1974). Open environment design for infant and toddler day care. *Journal of Applied Behavior Analysis, 7*, 529-546.

Venn, M.L., & Wolery, M. (1992). Increasing day care staff members' interactions during caregiving routines. *Journal of Early Intervention, 16*, 4, 304-319.

Vincent, L.J., Salisbury, C.L., Strain, P., McCormick, C., & Tessier, A. (1990). A behavioral-ecological approach to early intervention: Focus on cultural diversity. In Meisels, S., & Shonkoff, J. (Eds.) *Handbook of Early Childhood Intervention*. New York: Cambridge University Press.

Wimpelberg, R.K., Abroms, K.L., & Cataldi, C.L. (1985). Multiple models for administrative preparation in early childhood special education. *Topics in Early Childhood Special Education, 5*, 1, 1-14.

Winton, P., & McCollum, J. (1997). Ecological perspectives on personnel preparation: Rationale, framework, and guidelines for change. In Winton, P., McCollum, J., & Catlett, C. (Eds.), *Reforming Personnel Preparation in Early Intervention* (pp. 3-25). Baltimore: Paul H. Brookes

Winton, P.J., McWilliam, P.J., Harrison, T., Owens, A.M., & Bailey, D.B. (1992). Lessons learned from implementing a team-based model for change. *Infants and Young Children, 5*, 1, 49-57.

Wolery, M. (1995). Some concerns about process. *Journal of Early Intervention,* *19,* 1, 21-23.

Wolf, M., Kirgin, K., Fixsen, D., Blase, K., & Braukmann, C. (1995). The teaching-family model: A case study in data-based program development and refinement (and dragon wrestling). *Journal of Organizational Behavior Management, 15,* 1/2, 11-67.

Zlomke, L. C., & Benjamin, jr., V. A. (1983). Staff in-service: Measuring effectiveness through client behavior change. *Education and Training of the Mentally Retarded, 18,* 2, 125-130.

# SECTION 3:
# APPLICATIONS AND CONTRIBUTIONS OF ORGANIZATIONAL BEHAVIOR MANAGEMENT IN SPECIALTY SUPPORT AREAS

# Organizational Behavior Management: Applications with Professional Staff

## R. M. Schell

**SUMMARY.** Organizational behavior management (OBM) is an effective strategy for managing staff in developmental disabilities. Most studies in OBM involve individual or small groups of direct-service staff and their performance with clients in a variety of applied

R. M. Schell is affiliated with Western Carolina Center, Morgantown, NC.

Correspondence concerning this article should be addressed to R. M. "Duke" Schell, Department of Psychology, Western Carolina Center, 300 Enola Road, Morganton, NC 28655.

The author would like to acknowledge the influence of Jim Favell, Judy Favell, Martin Ivancic, Jon Bailey, Ginger Griffin, Tony Lybarger, Denny Reid and Judy Johnson for their encouragement of my initial interest in and continued commitment to OBM in developmental disabilities.

[Haworth co-indexing entry note]: "Organizational Behavior Management: Applications with Professional Staff." Schell, R. M. Co-published simultaneously in *Journal of Organizational Behavior Management* (The Haworth Press, Inc.) Vol. 18, No. 2/3, 1998, pp. 157-171; and: *Organizational Behavior Management and Developmental Disabilities Services: Accomplishments and Future Directions* (ed: Dennis H. Reid) The Haworth Press, Inc., 1998, pp. 157-171. Single or multiple copies of this article are available for a fee from The Haworth Document Delivery Service [1-800-342-9678, 9:00 a.m. - 5:00 p.m. (EST). E-mail address: getinfo@haworthpressinc.com].

settings. By contrast, few studies focus on the use of OBM with professional staff. This paper reviews investigations conducted with professional staff, reveals gaps that exist in the current research, and discusses future directions that need further study. The paper concludes with case illustrations of system-wide OBM applications that produced performance improvements by professional staff and meaningful gains for clients. *[Article copies available for a fee from The Haworth Document Delivery Service: 1-800-342-9678. E-mail address: getinfo@haworthpressinc.com]*

Organizational behavior management (OBM) has a long and effective history in developmental disabilities (see Reid, 1991; Sturmey this volume). In a description of the field of OBM in an editorial to the *Journal of Organizational Behavior Management,* Hall (1980) noted that OBM could "focus on the improvement of individual or group performance within an organizational setting . . ." in order to ". . . establish a technology of broad-scale performance improvement and organizational change so that employees will be more productive and happy, and so that our organizations and institutions will be more effective and efficient in achieving their goals." Fifteen years later this description is still a lofty goal for most organizational settings in developmental disabilities. By far the majority of efforts in OBM are with individual or small groups of staff and their performance with clients in a variety of applied settings (see Ivancic & Helsel, & Phillips, this volume).

While most of the studies of OBM in developmental disabilities focus on the behaviors of direct-service staff and their front-line supervisors (Reid, Parsons, & Green, 1989; Reid & Whitman, 1983), relatively little attention is paid to the use of OBM with professional staff in the same settings. This probably occurs because direct-service staff deliver the majority of the training and services to clients. For agencies that rely on the "kindness of strangers" (i.e., state or federal surveyors), the moment-to-moment interactions of direct-service staff with individuals are critical to continued participation in federal reimbursement programs like Title XIX. A second possible explanation for the lack of OBM applications with professional staff is that there is the widespread misperception that professional staff in developmental disabilities know what they are doing by virtue of their degree. Unfortunately few professional staff, other than special educators, typically receive training in working directly with people with mental retardation or other disabilities unless such training was required through some practicum or internship experience. If they did receive hands-on experience with clients, even fewer professional staff get any training in translating their expertise into effective use by other nonprofessional staff. A third reason for few OBM applications with professional staff, and the last one offered here, is that most researchers in OBM in developmental disabilities are primarily designing and conducting investigations from university-based research programs. Because of their dependence on graduate students as either the "staff" that directly provide the treatment procedures or the "supervisory staff" that provide the direct-service staff with performance feedback, university-based researchers typically do not have supervisory authority over the professional staff who work in those settings. This is in direct contrast to supervisors of professional staff working daily in applied settings (Reid, 1987). When students do not perform, data points are not collected–when professional staff do not perform, clients are not served.

## SUMMARY OF RESEARCH APPLICATIONS

In order to review OBM applications with professional staff it is necessary to define what the word "professional" means. The American Heritage Electronic Dictionary (1992) defines the adjective "professional" as: "(1.a) Of, relating to, engaged in, or suitable for a profession, (b) Conforming to the standards of a profession, (2) Engaging in a given activity as a source of livelihood or as a career, (3) Performed by persons receiving pay, (4) Having or showing great skill; expert." As a noun "professional" looks much the same: "(1) A person following a profession, especially a learned profession, (2) One who earns a living in a given or implied occupation, (3) A skilled practitioner; an expert."

Within the field of developmental disabilities the professional working in applied settings is further characterized by Thaw, Benjamin and Cuvo (1986) as staff who have "(a) standards of operation, (b) special language, (c) regulation and ethics, (d) specialized knowledge and technology, (e) presence of a power structure, and (f) overt symbolism." Perhaps a more accurate perception by administrative or direct-service staff of the professional is also offered: ". . . the sophisticated and well-trained (professional) who cannot translate his or her abilities into service usable and acceptable by direct care staff may come to be seen, and thus defined, by these staff as ineffective or unnecessary to the service operation" (Thaw et al., 1986, p. 151). Though harsh, this description of many professional staff may be realistic primarily because of the lack of skills acquired in bridging the gap between best clinical practice, or expertise, and its everyday delivery by direct-service staff.

In applied settings professional staff are typically administrators/managers, qualified mental retardation professionals (QMRPs), special education teachers, nurses, doctors, physical and occupational therapists, psychologists, speech pathologists, and social workers. Excluded from this group, and this review, are paraprofessional staff who frequently work for professional staff in some directly supervised capacity.

By far the most frequently studied professional staff are teachers (for a review of the use of OBM with teachers the reader is referred to Phillips in this volume). This is not surprising given that teachers are direct service providers in classrooms in much the same manner as direct-service staff in residential and work settings. In a recent bibliography of OBM research in developmental disabilities (Reid & Parsons, 1993) over 30 of the 244 studies cited involved teachers. By comparison 16 studies involved all other professional staff, usually nurses, QMRPs or habilitation teams, administrators/managers or other professionals. No studies specifically targeted doctors, psychologists, social workers or occupational therapists. However, some of these staff were members of habilitation teams that were selected for investigation.

Two studies targeted administrators/managers. Maher (1981) focused on training staff in program planning and evaluation. In this study managers were trained to evaluate IPP treatment goals and how they corresponded with training strategies. Hanel, Martin, and Koop (1982) trained staff managers to use self-instructional time management manuals. These two demonstrations of OBM strategies to improve administrative performance are useful simply because they are directly applicable to many of the regulatory-based settings in which people with developmental disabilities are served.

Three studies targeted various professional staff. Dowrick and Johns (1976) used videotaped feedback to train "therapists" to differentially focus their attention to the on-task behaviors of children with disabilities. Though constrained by the impracticality of videotaping in some natural settings, videotaped feedback can be extremely practical when reviewing complex skill acquisition, such as training fine discriminations by therapists. Videotaping also affords the trainer the possibility of reviewing skill acquisition many times for positive and corrective feedback. Bernstein and Karen (1978) reviewed types of preservice training for professional staff that would become behavior managers. Preservice training, as an antecedent strategy, improved only the in-class verbal repertoires of staff without generalizing the improvement to their work site. The authors suggested that the preservice training of professional staff, like that of direct-service staff, would only maintain within a reinforcing on-site work setting. Goncalves, Iwata, and Chiang (1983) used verbal feedback with audiotaped reviews to increase task-relevant evaluative statements and correct use of technical terms by undergraduate and graduate "supervisors" to direct-service staff. However, the investigators pointed out that the data were grouped so that specific effects on a given supervisor were unavailable and effects of the interventions were not measured for direct-service staff or clients.

Seven studies targeted QMRPs/case managers, and habilitation teams. Repp and Deitz (1979) improved the submission of timely records and comprehensive progress notes by supplying written feedback to individual professional staff. Hutchison, Jarman, and Bailey (1980) used public posting of attendance and punctuality by professional staff and others to increase attendance at habilitation team meetings. Interestingly enough, though attendance improved, tardiness did not. Coles and Blunden (1981) maintained the use of new procedures by providing staff with initial training feedback from several members of a multidisciplinary management team. This study incorporated both antecedent strategies, such as role assignments for staff in scheduled times and modeling in the living area, and consequences via publicly posted feedback. Fitzgerald et al. (1984) used skill modeling with practice and immediate feedback to train direct-service and professional staff to use manual sign language during daily routines for nonverbal clients. Feldstein and Feldstein (1990) improved the number of timely reports submitted for habilitation team meetings using written feedback on small posters and M&M candy to professional members of the team.

Two of the studies in this area targeted writing skills of professional staff. Page et al. (1981) used verbal feedback to habilitation team staff to improve the writing of habilitation goals and objectives. This study showed maintenance of the improvement in writing client IPP treatment goals following only an antecedent training intervention. Though not evident in other studies involving professionals, Page et al. (1981) suggested that the maintenance in the improvement of writing skills, in the absence of periodic feedback, may have occurred because professional staff were selected as participants instead of paraprofessional or direct-service staff. Another possibility was that there were sufficiently negative consequences for not completing the written assignments. Horner, Thompsen, and Storey (1990) also improved the quality of written IPP objectives with case manager feedback to staff.

*Three studies targeted nurses.* Ayllon and Michael (1959) described the first use of OBM with professional staff. They trained psychiatric nurses to respond differentially to the appropriate and "psychotic" behaviors of schizophrenic and "mentally defective" clients in a classic demonstration that the problem behaviors were under operant control. Patterson, Cooke, and Liberman (1972) used special comments in an agency newsletter to deliver written reinforcers to nurses as a way of publicly recognizing their performance. Marshall, Banzett, Kuehnel, and Moore (1983) described a system of services carried out by nurses that included positive social reinforcement by supervisors of the nurses' performance. Unfortunately, specific reinforcement procedures were not described. However, the "special prerogatives" that Marshall et al. (1983) listed, which could be seen as a noncontingent reinforcer menu, may also have impacted how well the system was implemented, aside from the social reinforcement of nurses' behavior.

In the only study that included professional staff as supervisors, with bachelor-level degrees or less in physical therapy or speech pathology, Page, Iwata, and Reid (1982) used verbal and graphic feedback to improve the training behaviors of both the selected supervisors and direct-service staff. This study deserves special note because it improved the delivery of training by direct-service staff through training and feedback provided to the professional supervisors in a pyramidal training fashion. The efficiency of this type of training to residential settings is important because it demonstrates effects with large groups of staff.

### Primary Conclusions

Studies with professional staff support the general findings in OBM in developmental disabilities that antecedent strategies alone, such as verbal or written instructions, generally do not sustain improved performance without some form of direct feedback as a consequence for behavior (Quilitch, 1975; Reid, Parsons, & Green, 1989). Both antecedent, consequence and combined strategies were used in different studies. In most cases investigators targeted a few key behaviors of professional staff, such as social or instructional interactions with clients, and less often selected outcomes of professional staff behavior, such as written work or client behavior change. With the exception of the finding noted by Page et al. (1981) regarding the maintenance of improvements in the IPP goal-writing by professional staff, initial treatment effects were sustained only with the inclusion of performance feedback or other reinforcers as consequences.

Interestingly, over 85% (14/16) of the studies were published before 1984–nine of those from 1980 to 1984–and only two studies have been published in this sub category of OBM since. Why? Though unconfirmed by data, it is possible that several factors have contributed to this trend. First, the mid-eighties were rocked by one of the most polarizing debates in behavioral psychology in the field of developmental disabilities regarding the use of aversive consequences for the treatment of severe behavior problems. While there was a renewed emphasis upon experimental/ functional analysis of severe behavior problems and their treatment with non-aversive antecedent and consequence interventions, many researchers were focusing on this crucial and controversial topic as opposed to OBM. Second, at the end of the eighties (June, 1988, to be precise) many applied researchers in larger service settings were retooling for the latest version of the federal regulations. In addition the revised regulations de-emphasized the standardized role of professional staff in service delivery and refocused on functional outcomes for clients. Combined with the push to downsize or close state residential facilities, there were fewer researchers ready to develop long-term research programs dependent upon these settings or external funding sources willing to support the improvement of services in these highly scrutinized settings. Or third, the technology of OBM in developmental disabilities is evident but research on the management of its application, and subsequent systems analysis, is too difficult to conduct for many applied researchers due to the many uncontrollable variables in the settings in which they work.

## Research Gaps

Rather than being pessimistic, it seems clear that much research remains to be done in applications of OBM with professional staff. There are several areas of study that are relatively untapped with professional staff in developmental disabilities that have already been explored with direct-service staff and teachers. It is clear that whether services are applied in large residential settings by departmental professional staff or in smaller community settings by consultant professional staff, the ecology of that service delivery needs further analysis (Willems, 1974; MacNamara, 1986; Wolf, Braukmann, & Ramp, 1987). There are only a few studies that have investigated the social validity or staff acceptability of professional staff training and programs (e.g., Maher, 1981; Fitzgerald et al., 1984) and fewer that have focused on the explicit use of participative management with professional staff rather than direct-service staff (Burgio, Whitman, & Reid, 1983).

Previous reviewers of OBM in developmental disabilities have also noted the paucity of large scale applications (Reid & Whitman, 1983; Reid et al., 1989). Outcome oriented and replicable service delivery systems must be available for the widespread adoption of the OBM technology and applied researchers need to develop these long-term demonstrations (Reid, 1992). Another area of research that needs more attention is the development of a technology that trains professional staff to translate their technical skills and procedures to practical use by direct-service staff with the clients they work with every day (Mager, 1982; McGimsey, Greene, & Lutzker, 1995).

### Future Directions

There are several future directions that research in OBM with professional staff can lead. One is the area of positive staff management (e.g., Daniels, 1994; Green & Reid, 1991; Reid & Parsons, 1995). Unfortunately, management by exception, or punishing mistakes and ignoring everyday acceptable behavior, is more the norm than the exception in many organizational settings in developmental disabilities. This probably occurs because it is more reinforcing to use punishment initially–there is an immediate change in behavior–and it is less effortful (Daniels, 1994). However, sustained skill acquisition and performance improvement require feedback and other forms of positive reinforcement. In order for professional staff to transfer their expertise to others they must become discriminative cues for reinforcement and develop the skills to deliver reinforcers effectively (Allen & Snyder, 1990; Crane, 1949; Ivancic & Schell, 1993).

Another area that warrants the attention of applied researchers is professional staff training. Because most professional staff are trained to deliver their services directly to clients during their practicum or internship experiences, developing the transfer technology for direct-service staff, including the development of more "user friendly" language to substitute for technological jargon (Lindsley, 1991), may appear daunting. However, OBM has already performed the analysis of the basics of training most acquired skills (cf. Ivancic & Helsel, and Phillips, this volume). The main challenge seems to be developing the necessary and sufficient curriculum for professional staff training that achieves the outcomes that the client and organization desire. It is important to remember that when valid curricula are created, practitioners of OBM in developmental disabilities must consider the issue of certifying acceptable procedures rather than people (Risley, 1975).

One way to improve the perception and the applicability of professional staff services is to link behavior to results with functional outcomes for clients and organizations. In other words, professional skills should be more performance-centered than behavior-centered. Worthy performance entails behavior and a valued accomplishment (Daniels, 1994; Gilbert, 1978). For example, a technically brilliant behavior analysis and support plan that fails to improve the behavior problems of the client for whom it was written is less than ineffective. It represents a trial of extinction or even punishment for the direct-service staff that are asked to conduct it. Whether or not an accomplishment is valued, or reinforcing, must be viewed from the perspective of the "customer." Professional staff are well aware that clients in the settings they serve are customers, but they often are not aware that those staff who implement professional programs are also customers from a marketing analysis perspective (Bailey, 1991). In order to be effective, both sets of customers must be satisfied.

An additional area in which OBM applications with professional staff can be strengthened is "behavioral self management" (Andrasik & Heimberg, 1982). The selection of one's own behaviors or outcomes to change and the arrangement of antecedent events and consequences that improve the selected behaviors or consequences defines this approach. Once professional staff leave their formal academic settings for positions in applied settings, attaining skills in areas such as time management for juggling busy schedules (Hanel et al., 1982), interpersonal relations for working with teams of staff (Carnegie, 1941; Crane, 1944) and developing colleagues with shared research interests (Reid, 1987), are all valuable self-management skills that will likely be reinforcing. These skills may be critical for new professional staff who are accustomed to large reinforcing effects in highly-controlled academic research projects. In less-controlled applied settings, similar reinforcing effects may be much more difficult to achieve. By way of paraphrasing a prominent OBM researcher, "a professional must find ways to reinforce him or herself without depending on others for reinforcement" (Reid, 1995).

As a final note in the discussion of future directions for OBM applications with professional staff, it may be constructive to look at past successes, particularly with systems-level applications (Bailey & Reiss, 1984; Parsons, Cash, & Reid, 1989). The Roadrunner Project at Western Carolina Center was developed in the late 1970s as a functional environment for persons with severe/profound retardation and multiple handicapping conditions prior to the arrival of the concept of "active treatment." Direct-service staff were given prescriptive checklists of daily tasks and regular performance feedback (Lattimore, Stephens, Favell, & Risley, 1984). Daily routines were often embedded in the context of small-group schedules that were posted as prompts for staff and supervisors. This management structure allowed for the natural flow of staff to different "zones" of activity (LeLaurin & Risley, 1972) to prompt client engagement and reinforce its occurrence. The creation of the Roadrunner unit as a "living environment" represented an early approximation to what an OBM perspective in developmental disabilities could offer (cf. Herbert-Jackson, O'Brien, Porterfield, & Risley, 1977).

In the early 1980s a different systems-level approach to the provision of day-program services was developed at the Thomas/Grady Service Center. In response to not seeing effective behavioral technology being applied on a basis consistent with expectations, a "behavioral systems management" approach was developed (Bailey & Reiss, 1984). The system components included: (1) the selection of a reasonable number of functional skills to be trained (no more than four per client per 13-week quarter); (2) public posting of scheduled training sessions with clients in staff classrooms; (3) data-based decision making facilitated by the public display of graphed training data on clients' objectives; (4) and quality control measures that included weekly feedback on training progress and client engagement by a staff supervisor (a nurse by training with a staff title of principal), monthly direct performance feedback to trainers from independent observers (graduate-level psychology students with staff titles of behavior specialist), and validation checks of training outcomes. The validations involved having the client perform a newly acquired skill with an independent observer after the completion of training. If the client completed the skill without help from the independent observer, the skill was "validated."

The introduction of the "behavioral systems management" components significantly improved the completion of training goals. The percent of objectives that were achieved continued to improve after the validations for each trainer were publicly posted on graphs in their classrooms (Schell, Allen, & Bailey, 1982). A final component of this OBM strategy was added by linking trainers' annual performance appraisals with their accomplishments with clients (i.e., the percent of achieved validations) and clients' levels of engagement with their environments when not in one-on-one training (Schell, Rogers, Griffin, Rubio, & Bailey, 1984).

A final case illustration of a systems-level OBM approach involving professional staff occurred at a public residential facility for persons with mental retardation called Winfield State Hospital and Training Center (Schell, Hudson, Caudillo, Hammock, & Lybarger, 1992). In 1987 the initial attention of the administration was focused on improving the facility's performance relative to annual surveys in the Medicaid Title XIX ICF/MR reimbursement program. An OBM system was quickly developed and implemented to meet the facility's need. The core components of the system included the following: (1) Staff responsibilities and client outcomes were defined in terms of measurable indices for each regulatory standard along with assigned responsibilities for collecting data monthly on each standard. Professional staff assigned these responsibilities included QMRPs, unit administrators, psychologists, social workers, physical and occupational therapists, speech pathologists and recreation therapists. (2) All staff that were assigned data collection responsibilities were trained in the definitions and measurements of the standards. (3) Both individual staff performance and aggregate unit performance were monitored. Over 50 of the standards were measured by independent monitors randomly reviewing client records and observing staff and client interactions across all three shifts. Data collected from direct observations, as well as self-reports from professional staff, were compiled in a monthly compliance report by unit. (4) The monthly reports were reviewed by administrative staff within two weeks of the end of the month. Performance feedback indicating the percent of compliance to each standard was compared against an expected percent of compliance, typically set at 90%. (5) In addition to verbal and written feedback by supervisors to professional staff each month as data were submitted for the monthly compliance report, performance consequences for compliance levels that were below expectations included the requirement of the submission of an action plan to improve the level of compliance. The effects of these action plans were then evaluated at the review of the next month's data.

The effects of the systems-level OBM intervention were immediate and significant. In the three years before the use of the OBM system, the percent of compliance with federal standards ranged from 55% to 65%. Within the first year of its implementation compliance increased to 87% and remained above 90% for the next three years. In addition to greatly improving the care and training for clients at the facility, the accomplishments of the systems-level OBM approach allowed for the development of a campus-wide staff recognition and reinforcement system. Recognition awards were created that prompted staff to "catch each other doing things right." The awards included the performer's and reinforcer's names, the behavior or outcome being recognized, and a statement that the recognition would be considered in that staff's annual evaluation. During the course of one year over 6,200 performance recognition awards were given. Direct-service staff gave 52% of the awards and professional, supervisory or administrative staff gave the remaining 48%.

These case illustrations remind us that large scale applications of OBM can be effective with professional and other staff. Their development took place over the course of several years and improvements initially gained were maintained while the systems were in place. However, the systems must be open ended to survive–continuing to adapt to changing internal and external situations and contingencies. They must be "user friendly" so that new staff can be trained to keep the system in tune. And with the trend toward deregulation and managed care in human services, large scale OBM applications must be effective and cost efficient for the clients/ customers they serve. The foundations of OBM in the core dimensions of applied behavior analysis are as powerful today as they were initially described over 25 years ago (Baer, Wolf, & Risley, 1968). Let's keep up the good work.

## REFERENCES

Allen, J., & Snyder, G. (1990). *I saw what you did and I know who you are: Giving & receiving recognition.* Tucker, Georgia: Performance Management Publications.
American Heritage Electronic Dictionary, 3rd Edition (1992). Houghton Mifflin.
Andrasik, F., & Heimberg, J.S. (1982). Self-management procedures. In L.W.

Frederiksen (Ed.), *Handbook of organizational behavior management* (pp. 219-248). New York: John Wiley & Sons, Inc.

Ayllon, T.A., & Michael, J. (1959). The psychiatric nurse as a behavioral engineer. *Journal of the Experimental Analysis of Behavior, 2*, 323-334.

Baer, D.M, Wolf, M.M., & Risley, T.R. (1968). Some current dimensions of applied behavior analysis. *Journal of Applied Behavior Analysis, 1*, 91-97.

Bailey, J.S. (1991). Marketing behavior analysis requires different talk. *Journal of Applied Behavior Analysis, 24*, 445-448.

Bailey, J.S., & Reiss, M.L. (1984). The demise of "Model T" and the emergence of systems management in human services. *The Behavior Therapist, 7*, 65-68.

Bernstein, G.S., & Karen, O.C. (1978). Preservice training of professionals as behavior managers: A review. *Behavior Therapy, 9*, 124-126.

Burgio, L.D., Whitman, T.L., & Reid, D.H. (1983). A participative management approach for improving direct-care staff performance in an institutional setting. *Journal of Applied Behavior Analysis, 16*, 37-53.

Carnegie, D. (1941). *How to win friends and influence people*. New York: Simon and Schuster.

Coles, E., & Blunden, R. (1981). Maintaining new procedures using feedback to staff, a hierarchical reporting system, and a multidisciplinary management group. *Journal of Organizational Behavior Management, 3*(2), 19-33.

Crane, G.W. (1944). *Psychology applied*. Chicago: Hopkins Syndicate, Inc.

Daniels, A.C. (1994). *Bringing out the best in people: How to apply the astonishing power of positive reinforcement*. New York: McGraw-Hill, Inc.

Dowrick, P.W., & Johns, E.M. (1976). Video feedback effects on therapist attention to on-task behaviors of disturbed children. *Journal of Behavior Therapy and Experimental Psychiatry, 7*, 255-257.

Feldstein, S., & Feldstein, J.H. (1990). Positive reinforcement for submission of timely reports by professional staff in a residential facility. *Education and Training in Mental Retardation, 25*, 188-192.

Fitzgerald, J.R., Reid, D.H., Schepis, M.M., Faw, G.D., Welty, P.A., & Pyfer, L.M. (1984). A rapid training procedure for teaching manual sign language skills to multidisciplinary institutional staff. *Applied Research in Mental Retardation, 5*, 451-469.

Gilbert, T.F. (1978). *Human competence: Engineering worthy performance*. New York: McGraw-Hill, Inc.

Goncalves, S.J., Iwata, B.A., & Chiang, S.J. (1983). Assessment and training of supervisors' evaluative feedback to their staff in an operant learning program for handicapped children. *Education and Treatment of Children, 6*, 11-20.

Green, C.W., & Reid, D.H. (1991). Reinforcing staff performance in residential facilities: A survey of common managerial practices. *Mental Retardation, 29*, 195-200.

Hall, B.L. (1980). Editorial. *Journal of Organizational Behavior Management, 2*, 145-150.

Hanel, F., Martin, G., & Koop, S. (1982). Field testing of a self-instructional time management manual with managerial staff in an institutional setting. *Journal of Organizational Behavior Management, 4*(3), 81-96.

Herbert-Jackson, E., O'Brien, M., Porterfield, J., & Risley, T.R. (1977). *The infant center: A complete guide to organizing and managing infant day care.* Baltimore, Maryland: University Park Press.

Horner, R.H., Thompsen, L.S., & Storey, K. (1990). Effects of case manager feedback on the quality of individual habilitation plan objectives. *Mental Retardation, 28,* 227-231.

Hutchison, J.M., Jarman, P.H., & Bailey, J.S. (1980). Public posting with a habilitation team: Effects on attendance and performance. *Behavior Modification, 4,* 57-70.

Ivancic, M.T., & Schell, R.M. (1993, May). Positive staff management. A workshop presented at the nineteenth annual conference of the Association for Behavior Analysis, Chicago, Illinois.

Lattimore, J., Stephens, T.E., Favell, J.E., & Risley, T.R. (1984). Increasing direct care staff compliance to individualized physical therapy body positioning prescriptions: Prescriptive checklists. *Mental Retardation, 22,* 79-84.

LeLaurin, K. & Risley, T.R. (1972). The organization of day care environments: "Zone" versus "man-to-man" staff assignments. *Journal of Applied Behavior Analysis, 5,* 225-232.

Lindsley, O.R. (1991). From technical jargon to plain English for application. *Journal of Applied Behavior Analysis, 24,* 449-458.

MacNamara, R.D. (1986). Forces in the administration of residential facilities. In J. Thaw & A.J. Cuvo (Eds.), *Developing responsive human services: New perspectives about residential treatment organizations* (pp. 51-82). Lawrence Erlbaum Associates, Hillsdale, NJ.

Mager, R.F. (1982). *Who did what to whom? II: Recognizing four behavioral principles in action.* Mager Associates, Inc. (Producer). Available from Research Press Co., 2612 North Mattis Avenue, Champaign, IL 61820.

Maher, C.A. (1981). Training of managers in program planning and evaluation: Comparison of two approaches. *Journal of Organizational Behavior Management, 3*(1), 45-56.

Marshall, B.D., Jr., Banzett, L., Kuehnel, T., & Moore, J. (1983). Maintaining nursing staff performance on an intensive behavior therapy unit. *Analysis and Intervention in Developmental Disabilities, 3,* 193-204.

McGimsey, J.F., Greene, B.F., & Lutzker, J.R. (1995). Competence in aspects of behavioral treatment and consultation: Implications for service delivery and graduate training. *Journal of Applied Behavior Analysis, 28,* 301-315.

Page, T.J., Christian, J.G., Iwata, B.A., Reid, D.H., Crow, R.E., & Dorsey, M.F. (1981). Evaluating and training interdisciplinary teams in writing IPP goals and objectives. *Mental Retardation, 19,* 25-27.

Page, T.J., Iwata, B.A., & Reid, D.H. (1982). Pyramidal training: A large-scale application with instructional staff. *Journal of Applied Behavior Analysis, 15,* 335-352.

Parsons, M.B., Cash, V.B., & Reid, D.H. (1989). Improving residential treatment services: Implementation and norm referenced evaluation of a comprehensive management system. *Journal of Applied Behavior Analysis, 22,* 143-156.

Patterson, R., Cooke, C., & Liberman, R.P. (1972). Reinforcing the reinforcers: A method of supplying feedback to nursing personnel. *Behavior Therapy, 3,* 444-446.

Quilitch, H.R. (1975). A comparison of three staff-management procedures. *Journal of Applied Behavior Analysis, 8,* 59-66.

Reid, D.H. (1987). *Developing a research program in human service agencies: A practitioner's guide.* Springfield, IL: Charles C. Thomas.

Reid, D.H. (1991). Technological behavior analysis and societal impact: A human services perspective. *Journal of Applied Behavior Analysis, 24,* 437-439.

Reid, D.H. (1992). The need to train more behavior analysts to be better applied researchers. *Journal of Applied Behavior Analysis, 25,* 97-99.

Reid, D.H. (1995, August). Supervisory survival skills: Self-motivation for supervisors. Paper presented at the *eighth* annual conference of the Developmental Disabilities Services Managers. Memphis, TN.

Reid, D.H., & Parsons, M.B. (Ad hoc Eds.) (1993). *Staff training and management: Bibliography of organizational behavior management reports in developmental disabilities and related human services.* Available from Developmental Disabilities Services Managers, Inc., P.O. Box 805, Morganton, NC 28655.

Reid, D.H., & Parsons, M.B. (1995). *Motivating human service staff: Supervisory strategies for maximizing work effort and work enjoyment.* Morganton, NC: Habiliataive Management Consultants, Inc.

Reid, D.H., Parsons, M.B., & Green, C.W. (1989). *Staff management in human services: Behavioral research and application.* Springfield, IL: Charles C. Thomas.

Reid, D.H., & Whitman, T.L. (1983). Behavioral staff management in institutions: A critical review of effectiveness and acceptability. *Analysis and Intervention in Developmental Disabilities, 3,* 131-149.

Repp, A.C., & Deitz, D.E.D. (1979). Improving administrative-related staff behaviors at a state institution. *Mental Retardation, 17,* 185-192.

Risley, T.R. (1975). Certify procedures not people. In W.S. Wood (Ed.), *Issues in evaluating behavior modification: Proceedings of the First Drake Conference on Professional Issues in Behavior Analysis* (pp. 159-181). Champaign, IL: Research Press.

Schell, R.M., Allen, L.D., & Bailey, J.S. (1982, September). Staff accountability: Increasing completed training objectives by publicly posting instructors' performance. Paper presented at the second annual conference of the Florida Association for Behavior Analysis, Orlando, FL.

Schell, R.M., Hudson, R.E., Caudillo, S., Hammock, R.G., & Lybarger, W.A. (1992). Performance management at Winfield State Hospital and Training Center. *Performance Management Magazine, 10*(3), 7-10.

Schell, R.M., Rogers, R.W., Griffin, G., Rubio, L., & Bailey, J.S. (1984, September). The design and implementation of a behavioral appraisal instrument for trainers of handicapped people. Paper presented at the fourth annual conference of the Florida Association for Behavior Analysis, Orlando, FL.

Thaw, J., Benjamin, E., & Cuvo, A.J. (1986). The professionals: Difficulties and directions. In J. Thaw & A.J. Cuvo (Eds.), *Developing responsive human services:*

*New perspectives about residential treatment organizations* (pp. 149-190). Lawrence Erlbaum Associates, Hillsdale, NJ.

Willems, E.P. (1974). Behavioral technology and behavioral ecology. *Journal of Applied Behavior Analysis, 7,* 151-165.

Wolf, M.M., Braukmann, C.J., & Ramp, K.A. (1987). Serious delinquent behavior as part of a significantly handicapping condition: Cures and supportive environments. *Journal of Applied Behavior Analysis, 20,* 347-359.

# A Review of Procedural Acceptability in Organizational Behavior Management

## Marsha B. Parsons

**SUMMARY.** Despite the documented benefits Organizational Behavior Management (OBM) applications can have on service provision for people with developmental disabilities, OBM is not widely practiced in service systems. One variable that may impact the utilization of OBM is how acceptable the associated procedures are to staff. The research on procedural acceptability in OBM is summarized in terms of two primary methods for determining consumer satisfaction with management procedures–rating scales and discrete choices. Results of acceptability assessments utilizing ratings scales have repeatedly indicated high degrees of staff acceptance for virtually all OBM procedures. However, when staff have been asked to choose among management procedures, clear and consistent differences in acceptability have been apparent. Suggested directions for future research focus on improving acceptability assessment methodology, developing guidelines for implementing effective OBM procedures in a manner that is most acceptable to staff, and involving supervisory and professional staff in acceptability evaluations. *[Article copies available for a fee from The Haworth Document Delivery Service: 1-800-342-9678. E-mail address: getinfo@haworthpressinc.com]*

Marsha B. Parsons is affiliated with the Carolina Behavior Analysis and Support Center, Ltd., Morganton, NC.

Correspondence concerning this article should be addressed to Marsha B. Parsons, Carolina Behavior Analysis and Support Center, Ltd., P. O. Box 425, Morganton, NC 28680.

[Haworth co-indexing entry note]: "A Review of Procedural Acceptability in Organizational Behavior Management." Parsons, Marsha B. Co-published simultaneously in *Journal of Organizational Behavior Management* (The Haworth Press, Inc.) Vol. 18, No. 2/3, 1998, pp. 173-190; and: *Organizational Behavior Management and Developmental Disabilities Services: Accomplishments and Future Directions* (ed: Dennis H. Reid) The Haworth Press, Inc., 1998, pp. 173-190. Single or multiple copies of this article are available for a fee from The Haworth Document Delivery Service [1-800-342-9678, 9:00 a.m. - 5:00 p.m. (EST). E-mail address: getinfo@haworthpressinc.com].

The research literature contains numerous demonstrations of the efficacy of Organizational Behavior Management (OBM) for improving staff performance along a broad continuum of services for people with developmental disabilities. Organizational Behavior Management procedures have been used to improve staff performance in residential (Parsons, Reid, & Green, 1993) and day programs (Fleming & Sulzer-Azaroff, 1992) serving children (Hundert, 1982) and adults (Sigafoos, Roberts, Couzens, & Caycho, 1992) in both the public (Suda & Miltenberger, 1993) and private (Boudreau, Christian, & Thibadeau, 1993) sectors of service provision. Research has documented the successful application of OBM procedures to a variety of staff performance problems frequently encountered in settings serving people with developmental disabilities including absenteeism, infrequent staff/client interactions, inadequate teaching skills, lack of active treatment, inadequate health care and unsatisfactory performance of administrative duties (see Reid, Parsons, & Green, 1989, for a review). Most importantly, research has also shown that improvements in staff performance resulting from OBM applications are accompanied by improvements in indices of client welfare (Fleming & Reile, 1993; Greene, Willis, Levy, & Bailey, 1978). In short, the beneficial impact that OBM strategies can have on services and supports for people with developmental disabilities has been well documented.

Despite the existence of an empirically-derived technology for managing staff performance, reports of staff performance problems have persisted in the professional literature (Reid, Parsons, & Green, 1989), the popular press (Reid & Parsons, 1995b) and in the legal system (Patrick, 1995). The apparent prevalence of reported inadequacies in staff performance is evidence that wide-spread adoption of OBM procedures has not occurred. The lack of adoption has led to calls for research to identify variables, in addition to effectiveness, that may influence the practice of OBM in human service settings (Reid & Whitman, 1983).

Consumer satisfaction with management procedures is one variable that can heavily influence the practice of any management approach (Demchak, 1987; Reid & Whitman, 1983). Consumer acceptability has been described as the consumer's perception of how much a procedure costs in terms of "effort, time, discomfort, and ethics" (Schwartz & Baer, 1991, p. 193). Acceptability specifically in regard to OBM has been defined as the extent to which consumers view a management practice as "fair, appropriate, nonintrusive, practical, consistent with standard practices, and unlikely to result in negative side effects" (Davis & Russell, 1990, p. 260).

Determining the acceptability of an effective management practice is important for two reasons. First, acceptability is closely linked to viability (Reid & Whitman, 1983). When supervisors view a management procedure as unacceptable because of inefficiency, the procedure is likely to be rejected even though it may be quite effective. To illustrate, a supervisor may not implement an inservice program for training direct support staff if the training requires staff to be away from their work site for several days. Similarly, a supervisor may not practice an effective management procedure if the procedure evokes additional, undesirable side-effects. For example, an effective group contingency for decreasing staff's use of unscheduled leave time may not be implemented if the contingency results in bickering among staff members.

The perceptions of staff whose performance is being managed can impact viability of management procedures as surely as the perceptions of supervisors. In settings with organized labor unions, staff can directly reject an unacceptable management procedure resulting in disputes and arbitration between labor and management (Greene et al., 1978). In systems where staff cannot formally reject a management procedure, the subtle, negative reactions of staff may serve the same function as more direct forms of rejection. That is, the unpleasantness of staff's negative reaction to a particular management procedure can function as a punisher to the supervisor, decreasing the likelihood that the procedure will be frequently or consistently implemented by the supervisor in the future. The punishing effects of an unpleasant interaction between staff and supervisor is well exemplified with performance monitoring. Performance monitoring is an essential component of OBM but unfortunately many staff immensely dislike being monitored (Favell, Favell, Riddle, & Risley, 1984). When a supervisor monitors a staff member's performance, the staff member may make a comment or facial expression indicative of displeasure at having his/her performance monitored. Staff's obvious displeasure, in effect, punishes the supervisor's attempts to conduct performance monitoring. As a result, many supervisors avoid punishment by monitoring as quickly and infrequently as possible. In essence, staff's serious dislike of a management procedure can critically undermine the procedure's viability over time.

A second reason consumer satisfaction with management practices is important relates to the detrimental impact unpopular management practices can have on staff motivation. Staff motivation has been conceptualized as staff working diligently and competently while also enjoying work (Reid & Parsons, 1995b). According to the latter conceptualization of motivation, the more frequently staff experience pleasant events at work relative to unpleasant events, the more staff's work enjoyment is enhanced. Conversely, management procedures which are unpleasant for staff detract from the work enjoyment aspect of motivation for both staff and supervisors. When staff are not motivated to fulfill their work responsibilities, staff performance problems become pervasive and ultimately agencies fail to accomplish their respective missions of service to clients.

Procedural acceptability research can play an influential role in determining the ultimate contribution of OBM in support systems for people with developmental disabilities. As the importance of consumer satisfaction with management procedures has become more clear, a number of investigations have included assessments of OBM procedural acceptability. This paper provides a summarization and critical review of the OBM procedural acceptability literature.

## FOCUS AND ORGANIZATION OF REVIEW

This review includes exclusively investigations addressing the acceptability of OBM procedures. Management procedures are defined as procedures for changing or maintaining staff performance. In keeping with the purpose of this special volume, the review includes only studies conducted in settings providing supports and services for people with developmental disabilities. In total, 25 studies were the primary basis for this review of OBM procedural acceptability.

The literature summary is organized according to the method by which consumer satisfaction was assessed. Organization of the review by methodology was due to recent calls for a more careful examination of the methodology for assessing consumer satisfaction with behavioral interventions in general (Schwartz & Baer, 1991) and OBM procedures in particular (Davis, Rawana, & Capponi, 1989; Reid & Parsons, 1995a). When methodological limitations are present, resulting evaluations of consumer acceptability can yield inaccurate and invalid results (Schwartz & Baer, 1991). By organizing the literature review in terms of methodology, results of investigations with methodological limitations can be viewed with appropriate caution.

Following a summary of the OBM procedural acceptability literature, apparent trends in results both within and across acceptability assessment methodologies are discussed. Although space limitations preclude critical comments regarding individual studies, weaknesses in the OBM acceptability research as a whole are noted along with suggestions for future research.

## RESEARCH SUMMARY

Evidence of consumer satisfaction with OBM procedures has been reported in a variety of ways including anecdotal comments, consumer responses to open-ended questionnaires, numerical rankings or ratings and consumer choices among procedures. However, the latter two me-thods–ratings and choice measures–have been the primary methods for objectively assessing OBM procedural acceptability.

## Consumer Responses to Rating Scales

The acceptance of management practices has been evaluated most fre-quently through the use of rating scales. The typical process for assessing acceptability using a rating scale involves the following basic steps. After experiencing a management procedure, staff are asked to respond to ques-tions on a written survey by marking a Likert scale at the point that most closely reflects the rater's opinion of the management practice. Rating scales have been used in this manner to assess acceptability of manage-ment procedures to improve staff and client interactions (Burgio, Whit-man, & Reid, 1983; Schepis & Reid, 1994; Suda & Miltenberger, 1993), behavioral teaching skills (Fleming & Sulzer-Azaroff, 1992; Hundert, 1982; Kissel, Whitman, & Reid, 1983; Parsons et al., 1993; Sigafoos et al., 1992; Singer, Sowers, & Irvin, 1986), basic client care (Korabek, Reid, & Ivancic, 1982), safety related skills (van den Pol, Reid, & Fuqua, 1983), supervisory feedback (Parsons & Reid, 1995) and work attendance (Bou-dreau et al., 1993). Rating scales have been utilized to assess procedures designed to assist staff in acquiring new work skills (Green & Reid, 1994; Hundert, 1982; Parsons et al., 1993; Parsons & Reid, 1995; Singer et al., 1986; van den Pol et al., 1983) as well as procedures to manage staff performance by increasing or maintaining the use of previously learned work skills (Burgio et al., 1983; Fleming & Sulzer-Azaroff, 1992; Greene et al., 1978).

*Acceptability ratings of multifaceted interventions.* The majority of in-vestigations utilizing rating scales to measure procedural acceptability in-cluded multifaceted interventions involving both antecedent and conse-quence management components (Fleming & Sulzer-Azaroff 1992; Green & Reid, 1994; Greene et al., 1978; Hundert, 1982; Kissel et al., 1983; Korabek et al., 1982; Parsons et al., 1993; Parsons & Reid, 1995; Schepis & Reid, 1994; Sigafoos et al., 1992; Suda & Miltenberger, 1993). When multifacet-ed management packages were utilized, acceptability was often reported in general terms regarding the total package of procedures (Hundert, 1982; Kissel et al., 1983; Parsons & Reid, 1995; Sigafoos et al., 1992; Singer et al., 1986). For example, following a multifaceted program for training teachers to write and implement behavior modification programs, partici-pants rated the total program in terms of applicability to the classroom, efficiency, enjoyment and benefits to pupils (Hundert, 1982). Reports of consumer acceptability for multifaceted interventions rated as a whole have generally reflected high levels of consumer acceptance.

Consumer acceptability ratings of procedural components within multifaceted interventions have also been reported. In comparing staff ratings of procedural components within multifaceted interventions, more variability in consumer satisfaction ratings across procedures has become apparent. In a multifaceted program for training staff to teach, staff found written homework assignments less helpful in improving their teaching skills than instructions, practice and feedback. Instructions and practice were rated by staff as the most helpful procedures in improving their teaching skills (Parsons et al., 1993). Within a management program involving instructions, self-recording, public posting and vocal feedback designed to increase the food intake of multihandicapped individuals, public posting of children's food intake and weights received the highest acceptability ratings and staff self-recording received the lowest rating (Korabek et al., 1982). Self-management procedures have been rated as less acceptable than instructions with goal setting, or feedback in a program for increasing therapeutic interactions by vocational staff although each procedure was rated as acceptable (Suda & Miltenberger, 1992). However, in the same investigation, acceptability ratings of self-management and feedback occurring two weeks after implementation were higher than the ratings received by the respective procedures immediately after implementation. In a peer management program for increasing the teaching interactions by staff in a vocational setting, staff rated peer feedback as more helpful than goal setting and graphing the number of teaching interactions (Fleming & Sulzer-Azaroff, 1992). Peer feedback was also more preferred than supervisory feedback or a combination of supervisory and peer feedback. Although rating individual management components within multifaceted interventions has resulted in more variability in acceptance ratings, this review found no component to be clearly rated as unacceptable.

*Comparisons of acceptability ratings of different management procedures.* Rating scales have been used to compare acceptability between two or more management procedures (or variations of procedures) implemented singularly rather than as part of a multifaceted intervention (Boudreau et al., 1993; Reid & Parsons, 1995a, in press). For example, requiring staff to notify their supervisor of an absence was compared to notifying a clerical staff member who arranged coverage for absences (Boudreau et al., 1993). Results indicated direct support *staff* had no strong opinion regarding whom they notified even though notification of the supervisor appeared to punish the use of unscheduled leave. However, two of the three *supervisors* participating in the same investigation had a strong preference to be directly notified of staff absences.

The acceptability of various formats for conducting performance monitoring and providing feedback have been compared in several investigations. In the context of a staff training program, both spoken feedback and spoken plus written feedback were rated highly acceptable by staff receiving the feedback (Reid & Parsons, in press). In the latter investigation, immediate spoken feedback and delayed spoken plus written feedback also received equally favorable ratings of acceptability. Acceptability ratings of performance monitoring were comparably high regardless of whether staff were familiar or unfamiliar with the system used to monitor their performance as part of a staff training program (Reid & Parsons, 1995a). However, performance observations occurring before staff were trained have been found to be less well-liked than performance observations occurring after staff were trained (Schepis & Reid, 1994). In the same study, staff were slightly more accepting of on-the-job observations when they received immediate relative to delayed feedback although delayed feedback was still rated as acceptable.

Differences in the relative acceptability of procedures were also apparent in a study by Burgio et al. (1983), although staff did not directly experience all of the assessed management procedures as part of the investigation. A multifaceted intervention comprised primarily of self-management procedures (i.e., self-monitoring, goal setting, self-evaluation and self-reinforcement) was effective in increasing interactions between staff and clients in a residential setting. Following the termination of the self-management program, staff who participated and staff who did not participate in the self-management program were asked to rate the acceptability of nine frequently used management consequence procedures on a 10-point Likert scale. The mean ratings ranked from high to low were as follows: increased lunch hour, contingent money, self-management, performance-based lottery, contingent supervisor praise, contingent preferential duties, publicly-posted feedback, contingent loss of compensatory time, and contingent loss of money. The mean rating of self-management by staff who had participated in the self-management program did not differ significantly from ratings of staff who had not participated in the program. Four procedures, publicly-posted feedback, contingent loss of compensatory time, contingent preferential duties and contingent loss of money, received an average rating below the acceptable range.

In three studies, staff rated the acceptability of several management procedures after exposure to the procedures in analogue situations (Davis et al., 1989; Davis & Russell, 1990; Miltenberger, Larson, Doerner, & Orvedal, 1992). The Acceptability Rating Scale (ARS), an extensive survey with reported reliability and validity, was initially used to determine the relative acceptability of instructions, reinforcement, self-management and punishment (Davis et al., 1989). Staff rated the procedures in response to written vignettes depicting work tasks that required two levels of staff work effort and two durations of staff/supervisor interaction time. Mean ratings showed instructions were the most acceptable of the four management procedures followed by self-management, reinforcement and punishment. The mean rating for punishment and for reinforcement ranged between points on the scale corresponding to "slightly acceptable" and "slightly unacceptable." Level of work difficulty and supervisory interaction time were not found to be significant variables affecting acceptability. However, staff with less education tended to rate all of the management techniques more highly than staff with more education. In a similar study, staff completed the ARS after participating in role plays of management procedures involving either instruction, reinforcement, self-management or punishment (Davis & Russell, 1990). Results were consistent with results previously reported by Davis et al. (1989) except that all procedures including punishment fell within the range of the scale indicating acceptance.

The acceptability of a larger and more varied group of management procedures was compared using the ARS (Miltenberger et al., 1992). Direct support staff and supervisors' ratings of acceptability were also compared. Participants completed the rating scale after reading a description of the management procedures applied to a specific staff performance problem. Mean acceptability ratings by direct support staff indicated "instructions" were most acceptable followed in order by "feedback and praise," "instructions and modeling," "instructions, feedback and praise," "self-management, feedback and praise," and "self-management." Interventions involving self-management were rated as significantly less acceptable than the other procedures by direct support staff. Supervisors, on the other hand, rated "instructions and modeling" as most acceptable followed by "instructions, feedback and praise," "feedback and praise," "self-management," "self-management, feedback and praise" and "instructions."

One similarity noted among three studies using the ARS in analogue situations to compare procedural acceptability is direct support staff tended to rate antecedent procedures as more acceptable than procedures involving consequences or self-management. Speculation regarding the reason antecedent procedures were more acceptable to direct support staff than procedures involving consequences was that antecedent procedures required less effort and accountability on the part of direct support staff (Miltenberger et al., 1992). One difference between two of the studies was that Miltenberger et al. found self-management procedures to be less acceptable and reinforcement-based procedures more acceptable to direct service staff than did Davis et al. (1989). Direct comparisons of the results reported by Davis and Russell (1990) with the other two studies using the ARS are more difficult because the average ratings for the management procedures in the Davis and Russell investigation were much higher for all procedures than the average ratings reported by either Miltenberger et al. or Davis et al.

The main finding among all studies utilizing rating scales to assess staff acceptance is that, with few exceptions, OBM procedures were acceptable to staff. Acceptability was found to be favorable whether staff were rating multifaceted interventions, components within multifaceted interventions, or different management procedures in actual or analogue situations. The only exceptions to uniformly high levels of acceptability based on rating scale evaluations have been procedures involving punishment (Burgio et al., 1983; Davis et al., 1989), self-management (Miltenberger et al., 1992) and publicly-posted feedback (Burgio et al., 1983). However, results of ratings indicating a lack of acceptance of specific procedures have been inconsistent in that procedures involving publicly-posted feedback (Greene et al., 1978; Korabek et al., 1982), self-management (Burgio et al., 1983; Davis et al., 1989; Davis & Russell, 1990) and even punishment (Boudreau et al., 1993; Davis & Russell, 1990) have also been found to be acceptable to staff.

## *Choice Measures of OBM Procedural Acceptability*

Although utilized much less frequently than rating scales, a second method of evaluating OBM procedural acceptability has been to provide staff with discrete choices regarding management procedures. The manner of choice provision has varied. One manner of choice provision has been to ask staff whether or not a management procedure should be continued. For example, when asked whether to (dis)continue a feedback system involving publicly posting management's responses to employee suggestions, 98% of the staff and 100% of the administrators responsible for managing the system recommended continuation of the suggestion system (Quilitch, 1978). More frequently than asking staff to choose to continue or discontinue a management practice, procedural acceptability has been measured by asking staff to choose between two or more management procedures to receive in the future. In an example of the latter type of choice, kitchen and living area staff in a residential facility were asked if they preferred announced or unannounced health inspections in their respective work areas (Quilitch, 1979). Results revealed that more than 80% of the staff members and 100% of the supervisors preferred unannounced rather than announced health inspections. In a more recent study, when given a choice of being either familiar or unfamiliar with performance monitoring systems, 78% of the staff chose to be familiar with future monitoring systems, 22% had no preference and 0% chose to be unfamiliar with systems for future monitoring (Reid & Parsons, 1995a).

Investigations of staff acceptability involving choice have examined staff preferences for various formats for receiving performance feedback. In regard to a preferred schedule for receiving feedback, two of three prevocational staff preferred to receive biweekly feedback rather than weekly feedback (Hrydowy & Martin, 1994). To evaluate the relative acceptability of feedback from different sources, staff were asked if they preferred to receive feedback concerning implementation of fire safety training sessions from a supervisor or from a staff fire-safety expert (Fox & Sulzer-Azaroff, 1989). Seventy-one percent of the staff had no preference regarding the feedback source.

Staff have also been given choices between temporal arrangements and presentation formats for performance feedback. As part of a program for training staff to teach people with severe disabilities, staff were asked if they preferred to receive immediate or delayed feedback in the future after exposure to both temporal arrangements. Seventy-three percent of the staff chose immediate feedback and no staff chose delayed feedback (Reid & Parsons, 1996). Within a similar training program, three times as many direct support staff members chose to be presented with a combination of spoken and written feedback rather than spoken feedback only (Reid & Parsons, in press). However, when immediate spoken feedback (more preferred temporal arrangement but less preferred presentation format) was compared to delayed spoken plus written feedback (more preferred presentation format but less preferred temporal arrangement), 90% of the participating staff chose to receive immediate spoken feedback, 0% chose delayed spoken plus written feedback and 10% expressed no preference between the two formats (Reid & Parsons, in press).

Although only a small number of investigations have involved consumer choice as a measure of procedural acceptability relative to the number of investigations utilizing rating scales, one important trend seems apparent. That is, when given a choice of management procedures, staff generally express a preference and often the expressed preference has been consistent for the majority of participants. In particular, based on the procedural acceptability research to date involving consumer choice, a strong preference for immediate rather than delayed feedback is becoming clear. In contrast, consistent differences regarding preferences for respective OBM procedures have not been reported within investigations relying on rating scale measurement methodology.

## *Comparison of Choice and Rating Scale Measures of Acceptability*

Two of the studies previously discussed conducted both rating scale and choice measures of OBM procedural acceptability, thereby allowing a comparison between results of both methods. Staff acceptance of monitoring was rated equally favorably when staff were either familiar or unfamiliar with the system for monitoring their performance. However, when given a choice between the two monitoring formats, staff were much more likely to choose to be familiar than to remain unfamiliar with future monitoring systems (Reid & Parsons, 1995a). Similarly, both spoken and spoken plus written feedback received uniformly high rating-scale scores of acceptability but when staff were given a choice of feedback formats for future observations, spoken plus written feedback was chosen significantly more often than spoken feedback only (Reid & Parsons, in press). In the latter investigation, rating scale scores for both immediate spoken feedback and delayed spoken plus written feedback reflected high levels of staff acceptance but when staff were given a choice regarding the two feedback formats, 90% chose immediate spoken feedback while 0% chose to receive delayed spoken plus written feedback. Results of studies comparing rating scale and choice measures of acceptability suggest that discrete choices between procedures may provide a more sensitive measure of procedural acceptability than rating scales.

## WEAKNESSES IN THE OBM PROCEDURAL ACCEPTABILITY RESEARCH AND SUGGESTIONS FOR FUTURE RESEARCH

### *Methodology*

The most pervasive weakness in the research literature regarding acceptability of OBM procedures has been the methodology. Investigations have relied primarily on rating scales to measure consumer satisfaction with OBM procedures. Among the studies included in this review, over 70% reported consumer responses to rating scales as the principal measure of acceptability. Consumers have, with very few exceptions, rated all OBM procedures as acceptable and most procedures as highly acceptable. However, there are indications that the consistently positive responses to rating scales may be somewhat misleading. One indication stems from results of investigations providing consumers with choices between management procedures as previously noted. In contrast to the lack of differences in acceptability among procedures based on the results of consumer ratings, in five of seven investigations involving a choice between procedures, staff consistently chose one of the procedures more than the other (Quilitch, 1978; Quilitch, 1979; Reid & Parsons, 1995a, 1996, in press). Moreover, in investigations directly comparing choice and rating scale measures of acceptability, choice measures revealed differences in the relative acceptability of procedures when rating scale measures indicated no differences (Reid & Parsons, 1995a, in press).

A second indicator that rating scale measures of acceptability may be spuriously high is the inconsistency between the positive responses to rating scales and anecdotal reports of staff rejection (see Reid & Whitman, 1983, for a similar discussion). For example, although peer training procedures received high acceptability ratings, both staff who participated in the peer training program declined the opportunity to train other staff when given a choice (van den Pol et al., 1983). A peer-management procedure received high acceptability ratings but two participants withdrew from the study expressing apprehension about giving and receiving peer feedback (Fleming & Sulzer-Azaroff, 1992). Similarly, an investigator had to assume the duties of instructing, goal-setting and giving feedback when observations revealed the supervisor failed to comply with experimental procedures even though staff had rated the procedures as acceptable (Suda & Miltenberger, 1992).

Anecdotal reports of actual rejection of effective management procedures coupled with the results of investigations comparing rating scale and choice measures of acceptability have led to questions regarding the validity of such positive ratings of OBM procedural acceptability. Therefore, interpretation of previous results stemming primarily from analyses utilizing only rating scales should be cautious. Although more research comparing choice and rating scale measures of acceptability with a variety of management procedures is warranted, if consumer choice continues to reflect clear and consistent preferences for specific management procedures, then future investigations of OBM procedural acceptability should utilize more discrete choice measures whenever possible.

Not all analyses of acceptability, however, allow the direct comparison of two management procedures by providing staff with choices between procedures (Schwartz & Baer, 1991). When rating scales are the only alternative for evaluating acceptability then several steps seem necessary to enhance the likelihood that rating scales will be as sensitive as possible to differences in acceptability. First, Likert-type scales should allow for a wide range of responses. For example, a 7-point scale may reveal more subtle differences in the acceptability of procedures that are not apparent when scales include 3- or even 5-points. In this regard, only a few studies have used 7-point rating scales (e.g., Burgio et al., 1983; Reid & Parsons, 1995a, in press; Schepis & Reid, 1994).

A second step which may enhance the use of rating scale measures of acceptability is to empirically determine what the numerical ratings actually mean to consumers (Wolf, Kirigin, Fixen, Blase, & Braukmann, 1995). Though not specifically addressing OBM procedures, Wolf et al. discuss the extensive surveys conducted to ascertain consumer satisfaction with the Teaching-Family model of services for troubled youth. When a particular aspect of services received a rating below 6 on a 7-point Likert scale, consumers were more likely to include negative comments regarding the same aspect of services. Any rating below a 6 was, therefore, considered an indication of consumer dissatisfaction. In order for rating scales to yield information that will be helpful in shaping a more acceptable OBM technology, researchers must determine more precisely when ratings reflect valid consumer (dis)satisfaction with management procedures.

Research to determine the validity of all verbal measures of acceptability, not only rating scale measures, seems imperative. In this regard, it is not clear how closely discrete choice measures of acceptability correlate with other behavioral indicators of actual acceptance or rejection of management procedures. For example, questions remain regarding whether or not management practices chosen by staff are more likely to be practiced than the procedures that were not chosen. Once there is reasonable certainty that respective verbal indicators are reliable and valid measures of acceptability, researchers can undertake the task of modifying unacceptable management procedures (Schwartz & Baer, 1991; Wolf et al., 1995). The experimental manipulation of acceptability variables represents another broad and essentially untapped area for future research.

## *Effects of Staff Experience on Management Procedure Acceptability*

Two issues pertaining to staff experience with a management procedure seem to warrant further investigation. One issue is the importance of direct experience with a management procedure prior to the assessment of procedural acceptability. Specifically, research is needed to determine if results of acceptability assessments obtained in analogue situations can be generalized to management practices in routine work settings. One study addressed this issue by comparing acceptability ratings by staff who directly experienced a management procedure to ratings by staff who only read descriptions of the procedure (Burgio et al., 1983). In the latter investigation, self-management received similar ratings by staff who directly experienced the procedures and by staff who only read descriptions of the procedures. Overall however, the extent to which results of analogue assessments of procedural acceptability can be generalized to routine practice has not been sufficiently evaluated.

A second issue is the effect *duration* of experience has on staff acceptance of management procedures. In one study, staff's view of self-management and feedback procedures was more favorable two weeks after the procedures were implemented relative to immediately after the procedures were initiated (Suda & Miltenberger, 1993). These results suggest duration of experience with a management procedure may effect acceptability, but additional research is required before definitive conclusions can be drawn.

### Acceptability Assessments Involving Supervisors

As discussed previously, the perspective of supervisors regarding the acceptability of a management procedure can be as critical to the viability of the procedure as the views of direct support staff. The OBM literature contains very few investigations of procedural acceptability involving supervisors. Among the investigations that have included supervisors (Boudreau et al., 1993; Green & Reid, 1994; Miltenberger et al., 1992; Parsons & Reid, 1995; Quilitch, 1978, 1979), three reported differences between the views of direct service staff and supervisors regarding the acceptability of specific management procedures (Boudreau et al., 1993; Green & Reid, 1994; Miltenberger et al., 1992). Although direct support staff did not indicate a strong preference regarding whom they notified when absent from work, two of the three supervisors indicated a strong preference that the supervisor be notified rather than a clerical staff person who arranged for coverage (Boudreau et al., 1993). Supervisors rated instructions as significantly less acceptable and self-management procedures significantly more acceptable than did direct service staff (Miltenberger et al., 1992). Supervising teachers rated corrective feedback as the least effective procedure though their assistants rated corrective feedback as the most effective procedure in a training program for assembling adaptive switches (Green & Reid, 1994). These results suggest that the views of direct support staff regarding management procedures may not necessarily be representative of the views of supervisors. It would be helpful in future acceptability research to obtain the perspectives of both direct support staff and supervisors whenever possible.

### Acceptability Assessments Involving Professional Staff

Another group of staff who have been infrequent participants in research on acceptability of OBM procedures is professional staff. The lack of acceptability research involving professional staff parallels the relative lack of OBM research involving professional staff (see Schell in this volume). When professional staff have been included in investigations of OBM acceptability, typically they have been teachers or vocational instructors (Fleming & Sulzer-Azaroff, 1992; Green & Reid, 1994; Hundert, 1982). The relatively few investigations conducted with professional staff have shown that professional staff, like direct support staff, generally view OBM procedures as acceptable. However, one investigation found an inverse relationship between education level and acceptability ratings in that staff with less education tended to rate OBM procedures as more highly acceptable than staff with more education (Davis et al., 1989). Considerably more research involving professional staff is necessary to determine if the view of direct support staff regarding OBM procedural acceptability can be generalized to professional staff.

## *Provision of Guidelines for Effective and Acceptable Practice of OBM*

If procedural acceptability research in OBM is to help shape a more useful technology of staff management, more research seems warranted to determine the most acceptable ways to practice *effective* management procedures. An example of how research can result in guidelines for using an effective OBM procedure in the most acceptable manner is developing in regard to performance feedback. A variety of formats for presenting performance feedback have been shown to be effective in improving staff performance (see Balcazar, Hopkins, & Suarez, 1985, for a review). The acceptability literature has shown which formats for delivering performance feedback are likely to be well received by staff. Based on the current literature, staff appear to prefer feedback from their peers relative to their supervisor (Fleming & Sulzer-Azaroff, 1992), delivered immediately rather than delayed several days following an observation (Reid & Parsons, 1996, in press; Schepis & Reid, 1994) and presented in a spoken plus written format relative to a spoken format only (Fox & Sulzer-Azaroff, 1989; Reid & Parsons, in press). Additional investigation seems essential to determine the most acceptable manner for implementing other basic components of an OBM approach. Managers could benefit from guidelines for specifying performance expectations, providing instruction, monitoring staff performance and delivering consequences in ways that are acceptable to staff.

Unless OBM procedures are routinely utilized by managers and supervisors, the positive outcomes of OBM applications documented in the research literature will be of little benefit to the vast majority of individuals with developmental disabilities. Therefore, one important focus for OBM research is to identify the variables influencing more comprehensive adoption of OBM in human service settings. In this regard, determining better methods for measuring as well as increasing staff acceptance of management procedures represent critical areas for refining and extending OBM research.

## REFERENCES

Balcazar, F., Hopkins, B.L., & Suarez, Y. (1986). A critical, objective review of performance feedback. *Journal of Organizational Behavior Management, 7*(3/4), 65-89.

Boudreau, C.A., Christian, W.P., & Thibadeau, S.F. (1993). Reducing absenteeism in human service settings: A low cost alternative. *Journal of Organizational Behavior Management, 13*(2), 37-50.

Burgio, L.D., Whitman, T.L., & Reid, D.H. (1983). A participative management approach for improving direct-care staff performance in an institutional setting. *Journal of Applied Behavior Analysis, 16*, 37-53.

Davis, J.R., Rawana, E.P., & Capponi, D.R. (1989). Acceptability of behavioral staff management techniques. *Behavioral Residential Treatment, 4*, 23-44.

Davis, J. R., & Russell, R.H. (1990). Behavioral staff management: An analogue study of acceptability and its behavioral correlates. *Behavioral Residential Treatment, 5*, 259-270.

Demchak, M.A. (1987). A review of behavioral staff training in special education settings. *Education and Training of the Mentally Retarded, 22*, 205-217.

Favell, J.E., Favell, J.E., Riddle, J.I., & Risley, T.R. (1984). Promoting change in mental retardation facilities: Getting services from the paper to the people. In W.P. Christian, G.T. Hannah, & T.J. Glahn (Eds.), *Programming effective human services: Strategies for institutional change and client transition* (pp. 15-37). New York: Plenum.

Fleming, R.K., & Reile, P.A. (1993). A descriptive analysis of client outcomes associated with staff interventions in developmental disabilities. *Behavioral Residential Treatment, 8* 29-43.

Fleming, R., & Sulzer-Azaroff, B. (1992). Reciprocal peer management: Improving staff instruction in a vocational training program. *Journal of Applied Behavior Analysis, 25*, 611-620.

Fox, C.J., & Sulzer-Azaroff, B. (1990). The effectiveness of two different sources of feedback on staff teaching of fire evacuation skills. *Journal of Organizational Behavior Management, 10*(2), 19-35.

Green, C.W., & Reid, D.H. (1995). A comprehensive evaluation of a train-the-trainers model for training education staff to assemble adaptive switches. *Journal of Mental and Physical Disabilities, 6*, 219-238.

Greene, B.F., Willis, B.S., Levy, R., & Bailey, J.S. (1978). Measuring client gains from staff-implemented programs. *Journal of Applied Behavior Analysis, 11*, 395-412.

Hrydowy, E.R., & Martin, G.L. (1994). A practical staff management package for use in a training program for persons with developmental disabilities. *Behavior Modification, 18,* 66-88.

Hundert, J. (1982). Training teachers in generalized writing of behavior modification programs for multihandicapped deaf children. *Journal of Applied Behavior Analysis, 15,* 111-122.

Kissel, R.C., Whitman, T.L., & Reid, D.H. (1983). An institutional staff training and self-management program for developing multiple self-care skills in severely/profoundly retarded individuals. *Journal of Applied Behavior Analysis, 16,* 395-415.

Korabek, C.A., Reid, D.H., & Ivancic, M.T. (1982). Improving needed food intake of profoundly handicapped children through effective supervision of institutional staff. *Applied Research in Mental Retardation, 2,* 69-88.

Miltenberger, R.G., Larson, J., Doerner, M., & Orvedal, L. (1992). Assessing the acceptability of staff management procedures to direct care staff and supervisory staff. *Behavioral Residential Treatment, 7,* 23-34.

Parsons, M.B., & Reid, D.H. (1995). Training residential supervisors to provide feedback for maintaining staff teaching skills with people who have severe disabilities. *Journal of Applied Behavior Analysis, 28,* 317-322.

Parsons, M.B., Reid, D.H., & Green, C.W. (1993). Preparing direct service staff to teach people with severe disabilities: A comprehensive evaluation of an effective and acceptable training program. *Behavioral Residential Treatment, 8,* 163-186.

Patrick, D.L. (1995, July/August). What the U.S. Justice Department is doing for people with mental retardation. *AAMR News & Notes, 8*(4), 6-8.

Quilitch, H.R. (1978). Using a simple feedback procedure to reinforce the submission of written suggestions by mental health employees. *Journal of Organizational Behavior Management, 1*(2), 155-163.

Quilitch, H.R. (1979). Applied behavior analysis studies for institutional management. In L.A. Hamerlynck (Ed.), *Behavioral systems in the developmentally disabled: II. Institutional, clinic and community environments* (pp. 70-81). New York: Brunner/Mazel.

Reid, D.H., & Parsons, M.B. (1995a). Comparing choice versus questionnaire measures of the acceptability of a staff training procedure. *Journal of Applied Behavior Analysis, 28,* 95-96.

Reid, D.H., & Parsons, M.B. (1995b). *Motivating human service staff: Supervisory strategies for maximizing work effort & work enjoyment.* Morganton, NC: Habilitative Management Consultants.

Reid, D.H., & Parsons, M.B. (1996). A comparison of staff acceptability of immediate versus delayed verbal feedback in staff training. *Journal of Organizational Behavior Management, 16*(2), 35-47.

Reid, D.H., & Parsons, M.B. (in press). Differential effects of choice versus questionnaire evaluations on the acceptability of feedback procedures in staff training. *Journal of Organizational Behavior Management.*

Reid, D.H., Parsons, M.B., & Green, C.W. (1989). *Staff management in human services: Behavioral research and application.* Springfield, IL: Charles C Thomas.

Reid, D.H., & Whitman, T.L. (1983). Behavioral staff management in institutions: A critical review of effectiveness and acceptability. *Analysis and Intervention in Developmental Disabilities, 3,* 131-149.

Schepis, M.M., & Reid, D.H. (1994). Training direct service staff in congregate settings to interact with people with severe disabilities: A quick, effective and acceptable program. *Behavioral Interventions: Theory & Practice in Residential & Community-Based Clinical Programs, 9,* 13-26.

Schwartz, I.S., & Baer, D.M. (1991). Social validity assessments: Is current practice state of the art? *Journal of Applied Behavior Analysis, 24,* 189-204.

Sigafoos, J., Roberts, D., Couzens, D., & Caycho, L. (1992). Improving instruction for adults with developmental disabilities: Evaluation of a staff training package. *Behavioral Residential Treatment, 7,* 283-297.

Singer, G., Sowers, J., & Irvin, L.K. (1986). Computer-assisted video instruction for training paraprofessionals in rural special education. *Journal of Special Education Technology, 8,* 27-34.

Suda, K.T., & Miltenberger, R.G. (1993). Evaluation of staff management strategies to increase positive interactions in a vocational setting. *Behavioral Residential Treatment, 8,* 69-88.

van den Pol, R.A., Reid, D.H., & Fuqua, R.W. (1983). Peer training of safety-related skills to institutional staff: Benefits for trainers and trainees. *Journal of Applied Behavior Analysis, 16,* 139-156.

Wolf, M.M., Kirigin, K.A., Fixsen, D.L., Blase, K.A., & Braukmann, C.J. (1995). The teaching-family model: A case study in data-based program development and refinement (and dragon wrestling). *Journal of Organizational Behavior Management, 15, 1/2,* 11-68.

# Author Index

Abroms, K. L., 140,155
Accardo, P., 134,153
Adams, H. E., 111,127
Adams, K., 80
Agnew, J. L., 23,27,45,56
Alavosius, M. P., 64,68,76,113-115,
    124,125
Albin, J. M., 45,49,56
Allaire, A., 128
Allen, G. J., 69,78
Allen, J., 164,167
Allen, L. D., 166,170
Amado, A. N., 99
Ames, H. N., 117,127
Anderson, D. C., 135,139,145,
    149,153
Anderson, D. J., 99
Anderson, S. R., 36,57,93,99,
    109,128
Andrasik, F., 165,167
Andrews, J. R., 150,153
Andrews, M. A., 150,153
Arco, L., 73,76
Ard, W. R., 93,99
Ashbaugh, J. W., 62,76
Austin, J., 64,76
Ayllon, T., 104,126,161,168

Babcock, R. A., 33,41,56
Bachelder, L., 84,97
Baer, A. M., 120,128
Baer, D. M., 17,27,49,50,52,59,
    120,128,134,135,153,167,
    168,174,176,184,185,190
Bailey, D. B., 131,132,137,145,150,
    153,155

Bailey, J. S., 29,37,57,59,64,67,69,
    71,76,78,81,112,123,126,
    127,161,165,166,168-170,
    174
Baker, B. L., 76,94,97
Bakken, J., 68,77,91,98
Balcazar, F., 187,188
Banzett, L., 162,169
Barnett, C. D., 8,16,27
Barrett, S., 28
Barton, L. E., 40,59,66,80
Basit, A., 76
Bauman, K. E., 29
Baumeister, A. A., 14,16,18,28,32
Baumgart, D., 117,128
Bearden, L. J., 18,27
Bellamy, G. T., 85,97
Benjamin, E., 159,170
Benjamin, Jr., V. A., 156
Bensberg, G. J., 8,16,27,81
Berg, W. K., 67,81,128
Berger, D. C., 52,57
Bernheimer, L. P., 136,153
Bernstein, G. S., 9,27,104,129,
    160,168
Bersani, H. A., 14,27
Bible, G. H., 72,76
Bijou, S. W., 134,135,153
Blae, K. A., 42,43,64,74,77,82,
    156,185,190
Blakelock, H., 80
Blaney, B. C., 62,76
Blindert, H. D., 9,27
Blue, S., 105,126
Blunden, R., 35,40,41,56,73,76,
    161,168
Bogdan, R., 95,101
Boles, S., 85,97

   *191*

# Subject Index

absenteeism, 23,64,95,174
abuse, 14,24,62
acceptability (of management
    procedures), 10,19,39,
    49-52,115-117,125,163,
    173-188
Acceptability Rating Scale, 179-180
accidents, 64
Accreditation Council, 17,41
Achievement Place, 64,74
active treatment, 18,20,38,44,
    165,174
*Administration and Policy in Mental
    Health* (journal), 86
administrative research, 25,36,63-64,
    160
age appropriateness, 69,108,120,132
*American Journal on Mental
    Retardation*, 86
American Society for Quality
    Control, 46
antecedent interventions, 105,
    106-108,112,118,123,
    141,143,160,177
    instructions, 10,108,180
    modeling, 14,22,40,161,180
    prompting, 10,22,35,36,121,165
    scheduling, 38,69,161
applied behavior analysis, 8,52-53,
    104,110,120,133
autism, 121,140

behavior-centered skills, 164
behavior disorders, 11,107,121
behavior modification, 147,177
*Behavior Modification* (journal), 86
*Behavioral Interventions* (journal), 34
*Behavioral Residential Treatment*
    (journal), 34

behavioral systems analysis,
    151,165-166
burn out, 70,94,95

case managers, 122
checklists, 72,138,165
child-centered supports, 74-76,
    133-134,144,150
choice (of management procedures),
    173,181-183
coaching, 139
community living arrangements,
    15-16,39,63,83-97
conditional probability analysis, 48
consequence interventions (see also
    feedback), 108,114,123,177
    lotteries, 10,179
    monetary, 39,73,179
    natural, 124
    praise, 39,108,179,180
    punitive, 23-24
consultation skills, 39,122
consumer satisfaction, 46,48-52,
    174,176,178
consumer-driven quality, 45-46
consumerism, 16
contingency learning, 17-18,23
Continuous Quality Improvement,
    20,24,25-27,34,44-45
control charts, 53-55
correlational research, 94-95
cost-benefit analysis, 148
cultural evolution, 16,17,23

day care centers, 138-139,142,144
developmental perspectives,
    133-134,146

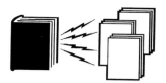

# Haworth
# DOCUMENT DELIVERY
# SERVICE

This valuable service provides a single-article order form for any article from a Haworth journal.

- *Time Saving:* No running around from library to library to find a specific article.
- *Cost Effective:* All costs are kept down to a minimum.
- *Fast Delivery:* Choose from several options, including same-day FAX.
- *No Copyright Hassles:* You will be supplied by the original publisher.
- *Easy Payment:* Choose from several easy payment methods.

*Open Accounts Welcome for . . .*
- Library Interlibrary Loan Departments
- Library Network/Consortia Wishing to Provide Single-Article Services
- Indexing/Abstracting Services with Single Article Provision Services
- Document Provision Brokers and Freelance Information Service Providers

## MAIL or *FAX* THIS ENTIRE ORDER FORM TO:

Haworth Document Delivery Service
The Haworth Press, Inc.
10 Alice Street
Binghamton, NY 13904-1580

**or FAX:** 1-800-895-0582
**or CALL:** 1-800-429-6784
9am-5pm EST

PLEASE SEND ME PHOTOCOPIES OF THE FOLLOWING SINGLE ARTICLES:

1) Journal Title: _____

   Vol/Issue/Year: _____ Starting & Ending Pages: _____

Article Title: _____

_____

2) Journal Title: _____

   Vol/Issue/Year: _____ Starting & Ending Pages: _____

Article Title: _____

_____

3) Journal Title: _____

   Vol/Issue/Year: _____ Starting & Ending Pages: _____

Article Title: _____

_____

4) Journal Title: _____

   Vol/Issue/Year: _____ Starting & Ending Pages: _____

Article Title: _____

_____

**(See other side for Costs and Payment Information)**

*COSTS:* Please figure your cost to order quality copies of an article.

1. Set-up charge per article: $8.00
   ($8.00 × number of separate articles) _____

2. Photocopying charge for each article:
   1-10 pages: $1.00 _____

   11-19 pages: $3.00 _____

   20-29 pages: $5.00 _____

   30+ pages: $2.00/10 pages _____

3. Flexicover (optional): $2.00/article _____

4. Postage & Handling: US: $1.00 for the first article/
   $.50 each additional article _____

   Federal Express: $25.00 _____

   Outside US: $2.00 for first article/
   $.50 each additional article _____

5. Same-day FAX service: $.50 per page _____

   **GRAND TOTAL:** _____

---

*METHOD OF PAYMENT:* (please check one)

❏ Check enclosed   ❏ Please ship and bill. PO # _____
(sorry we can ship and bill to bookstores only! All others must pre-pay)

❏ Charge to my credit card: ❏ Visa;  ❏ MasterCard;  ❏ Discover;
❏ American Express;

Account Number:_____ Expiration date:_____

Signature: *X* _____

Name: _____ Institution: _____

Address: _____

_____

City: _____ State:_____ Zip:_____

Phone Number: _____ FAX Number: _____

---

## MAIL or *FAX* THIS ENTIRE ORDER FORM TO:

Haworth Document Delivery Service
The Haworth Press, Inc.
10 Alice Street
Binghamton, NY 13904-1580

**or FAX:** 1-800-895-0582
**or CALL:** 1-800-429-6784
(9am-5pm EST)

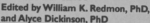